Flying with One Wing

Flying with One Wing

✦

A Family's Triumph in the Tapestry of 20th Century America

Barbara Heeter

iUniverse, Inc.

New York Bloomington Shanghai

Flying with One Wing
A Family's Triumph in the Tapestry of 20th Century America

iUniverse books may be ordered through booksellers or by contacting:

iUniverse
1663 Liberty Drive
Bloomington, IN 47403
www.iuniverse.com
1-800-Authors (1-800-288-4677)

Because of the dynamic nature of the Internet, any Web addresses or links contained in this book may have changed since publication and may no longer be valid.

The views expressed in this work are solely those of the author and do not necessarily reflect the views of the publisher, and the publisher hereby disclaims any responsibility for them.

Library of Congress: txul-331-772

ISBN: 978-0-595-45713-7 (pbk)
ISBN: 978-0-595-62306-8 (cloth)
ISBN: 978-0-595-90014-5 (ebk)

Printed in the United States of America

To my granddaughters, Sonja, Amanda, and Mariah, the fourth generation in the new country. They have given me wing through the music of their lives.

Who will tell the tale of a family, its love, its heartache? Who will recognize the struggles for dignity and importance and through the telling, make them important to others?

—Christopher R. Baker

Contents

1

The House

It was never a house. By forever calling it "*the* house", the residents implied there was no other and, without forethought, bestowed on the dwelling a name forever lost in the dust of category. Rather than saying, "I'm going home" they would casually note, "I'm going to the house." None of them tried to understand how such a simple statement separated this space from others of its kind. They were all too close. Everyone they loved lived there. And most of the important events of their lives unfolded there. Only their unconscious understood the crucial difference that caused them to remain at the house for lifetimes.

In the beginning, Anna moved into the house with her brood of six and a one-year lease. Sixteen years later, her wake took place in the living room. Never a demanding person, she had strong feelings about her death and made her wishes known well in advance. She disliked the cold formality of funeral homes where lifeless bodies move along a shifting belt of strangers and requested a wake at the house—and a female mortician. In her homeland, the dead were only touched by those who loved them in life, from the moment of death until commitment back to the earth. So, promising that the house would be the place of their last moments with her, Anna's children remained true to their word and eliminated the dreary wake common even in those days in professional funeral *homes*. Soon to be returned to the earth and never seen again, bodies lie alone in the dimmed light of such establishments throughout the night.

But in the living room of the house, the body was never alone as it awaited the burial.

Though not nearly as large as the third generation now recollects, the room was of ample size and easily converted to a space for those who came to share the pain of death with the living. The room had never been as crowded, nor would it be again, as when it held her casket. Constantly coming and going in those hours of goodbye, friends and loved ones filled the house. Small gatherings could be found in any room, though only on the first floor. Guests only fluttered to the second floor to use the single bathroom; none invaded the privacy of the upstairs bedrooms, though it seemed that no one slept for the four days and three nights of the wake.

The time touched every human sense. The many flowers, mostly from friends of the living combined with burning incense produced a unique smell that mingled with salty tears as her body left the house for the last time. But even then, the family knew that Anna's spirit would remain at the house, just as they hoped would theirs, when that fated day arrived.

Those wakeful days of vigil laid bare an army of feelings. Though such sentiments always ran underground at the house. Just as the old adage advises, feelings were best expressed in actions rather than words. These six children of immigrant parents were cautious with their feelings, even as they buried their beloved mother. This first generation in a new land saw feelings as unsafe, making them vulnerable in a culture unfamiliar to their parents. Feelings would hinder their determination to succeed in the bustling land, so they were careful to reveal them only in the strictest order. Fear, the most difficult of all, was followed by sadness, joy and anger. As their defense, anger came most easily and occasional bickering could be heard throughout daily life at the house

After the burial, they longed to return to the routine of their lives. And what *was* normal at the house? Even with Anna gone, a *nest* describes it best.

When she moved in as a widow, four of her children were in their twenties, and the two youngest attended high school. So none were fledglings. Still, only one ever chose to leave. In addition to Anna's six, there was also Kate, who became part of the story. Though not blood, Kate came to live at the house shortly after the move and increased the number to eight.

Eventually two of the grown children left then one returned with a spouse so the numbers remained unchanged, but when a second sister returned with her spouse, space became a problem. The structure had been made into a duplex by the owner when the Depression began to take hold, and Anna and her clan had moved into the larger space, two-thirds of the entire structure. So the smaller section, housing strangers, had to be reclaimed when the sisters started returning with partners. A third sister eventually made her residence a half block away, and though the space provided a convenient alternative to the house, catching the overflow when necessary, it never replaced the house—even to her.

At the high end, thirteen people lived there. Though three of these were part-time residents, thirteen is high for a fifty-year-old, two story frame structure. And one might guess that someone would have worried about fire extinguishers, fire codes, and, finally, smoke detectors, but no one did. In the minds of the residents, the house was not subject to either natural or man-made disasters, like the rest of the world. Though fire did finally fell the house, no one of that first generation remained to witness its collapse.

To understand it all became the lonely task of the second generation.

ଓଃଓଃଓଃଓଃଓଃଓଃଓଃଓଃଓଃଓଃଓଃଓଃଓଃଓଃଓଃଓଃଓଃଓଃ

Of the second generation, I was one of the part-time residents and saw the house differently than the third generation who never lived there and knew the house only as children, when most things are larger than life. They inflate beyond reality and innocently exaggerate with tales of a grand structure with large ornate rooms, remote on a mountain top. Likely, these flourishes spring from the unspoken dreams of my grandmother and her children, who before the move had only cleaned such homes for income. Her six children, the first generation in a land foreign to their parents, had known only tenements their entire lives, until they moved to the house.

The house did sit on a hill—that proved a solid hike for me as a kid and for those in the family who in the early years could not afford cars. Surrounded by an average city neighborhood, it eventually held elaborate furnishings spawned by the owner's remodeling scheme. Still, unlike the fourth generation who now only knows the house from family tales, the third generation *was* once there, eating the ancestral foods and tearing up the long stairway to the second floor where they could actually enter the other side through the odd doorways that served as partitions when strangers had lived there.

My memories are of smaller things like the old vertical windows that opened inward as though inviting the summer breezes and—early ones like the mutt Brownie. Though belonging to the owner of the house, Brownie knew everyone and devotedly walked each to work. As a kid, I had no regular destination and only played with him, but the others had daily schedules, so he would accompany one and then find his way back to trot down the hill again at the side of the next one. The busiest of dogs, Brownie waited to escort residents home at the end of their workdays and was rewarded with affection as well as a doghouse close to the kitchen door where he was assured of the best of scraps.

In the end, the city updated their leash laws and, finding Brownie with excessive freedom, put him to sleep before any of the residents could come to his rescue. I remember that the loss was so traumatic that no one at the house even hinted at the possibility of another pet as a replacement. Finally, many years later, they got a shepherd named Sheba, but it was never the same. Even a fancy-named pedigree, actually bred to herd as Brownie had once done so masterfully, could not find her way into their hearts. Today, I find no fault with the shepherd; the years between the two dogs had changed the residents.

I was there, too, for the wakes of that first generation. Less memorable than the wake in the living room of the house were those of the six who followed the modern mode of funeral homes, and I viewed each of the bodies with the same question. My eyes immediately focused on their hands when I first saw them in their eternal caskets. Confronted six different times with the archaic practice of the open casket, a throwback to days when mourners were unsure if spirits had truly left the lifeless bodies, I studied the hands I had known so well in life. Unconsciously, I had come to know each resident best through these vital extremities that clearly distinguish us mortals, and I felt compelled to learn what death and the mortician had altered. But their hands, though still now, remained unchanged, so I recognized them all just as I had in life, by their hands.

CRCRCRCRCRCRCRCRCRCRCRCRCRCRCRCRCRCR

With people sounds forever fluttering through the house, no resident ever felt alone there. An adult calculation today would conclude that the only silence came between three and six, in those wee hours that precede the dawn. The living hours of so many vary, and the late people generally missed the early people. The late ones had barely closed their eyes when the alarms went off for the early ones. And then there were the shift people whose work caused their hours to change from time to time; this group sometimes slept in the afternoons and ate dinner at times ordinarily classified as bedtime. Only on Sundays did more than three of them sit down to a meal together. But in the end all the shuffling worked; those taking their meals at regular times often visited with ones who ate alone at odd hours. And unplanned forays into each other's lives occurred in these casual moments. What might have appeared as discord only gave the house its energetic rhythm.

When life got too hectic for someone, the front porch provided respite, though only in the summer months. Located in western Pennsylvania, the house sported a front porch common for the times. It served for relaxation and personal reflection, but with thirteen active beings within the same walls, time alone even on the porch was scarce. Mostly, the front porch supplied another gathering place and a box seat on the neighborhood. Front porches have made a comeback in the twenty-first century; homeowners across America have found that the entire street provides a vast conversation piece, unknown in the private, though often lonely, back-decks.

Residents could sit on the front porch and comment among themselves on the neighbors' comings and goings without interplay with the characters, except of course the occasional friendly wave. Also equipped with porches of their own, the neighbors had a similar opportunity to mull over happenings at the house, where with its many residents much could be surmised and enhanced with imaginings of their own. Equity in the idle gossip of the neighborhood existed and provided commercial-free entertainment.

Majestic, too, from the front porch were the fires from the local steel mills. Urban and located only a mile from the main industry, the house could not be separated from the city's livelihood. The steel mills spewed a distinct odor and constantly displayed an awesome fire from the blast furnaces. Both the fires and the smell could be identified for miles around. The prevalent smell that quickly filled the nostrils was created by mixtures of iron ore, coke, and limestone heated in the furnaces to 1600 degrees Fahrenheit. Not repulsive, this smell today can instantly return the second and third generations to the house. The orange glow from the furnaces lit the skies and testified to the fire's intensity. Forever visible, the fires deprived night of its true darkness.

Today the gases would likely be found physically harmful to humans, but then such worries were unknown. Though the mills also delivered a thunderous roar as well as a dust that reappeared daily on the windowsills of all the homes of the city, it is only the odor and light that now linger, wedging their way into the story. The steel mills added character to the house, so their demise matched the fall of the other. With both the original residents and the city's livelihood gone, the house became as poor as it had once been rich—in ways far greater than money.

2

The Long Journey

Anna moved to the house as a widow in the infamous year of 1929. Mirrored now in memories of the third generation that far exceeds the realities of the space, it was a ray of hope to her and her family. The stock market made its historic plunge that year and the failing American economy left prices, wages, and jobs at record lows. America was now crippled by the Great Depression that enveloped the lives of all its citizens. Thirty years earlier when Anna made the journey for an arranged marriage to escape the poverty in which she had been raised, America had appeared on the brink of something bigger than the turn of a century. Excitement over the hopes of boundless prosperity vibrated across the land and matched her dream. Why else would a young woman hazard such a journey?

Without literacy in any language, she carried only the customs and citizenship of Galicia when she boarded the S. S. Kensington—Red Star Line in 1897 in Antwerp, Belgium, a thriving seaport over seven hundred miles from her home. Embarking the large vessel for the thirty-five hundred mile voyage to America, Anna saw the difficult part of the journey behind her. Her quest had begun a month earlier. The seven hundred mile trip from Galicia to Antwerp was made on foot with occasional kind offers from travelers in horse drawn wagons.

The ship's manifest lists her as a steerage passenger, a "laborer without luggage", meaning she rode in the lowest level of the ship, which held its steering mechanism; the purpose of this space was hardly passenger comfort and serves now as a stark sign of her dire poverty. On this particular voyage, the S.S. Kensington carried seventy-four passengers, half of which were cabin travelers: merchants, students, and voyagers who could afford decent accommodations. Of all the passengers, during the month-long crossing to America, fourteen died on board.

Anna survived the crossing and became one of the many immigrants cascading into America from central Europe at the close of the nineteenth century. Searching for a better life, she abandoned everything she had known in her twenty-four years. When the subject of her native land arose in the future, she forever called it "the old country", perhaps from the common reference at the time to the *New World,* as Columbus had dubbed it; but puzzlingly, she never called America the "new country". Now part of another world order and determined to make this land her own when the boat docked in New York Harbor, she had one remnant of the old country left. Her younger sister, Rosalie, also in an arranged marriage, had preceded her in this exodus and had encouraged Anna to share the dream.

A formal form of reception for immigrants was a local flyer published and freely distributed in the teeming city; the paper held answers to refugees' pressing questions. But Anna could not read. Other forms of welcome such as the present training in E.S.L. (English as a Second Language) were unknown then. Though determined, Anna needed reassurance in this foreign land, and eventually the house became that abiding comfort—years after her arrival on the S.S.Kensington

Her quest came at a time when the culture, like Anna herself, was exploring new ways of life. The Industrial Revolution had been underway for a century before her birth, but the discoveries in her lifetime of seventy-two years remain astonishing: the box camera, automobile, telephone, motion picture, x-ray, telegraph, airplane, radio, vitamins, air-conditioning, insulin, quick-frozen foods, penicillin, phonograph, the combustion engine, microphone, fountain pen, cellophane, rayon, nylon, the helicopter, guided missiles and the atomic bomb.... to name but a few of the better known inventions. Such dramatic creations may have spurred the young immigrant to become part of the human search.

The oldest of five children, Anna had been raised by peasants in the now forgotten land of Galicia. Galicia, south of present day Poland and seven hundred miles southwest of Moscow, is now called Slovakia. Known as Austria-Hungry during World War I, the tiny country was nearly obliterated by the fighting. The assertive Rosalie never learned what had been realized by her insistence that her sister join her. Illiterate and unable to communicate with the family they had left behind in the old country, the two had no means of knowing the Galician history that followed their departure. Tucked away in the new country, neither learned of the Austro-German Army offensive that pushed the Russians back in the battles of World War I. The conflicts raged across the Carpathian Mountains in Galicia in 1917 and likely extinguished the sisters' family. Those who managed to flee the ravages of war were likely eliminated by Hitler's invasion of Poland in 1939. With her insistence to migrate, Rosalie had given her sister more than a new life. She had given her life.

But the year 1917 delivered its own blow to Anna. Her husband Alex died of a lung disease brought on by long hours below ground in the coalmines of western Pennsylvania. Strikes in the mines several years before his death had failed to raise the working conditions, at least in time for him. Leaving his wife with six children, ranging in age from three to sixteen, he remains a mysterious figure to his descendants, with no remnants in the form of snapshots or even family stories. Even the location of his unmarked grave continues today as a question. At the time of his death, money to mark the grave proved impossible for the family, who managed only to scrape enough together for a pine box. Had it not been for the parish priest's special collection in the congregation, Alex would have been thrown into a mass grave of paupers.

He did leave one material item behind, a single sheet of paper that supported his repeated claim to land in his native Russia. At the beginning of the twentieth century, land ownership was everything. (Originally, the "unalienable rights" as described in the Declaration of Independence were "life, liberty, and *property*." Land granted voting rights to citizens in many countries, but at the time of Alex's death, the requirement for the privilege of voting in the new country was merely that the voter be male.) Though often hearing his claim to land ownership, Anna had had no evidence of such an asset in the eighteen years of their marriage. The duties of wives then were confined to bearing and caring for children, preparation of food, and housecleaning. Not permitted to vote even in the democratic country of America, most women remained exiled from money matters. Unless an emergency arose. And the death of the breadwinner who left an illiterate widow with six underage children constituted such a crisis.

So Anna's two oldest daughters, with a decade of schooling behind them, deciphered the paper, which proved to be a deed for land in Russia just as Alex had claimed. And through mailed correspondence, the women quickly sold the property. Uneducated in the details of such matters, the three hardly disputed the first price they were offered for the unknown land. The proceeds allowed Anna to buy a small life insurance policy for her and each of the six children. Such an act assured money with which to be buried, a grave concern for poor families whose finances forbade both luxury and comfort beyond survival. Existence for immigrants like Anna was truly a matter of life or death, with little in-between.

Though feeling safer with policies that insured proper burials, Anna remained thousands of miles from her homeland, faced with life in America as a penniless widow, ironically as destitute as she had been in the old country. But *home*, regardless of circumstances, provides security, so Alex's early death caused her to now reflect on the immensity of the decision to follow her sister to America. But the luxury of reflection had never been hers so she quietly assumed the burden. A woman who appreciated the different forms of wealth, she recognized that her choice to journey to America had endowed her with six healthy children, who now had the hope of futures far different than those they would have known in the old country. That her decision had also saved her from the ravages of war in her native land, a notable comfort, remained unknown.

The needy widow began to scrub floors in the homes of the upper class; in 1917, twenty percent of all households had domestic help. Her life as a Galician peasant had endowed her with an inner strength and forced her to accept manual labor at an early age. Never accustomed to a life of privilege, she adapted to her destiny as an illiterate widow with six mouths to feed. This meant she was both breadwinner *and* mother, endlessly working without complaint. Only in the pictures of her that survive is the pain evident.

In the snapshots, the few taken when a camera finally became available to the family, she looks neither angry nor sad, simply depleted. At age fifty, she appears eighty and too drained to stand. Seated in an old kitchen chair, Anna has her auburn hair, a gift of nature, tied and hidden in a bun. The long, shiny hair remained unaffected by age and the lack of protein in her starchy diet. Even with the harsh Castile soap that she used as shampoo, her hair had never lost its original color.

Once while toiling on her knees in a workplace after her husband's death, Anna was asked by her employer if she would be willing to sell her striking hair.

"No, I von't" came her immediate reply. The answer, though docile, was firm, in spite of the fact that selling one's hair was a common practice of the day.

"I will pay you well" replied the hopeful owner.

"No."

Given her life at the time, this response to a superior contrasts Anna's spirit in a different way than her exhausted body. The incident became a family tale that continued long after her death and is accompanied today by a lovely braid. One of her daughters had kept her mother's hairs, collected from a hairbrush, and had it braided. And the keepsake discloses the quiet vibrancy of a spirit that no camera could capture.

Tested by all the standards of a life, Anna's spirit was strengthened by her devotion to the Russian Church. Though she had her younger sister, who lived with her own brood a short distance away, Anna's connection to the Russian Church, a sector of the Greek Orthodox faith, sustained her in ways that even a sister could not. The Church provided a link to the old country and was vital to the tapestry of her new life. In a letter scribed by a literate friend, Rosalie had encouraged her older sister's journey to America with the one fact she knew would affect Anna; their church had expanded into the new country! The note assured the hesitant sister that the Russian Church remained unchanged in America. And when Anna finally considered an arranged marriage, the religious allegiance of her future partner was her first question, followed by the ordinary questions of his age and work. Assuring her of his own devotion to the faith, Alex married Anna in the Russian Church of the new country. And quickly the couple connected with a congregation within walking distance of their dwelling.

The Church provided a familiar culture to the couple and served in the bonding of the new union. As in the old country, replete with ritual that included rich incense and countless candles, the liturgy was in Anna's native tongue; the stained glass windows and priests in gold embroidered robes were identical to those she had forsaken in the old country. Like all Russian churches, murals replace statues in the sanctuary, because in the Bible, God forbids graven images.

When she entered this place of worship in the new country for the first time, the familiar three-barred cross on the steeple and the Byzantine art at the altar put Anna more at home than she had been since her arrival. Even the sight of Rosalie awaiting her boat as it docked in New York Harbor had not comforted her as the Church now did. The intimate nature of this space enveloped her as it had through her childhood, duplicating the security of old slippers that have molded to familiar feet after years of wear.

But now at Alex's death, with young children to feed and shelter, Anna did not leave the Mass sustained by thoughts that her present life would improve. The Church taught that only death brought a life free of earthly pain. According to its teachings, Alex now dwelt in a paradise that awaited her. Though the temporary splendor of Sunday Mass masked the outside world with stained glass windows and separated the worshippers from the drabness of their everyday lives, the service offered only hope of a glorious heaven where life at last would be joyful. As a child in Galicia, Anna had learned through her faith the certainty of human weakness and the superiority of men. Messages that now hindered the struggling mother of five daughters and one son.

Still, the Church gave structure to the seven lives and proved invaluable to the destitute family. Other teachings, though more subtle, suggested that life had terms that could not be violated with impulsive behavior, that sacrifice was often necessary for a greater good, and that there exited a Life Force much larger than their own egos. These teachings led to a discipline that when taken to heart, as they were by Anna and eventually her children, helped the fatherless family to forge ahead even at the lowest of times. And influenced even the less devout of the generations to come.

Disagreements on Sunday Mass could be heard throughout the house.

"Soondays beegin vith Mass. My children no be idle in God's eyes!" In her broken English, Anna argued nearly every Sunday.

"Mama, Sunday is my *only* day off. I want to sleep now! Next Sunday. I promise."

"Go ta bed early. Now git up."

"I can't."

"In bed vhen ve can be vith God is deevil doing. And no vork in house on Soonday. So ya vill go to church."

In her broken English, Anna argued with any of the six—technically all were of age—who dared to put on trial one of her stanch rules around the holy day. On other days, the disputes were usually about the late hours kept by anyone of the six who, unlike their mother even in her youth, found excitement in the wee hours of the morning. But her rules, carved from a lifetime of physical work, never changed and finally, though often tested, were never broken.

Church also gave Anna a chance to share customs with fellow immigrants, people who, like her, had led a simple life and abandoned their homelands for this country where, reportedly, *streets were paved in gold*. The traditions around the foods that nurtured the hopeful immigrants became a basis for friendship among them. Generally meatless because of cost rather than health, meals were made with simple, low-cost ingredients. The real expense lay in the labor of preparation. Hours were spent in the kitchen creating soups and dishes of the past—from memory. Mushrooms, caraway seeds, corn meal, and cabbage were combined in a variety of ways with root vegetables such as potatoes, beets, parsnips and horserad-ish. Legumes such as lentils and lima beans offered novelty as well as a bit of protein. Buttermilk, the inexpensive residue after the butterfat in milk has turned to butter, proved a popular source of protein for Anna and her family. White flour evolved to homemade dumplings and crusts of all sorts. More expensive ingredients such as garlic, honey and a particular variety of black mushrooms were carefully reserved for the highest of the Church's holy days, Easter and Christmas.

Preceded by weeks of Lent or Advent, Easter and Christmas celebra-tions required preparation. Food was mysteriously woven into Church teachings, and both periods of readiness for these holidays advised sacrifice in diet that eliminated not only meat but also the products of animals, such as milk and butter. According to the teachings, elimination of these foods cleansed the body, preparing it for the holiday celebrations. Reflected in the strictest of menus for the eves preceding these holidays, the spiritual nature of the two nights exceeded the holy days themselves. Saturday night before Easter Sunday, baskets filled with ham, homemade breads known as *pascha*, special horseradish mixed with cooked beets, salt, and raw eggs were taken to church for a special blessing at Midnight Mass. Then they could be eaten as the first foods at the end of the Lenten fast—at two o'clock on Easter morning. Christmas Eve dinner required honey for the sweetness of life and garlic for its bitter parts, followed by mushroom and lentil soups and a wonderful combination of browned cab-bage and noodles.

These religious rules around food extend back to Jewish roots. Milk, from cows that walk the earth, is never taken with fish, which originate in the sea. And the foods of "animal origins" are sacrificed every Friday in the name of God. Though the expense of meat made it a luxury on *any* day for Anna and her children. These traditions around food proved difficult after her husband's death, as she felt fortunate to have much of anything to put on the dinner table. Still, Anna faithfully followed the teachings as best she could.

CR CR CR CR CR CR CR CR CR CR CR CR CR CR CR CR CR CR CR CR

My favorite was her kummel soup, made with inexpensive caraway seeds. For good reason, soup was my grandmother's specialty. An entree, which when accompanied by black bread could easily be stretched among the hungry family, soup offered a healthy meal. And the ingredients were cheap. At the end of a full day atop the stove, most of the soups were flavored with flour that had finally browned after frequent stirrings. Mixed with water, the paste-like flour—a roux known as *zaprushka*—thickens the soup and is added at the end. For kummel soup, the roux is added before the egg dumplings. As I sat eating the soup, she often stroked the top of my head in affection. And the touch remains with me still.

Unlike her, I have a variety of bowls to serve my own soup today, depending on the type of broth. But the bowls are only presentation, all about the kind of show that my grandmother had neither the money nor desire to secure. She never knew variety of any kind in her life; one of anything was sufficient for a lifetime. And finally the taste of a bowl's contents depends on skill. Though many of my soups are good, my kummel soup never tastes like hers once did. Still, I make it for the marvelous smell that immediately transports me back to the house.

CR CR CR CR CR CR CR CR CR CR CR CR CR CR CR CR CR CR CR CR

In her final days, Anna, too ill to cook the traditional Christmas Eve dinner celebrated on January 6 under the old Julian calendar the Russian Church chose to keep, passed on the many recipes from her homeland that she had never put down on paper. Her devoted daughters made repeated trips up the steps to the sick room to get their mother's approval on their fledgling attempts at this solemnest of meals.

"Mama, I don't think it tastes like yours."

"It goood. No vorry."

Requiring the same reassurances that Anna herself had once needed from fellow immigrants, the daughters conveyed to their dying mother that Christmas Eve of 1944 that the family would remain together. Even as the new country was torn apart by another world war.

Anna had been ailing for over a year. The sickness had been diagnosed as irreversible, so no doubts about outcome clouded the minds of her six children. In the final days of the illness, her youngest daughter, now a part-time resident of the house, had to leave for her own child's schooling in another state. When she came to take leave of her ailing mother, the brief exchange, so intense in its simplicity, remained with the young woman for the remainder of her life.

"I vouldn't mind ta sa 'goo-bye' if I can sa 'ello' again," Anna said as her daughter bent over the bed to kiss her mother—unknown to her, for the last time.

Even with the family's acceptance of her impending death, the night of February second struck a blow to everyone at the house, a blow that even members not present also felt. As her condition worsened, Anna had been moved the previous month of course not to a hospital, but merely to a larger bedroom in the house. The change accommodated her visitors, which included the family doctor and priest who frequented her bedside. This larger room had more table space for food and medication and more windows, which offered the patient a view of the large oak tree on the front lawn; her previous room in the back of the house had given her only a view of the empty garage. As the night of February second wore-on, Anna's attending daughter became aware that her mother repeatedly asked the time.

"Vat da time is?" Anna asked in earnest.

Later, the persistent question became part of the discussion at her wake. All wakes provide opportunity for such dialogue, and Rosalie, the only one with a sense of Anna's life in Galicia, supplied the answer by repeating an old Russian myth that described death as directed by God; spirits that leave the body when the second hand of the clock passes the six and heads up towards twelve are quickly welcomed into heaven.

Officially, Anna's death is recorded as 7:40 p.m., sixteen years after her move to the house.

Her spirit demanded more in death than she ever had in life. Accepting the gravity of her illness from the beginning, Anna had made her wishes clear. Requesting slippers on her feet—she had gone barefoot in Galicia—and a burial site on a hill near homes warmed by children, she desired in death to be surrounded by the comfort of family as well as a view of the city that had become her home nearly twenty years ago. Though an unusual appeal by someone devoted to the teachings of a heaven, Anna's request held the essence of a woman who had known much of life on earth. And chose to hold onto to some of the beauty she had found there.

The traumatic moments of the wake came with the removal of her body from the house—on two different occasions. Immediately after death, the covered stretcher was carried by the mortician's aides. And later, the casket, borne now by pallbearers and led by the priest, made its final journey down the steps of the house and into the hearse for the short trip to the burial Mass. Both inside and out, the smell of frankincense filled the air as the priest swung the thurible, a vessel of burning incense designed to mask earthly smells at this solemnest of moments; the burning also produces smoke that is said to carry prayers more quickly to God. Her children watched and struggled to hide their grief, a sentiment the Church taught was wrong at such a time. Death was viewed as God's will and heaven anticipated with great joy rather than sadness. At the end of the Mass, the casket was closed forever. And her adult children, the first generation born in the new country, returned to their lives together. At the house.

3

The Residents

Anna's first child was christened Anna after her mother, a common practice in those days. Naming children after older family members or saints meant that the attending adults had previous links with the namesake, even if distant as in the case of church saints. Though the custom bestows an honor, it also implies that the new being will display the nature of the namesake. But names hardly guarantee identities. And Anne—the Americanized version of Anna—proved to be nothing like her mother but was instead, like her Aunt Rosalie, who eventually became the namesake of Anne's younger sister. Aunt Rosalie could afford an air of elegance that provided a different model for these two sisters.

Even when she could not afford the luxury, Anne focused on appearance and charm, qualities that her mother had neither time nor energy to consider. Anne's life secret lay in blending her own joy with what eventually became her profession. As a beautician—the old word for the modern "hair stylist"—she made others look good, just as she herself always did. Though the effort to make her beautiful was minimal. She was the acknowledged beauty in a family of attractive women.

Quitting school at age sixteen, she worked hard in her early life and managed to open her own business eleven years later. But her toil never reflected in a personality that was forever free of both complaints and vengeful moods. Never moody, her nature remained easygoing and happy. Her chosen career came so naturally that life was less stressful for Anne than to most. Or perhaps she smartly avoided the unwelcome thoughts that distress humans.

Contrary to the attitude of the times and the virtue of her good looks, Anne never sought wealthy men for the safety of marriage. The mere energy of the Suffrage Movement, well formed when she came of age, influenced her, though she had no time to give to the effort. Helping her mother and younger siblings, Anne had survival to motivate her. Far from an activist for women's rights, she *lived* the essence of the Movement. Still, had the local steel mills not strengthened the economy of the city, her own power might not have been sufficient for her early endeavors. Because of steel production, small enterprises such as Anne's prospered in their city even under the ravages of the Great Depression. Feeling the burden of her father's death, and recognizing that her mother had the deck stacked against her, she set out determined to ease the family's financial woes. Becoming a widow with six underage children is one kind of woe, but as an immigrant who could neither write nor read in a foreign land, at the beginning of the depression, her mother carried an unspeakable burden.

Even as a new beautician with family responsibilities far beyond her years, Anne guaranteed herself freedom to enjoy life. More than success, she searched for wonder in life, a goal high on her list. Determined not to be entrapped by servile tasks, she boldly broadcast her values with statements such as, "The dirt will always be here tomorrow." Housework, cleaning of any sort, never proved a priority in Anne's life, which shocked her four sisters who fretted over the spotlessness of the many rooms of the house.

Other than the tiny sitting room, there were no *spare* rooms there, no extravagant spaces such as mudrooms, pantries, studies or guest rooms. Studies, spaces in large homes that appeared much earlier than the nineteenth century era in which the house was built, may have been sacrificed when the temporary partitions went up at the start of the Depression. Or perhaps the house failed to meet the social class of such a prestigious space known as a *study*. But worries over neither fashion nor dust troubled Anne.

Early marriage was the custom of the day. But bothered by the load she saw her mother carry, she refused to marry at an early age. At the time, for a woman, "late in life" arrived when she reached her mid-twenties, and Anne had long passed this benchmark when she finally married. To say that she left the house when she married sounds natural, but in Anne's case, such a statement proves misleading. Her only nuptial took place after she had lived at the house as an adult for sixteen years, so her departure to a house a stone's throw away, was minor.

Though enchanted by men, Anne never allowed herself to be lured by the gold band of marriage. But with her looks and charm, boyfriends proved plentiful. Easy to conclude in hindsight that her favorite suitor was her husband, this deduction too may be flawed. Likely, he finally got her hand because he was the most patient and faithfully stayed around—until Anne was ready for the marital bliss that might curb her adventures.

Anne often declared, "I'll give it a try," welcoming ventures of all sorts.

Interested in all the excitement life had to offer, she placed travel near the top of her list and gambling a close second, especially when it held the hope of monetary return. Low risk, high return was her goal long before modern investment firms adopted the slogan. Aligned with her interest in gambling was Anne's strong belief in luck, and she had several practices that enhanced her chances at winning—especially when all the siblings played poker in the kitchen of the house. Eventually, Anne experimented with bigger stakes in horse racing, casinos, and finally the stock market. Her optimistic nature dictated that she would eventually win back any incurred losses. And in the end, her winnings outdistanced the losses.

Though organized crime held her attention only in the fantasy of fiction, Anne harbored a nature not far removed from Mafia members. From a first generation of poor immigrants, she gave her allegiance to family with the staunch belief that gambling could secure the money to make them safe: that strangers in a new land needed to protect themselves in ways that government would not.

With a natural quickness, she often proclaimed: "You can't fly with one wing." For Anne, the family provided the other wing. Just as the fact that the second log in a fire causes the first one to burn brighter, so her family enhanced her life

In addition to this dictum, Anne had other rules in her life scheme that could not be broken. Demanding peace when disagreements arose in the family, she was quick to compromise and carried a sense of fairness difficult to ignore. With priorities that never wavered and an elegant style, she held a philosophy that included one requirement. Life must be enjoyed.

Different than Anne in every way except family devotion was the *second* born, her sister Marie.

Marie's given name was Mary after St. Mary, but it mysteriously evolved to Marie and finally Mame, long before Broadway's showy Auntie Mame came into prominence. Aptly, she answered to all three names as each was reserved for use by different members of the family.

Her mother called her Mary, appropriately the saint, while her siblings called her Marie, the more formal variation of Mary. Finally, the more affectionate Mame belonged to her husband and members of the second generation. Reflected in this trilogy of names, the variety offers different views of the enigmatic second-born.

A competitive nature often appears in the second child of a family, especially when the first is of the same sex. And thus were Marie's feelings towards her older sister. Faulting Anne's time spent in front of the mirror as well as her other leisurely pursuits, Marie recognized from the beginning that she would have to find something other than beauty to come out ahead of her older sister in the sibling race. With this directive in her life, she managed everything on a grand scale—her clothes, the house, its furnishings and her enterprise. Laboring endlessly to save money, she eventually bought a small newsstand that she converted to an eatery. Strategically located close to the city's steel mills, the business grew from her creative nature, extraordinary by any definition. Though such drive is rewarding, Marie's inspirations never allowed her to relax. Her creativity, linked to the desire to aid her destitute family and mingled with sibling rivalry, produced a woman who stayed constantly in motion, physically and emotionally.

Even laundry—which eventually she could have afforded to have done by hired help—Marie often did herself, less to save money than simply to expend the energy that forever coursed through her thin body. In her youth, she did the laundry by hand on a cruel washboard in cold water and later in the basement of the house with a wringer-washer. The large basement of the house served the purpose well. Though rough, the space sported a single toilet, which eliminated trips up two flights of steps to the full bathroom. Never used by guests, the facility allowed a resident to step into laundry day and not be sighted for hours at a time. Washdays were always on Mondays, except for days when Marie took on the task. Because of her business enterprise, she could only do the job on Sunday evenings.

Following her mother's rule of no work on the Sabbath, she would wait until the sun had set and then would don a *bathing suit*. No hope of a tan existed; she simply accepted the fact that her submersion in the chore of washing clothes with the wringer-washer would eventually lead to wet clothes on her body. Even in mid-winter, she wore the suit. Such behavior perhaps reduced the stress of the week for her, but the flamboyant act resembled the classic manner of the theater's Auntie Mame.

Not surprisingly, it was Marie who leased the house fifteen years after her father's death and turned it into a nest. Attempting to form a womb that would eventually shelter them all. She built her business with similar motives and eventually employed two of her sisters. Marie was also the first to move her husband into the house, encouraging her sisters to follow suit.

Immediately taking the reins at her father's death, she became the *patriarch* of the family rather than the feminine matriarch. Males were still the dominant heads of households in the twenties, and her aggressive personality fit such a role.

Marie had no children to help absorb her endless energy. No offspring of hers ever ran through the halls of the house. Though it was obvious to all that she adored children. Early in life, most likely when she assumed the mantle of patriarch, she accepted that motherhood could never be hers. With so much to do and watching her mother give birth every other year in a poverty-stricken home convinced Marie of the enormity of such choices. Impossible now to conclude that she *willfully* chose childlessness, it is known that she relied on her younger sister to shoulder a job Marie considered significant, in moderation. She had huge goals from the beginning of her patriarchy and that the nest would eventually nurture the second generation proved one of them. But motherhood would never be her role.

While encouraging the nest at every turn, her tastes and interests were different than her sisters. While they traveled, read, and discovered the new entertainment known as motion pictures, she chose dances, amusement parks, and circuses, places where things were constantly in motion, just as she was. The only teetotaler among the sisters, Marie eventually sold alcohol at her place of business, but spirits remained *hooch* to her and forever off-limits. For a time following the cigarette smoking rage of the thirties and forties, all the sisters—except Marie—smoked. But the thing that projected her into a whole different category, at least in her sisters' eyes, was her driver's license. She obtained it in 1925! Eventually sharing the dubious title *woman driver* with her youngest sister, Marie was the first among them to own a car.

When at last she could afford such luxury, she enjoyed dining out. And though she seemed to relax at such times, even this act proved only office talk. She liked to explore new foods on menus and enjoyed observing how others ran establishments similar to her own. Another pastime caught her fancy for a time when grocery stores began their climb to gigantic spaces. Marie excitedly food shopped for the house and her business; this was a job she could have delegated, but as with the laundry, the task reduced stress brought on by a drive that never rested. Her one demand, whether shopping for the house or for her business, was that all items be *fresh.* Whether eating at a new restaurant, shopping, or planning the menu at her enterprise, Marie always searched for fresh meats and produce. Undoubtedly this lifelong worry over freshness reflected the poverty of a youth where food, when available, was far from fresh.

Marie's opinions were as active and colored as her physical movements, both fueled by an extraordinary drive to succeed. Seldom keeping her convictions to herself, she disagreed most with her younger sister Rose, whom she always argued failed to move up the corporate ladder.

Rose, true to her namesake, mirrored Aunt Rosalie's sophistication. Forever advising residents of the house to *relax*, she displayed a calm demeanor that belied her own energy. She had excess energy to donate both to the needs of the house and her lifelong career. Getting jobs done absorbed her, so that others often labeled her *aloof,* but such was not the case with those who knew her well.

"God helps those who help themselves," Rose liked to quote. And then proceeded to complete the entire job with only spiritual assistance.

Though burdened by the same financial despair in the early years of her life as her older siblings, Rose possessed what they did not: the security of their determination; she knew that they would never allow their mother and the younger ones to go hungry so she had more latitude than they in her job search. Her work life took a different turn and cast her farther from home. Her siblings had been working for three years when Rose quit school to lessen the family's financial despair. But unlike them, she left her own prosperous city and sought work in the nearby metropolis of Pittsburgh, commuting daily by train to a large department store there. Though sales work of this kind is seldom seen as a career, it was a job that Rose took very seriously, working for the same company at the same job for many years. The store records show that when she left the job, she had taken no sick days, though she had used personal days—for family matters.

In the atmosphere of the large city, Rose's job endowed her with a lifestyle different than her sisters, if only during work hours. Cherishing her nightly return to the house, she had the sitting room, the favorite gathering place of all the residents, to comfort her after a long day's work.

Although difficult to conclude why a particular room in any home becomes a favorite, the sitting room lured them all. Squeezed between larger, otherwise forgotten rooms, it held a puzzling appeal. Appearing a space where the builder had run out of ideas, an area unaccounted for in the original plans, the sitting room by its size and location felt as though someone had been forced to wing it in the end. Hardly more than an unusually wide hallway, it became the choice of everyone during their free moments. Its strategic position next to the kitchen allowed for convenient snacks during conversations, and family members there could easily converse with those in the kitchen who, as Rose often did, ate their odd-hour meals there. Still, the sitting room's popularity remains puzzling, especially when compared with the large living room. Perhaps the childhoods of this first generation—spent as they were in cramped quarters—influenced them, and they forever gathered in the tiny room.

Her job in Pittsburgh reinforced the sophisticated persona that Rose had assumed. While in the large city, she pampered herself with personal services, in ways foreign to her sisters, who occasionally called her a snob. Her refined manner was forever evident in both appearance and personal choices, but curiously, her image was never expressed in material goods. Her minimal wardrobe, tucked away in the closet adjacent to her bedroom, comprised all her personal possessions. Content to live at the house with little that was solely hers, Rose declined to even decorate her bedroom, claiming to like the space just the way it was, with its old-fashioned, six foot windows that awkwardly opened across her bed.

"The best air-conditioning system in the world cannot match these windows on a hot summer's night," she often proclaimed in a casual salute to the house and all its oddities.

Most of her years in the department store, Rose sold coats. Although not professional by definition, the job became classy by her style. Managing honesty and a genuine interest in the needs of her customers, she offered them all a welcome lift as they walked away with their purchases. She cherished this life that allowed her to sharply divide work and home. And the unusual design evidently filled her needs, for she lived a long life. Daily, she commuted on the train—considered elegant transportation for the day—smoking the most expensive of cigarettes while casually chatting with professionals. She had her long nails and beautiful dark hair professionally done weekly—"intown." Her use of *intown* separated their own city and placed the metropolis in an exclusive category. And ruffled her sisters.

Rose's world was divided perfectly into halves. And though she maneuvered in both, friends found the lifestyle difficult to decipher. Why didn't she *move* to Pittsburgh, they wondered.

Rose did occasionally ponder over her destiny. Had things gotten confused and landed her in the wrong family? Whenever she said this aloud, she had a twinkle in her eye as though she had spoken in jest. But at times, she seriously wondered over fate. And though she never expressed a desire to leave the house, she seldom sat down to eat with the others, in those rare times when everyone was seated at the same table. Even cooking the entire meal on Sundays, her one day off from work, she found convenient reasons not to join in the repast. Though she made exceptions on Church holidays when the family ate in the spacious dining room. But with so many comings and goings at the house as well as the limited space at the kitchen table, her absence went unnoted and was finally taken for granted.

Unlike Marie who forever worried over the freshness of food, Rose's concern was quantity. To her, refined people ate small amounts, a simple rule that, for her, immediately excluded the future "All you can Eat" enticements.

Still, such differences hardly prohibited Rose from honoring family ties with both money and devotion. Lacking all hesitation, she even took on the family wash in the basement when necessary. Though never in her bathing suit.

And she was the best source of family history—the only one to ever speak of their brother Nathaniel or the fire. As the sole keeper of the scrapbook filled with significant family memorabilia,—their mother's ticket on the boat that brought her to the new country—Rose searched for her *place* in the family. Though at times, they labeled her snooty, she lovingly cared for her young nieces during the age of bathroom clashes. Enduring those squabbles with close-age siblings, bathing in the same tub.

CRCRCRCRCRCRCRCRCRCRCRCRCRCRCRCRCRCR

I remember these fights to be great fun, but looking back, they were surely frustrating for my patient aunt whom I called "Ro." Hardly sophisticated in the middle of these water battles between my sister and me, she volunteered for the chore after a day's work. Giving no thought to her newly manicured nails.

CRCRCRCRCRCRCRCRCRCRCRCRCRCRCRCRCRCR

During her paid vacations, Rose claimed a second glamorous city, Atlantic City. While her sister Anne *traveled,* demanding that the cost of her trips be returned through her personal education, Rose *vacationed,* insisting instead on luxury away from the routine of her life. Their mother had not known of either vacations or travel—those forays into the world of the middle class. But Anne and Rose had come to identify with Aunt Rosalie, who knew more of such pastimes.

Outwardly Rose had most in common with Anne, but inwardly she was drawn to Maggie, her younger sister closest to her in age.

Maggie, a shortened version of Margaret, was named after a saint, and the angelic origin proved correct; Margaret means pearl. The invaluable mainstay of the house, she had a prevailing presence there. Which, as these things often are, was taken for granted by her siblings. Her nurturing ways were available to all—except perhaps to her. She forever fretted over the well-being of the others, and as expected, it was Maggie who immediately took over the constant care of their dying mother, never leaving her bedside in the months preceding the certain death.

When Maggie was only twelve years old, it seemed to her that everyone in the family had suddenly left to assume paying jobs. Understanding that her father had left them forever,—he was now with God—she was too young to link the exodus of *five* family members with his death. Stunned by the serial events, Maggie quickly assumed responsibility for keeping house. And caring for a rowdy kid sister. As such traumatic happenings do, this period shaped her identity; the role she would play in life presented itself to her early. In adulthood, Maggie continued the caretaking duties she had assumed at twelve. With a work ethic that equaled her siblings, she assumed the non-paying job, and sometimes referred to herself as a *workhorse*, though never in a weary tone. She took pride in the work that focused on those at the house and eventually became the full-time housemother. Protecting them all in her maternal way, she carried concrete proof of the script on her left leg. A scar, obvious years later as a human bite, came about during a childhood fight, when Maggie stepped in to protect her sister.

The sister who moved back to the house with her husband when the tenants departed and the partitions fell, Maggie increased her family size to twelve in one swift stroke. During her mother's illness, she vaguely planned a return to the apartment that she shared with her husband. But in the end, the allure of the house proved too great.

In her twenties, she waitressed for a time at Marie's establishment and, for the first time, was paid for her hours of hard work. Her personality, good looks, and flair for clothes made Maggie the model for such work. Forever looking as though she had just *stepped out of a bandbox*—an old phrase for looking great—Maggie enjoyed both clothes and the shopping that naturally preceded them.

But what distinguished Maggie in the family was her attraction to *people*, which did not end with her waitressing job.

More social than her sisters, Maggie would stop to chat with distant acquaintances at every opportunity, never too busy to hear of their lives and share the feelings behind their words. Attracted to people of all sorts, she would have welcomed the use of her talents for entertaining guests in the home. But guests posed problems in the house where so many others lived. Also, each resident had their own schedule, and the resulting synchrony would have been disrupted by strangers, Maggie soon concluded.

How would have outsiders fit into the tiny sitting room that met the social and practical needs of the family? In addition to the sofa and two chairs—too few for a real gathering space—the sitting room held a small desk, though no evidence of bills or accounting of any sort ever appeared on or in it. The desk did sport a phone, the only one throughout the house of thirteen people. In addition to this surprising detail in a day when cell phones fill every other hand, the one telephone was wired into the wall! Like the house itself, the sitting room flowed on its own, visibly free of the world's accoutrements—and without the need for guests. So in the end, Maggie entertained no visitors. Instead, she used her energy for the good of the house, directing traffic and keeping a sense of order.

The romantic among the sisters, she found joy, and sometimes escape, in the new form of entertainment known as motion pictures. She could name any actor, regardless of their vintage and enjoyed seeing the same movie when it was later replayed on the even newer marvel of television. Long before movies became available on video, she excitedly watched the same *picture show*, as they were known then, on television—in the sitting room of the house.

Several years after moving to the house, Maggie suggested that the sisters have "a movie night out," and her idea caught on and turned into a commitment for everyone except Marie who, contrary to the others disliked the fictitious nature of movies. Neither friends nor partners of the four sisters were included in the weekly event, so the time guaranteed that the four would socialize with each other, catching up for the week, at a neutral gathering place. This delightful Thursday night tradition lasted for ten years.

Maggie's nature to herd her sisters together in the domestic harmony she cherished developed when two-thirds of the family suddenly left "for work". And by the time she reached adulthood, she was experienced at such endeavors. Her personality, a natural blend of her mother *and* Aunt Rosalie, proved a bridge that united the two groups into which the other four sisters had divided themselves. The two with personalities similar to Aunt Rosalie and the other two who were like their mother connected through Maggie.

In addition to the male stars of the silver screen, Maggie nurtured a practical side that freely expressed her attraction to the everyday human males who crossed her path. Her ultimate compliment was to label a man "the cat's meow." With a shy grin, she would add, "He can park his shoes under my bed any day." This rather risqué comment likely arose from the fact that gender stereotypes were beginning to crumble in the twenties. "Demure" ceased to be the only adjective that defined women; now they could at least *hint* of their attraction to the opposite sex.

Though her morals were too strong to allow for trysts, Maggie owned the fanciful bent among the sisters. In fact, at one point, she was literally *in* love with Love—a man whose given name was actually Love. Clark Gable, one of many leading men she found dashing and desirable, bore a likeness to Love. Which swayed her.

Watched over by Maggie in those early days of childhood, Billie was the "rowdy kid sister," and this fate created a bond between the two, which proved greater than the genes they shared.

Christened Helen at birth, after Saint Helena, Billie never used the name. More precisely, *others* never called her Helen; the name only served to meet Church standards. At least in 1914, a female could not be baptized in the Russian Church with a male name. But after four daughters and two sons, one of whom survived for less than two years, the family longed for a male. And during Anna's last pregnancy, they named the baby William—*before* the birth. The premature designation lasted a lifetime. "Billie", not a particularly feminine name but several notches above William, suited her personality.

But the reverse proved the case. It was the unusual name that directed who Billie was. Preceded in life by the name "William", she became the daring tomboy among the sisters. With such expectations *before* her birth, there should be no surprise in such an outcome. Billie reveled in challenges of any sort, and, befitting the last in a family of primarily females, her ardor often targeted her sisters. Forever attempting to convert them to her thinking, which often proved on the cutting edge, she overwhelmed them with her passions.

"Calm down, now. Lower your voice," even Marie, whom Billie was most like, would caution whenever her sister's fervor got out of hand.

"If you don't feel strongly about something, then anything can sway you." Billie would reply.

Still, her passionate nature created a strength of character that often comforted even strangers. When Billie assured someone that, "It will be all right," regardless of the circumstance, they immediately felt better, even when she had no new facts to support her claim. "How could anyone who felt so intensely be mistaken?" everyone reasoned about her support.

Though a reassuring presence to those in need, she had little patience for those she considered *namby-pamby*—people unwilling to throw their energies into pursuits of any sort. The nature of a goal mattered little to her; only the intensity behind the intent drew her attention. This lack of tolerance to those with less determination than Billie gave her a strong identification with Scarlett O'Hara, who became her heroine when *Gone With the Wind* made its debut at the end of the thirties. Once Scarlett made up her mind, she could conquer anything, an attitude consistent with Billie's own intensity. In this same resolute manner, when evidence of the harmful nature of cigarettes emerged in the sixties, she quickly stopped smoking. With neither slow withdrawal, patches, nor nicotine gum, she cut the habit from her life—in one day. In her philosophy, if something needed to be done, one did it without excuse. Though she still experienced life's pain to reach her goal, she managed to keep her eye on the ball rather than the difficulty.

But even *her* daredevil nature never allowed Billie to compete with her sister Marie. Daunted and awed by her older sister's drive for as long as she could remember, Billie concluded early that she had met her match in her second sister. She worked for Marie, even when she had to make a five hour commute—not a simple task. The job linked her to the house, even though she was the only family member who chose not to live there full-time. Her most rebellious act.

Filled with life, Billie drew others to her without effort. Throughout high school and the years before her marriage, she found herself surrounded by friends of both sexes. Her exploits were often accompanied by official dates with men, but locals never satisfied her desire for the exotic. Even friends were not among the necessities of her life. Her favorite activities, swimming and diving, were interests that satisfied her need to defy nature. Baseball held her interest through the local Pirates team until the players' strikes for higher salaries—unrealistic demands in Billie's mind—abruptly ended her fascination with the game. Angered by such greed, she lost interest in the team just as she did when her favorite singer, Bing Crosby, remarried too quickly after his wife's death. Her ideals would not be compromised, regardless of the appeal.

Living at the house only until she married, Anna's last child appeared to be the only one who would leave the nest. Marriage seemed the cut-off point for Billie, if not for her siblings. Though she was the rebel among the five sisters and her departure ought not be surprising, she was as devoted to the family as were the others. Whether for a long, summer vacation or a short Easter weekend, she packed her suitcases and made the round trip of five hundred miles to return to the house. Talk of her permanent return could often be heard among the family.

Andrew was eclipsed by his five sisters. Never their intention to deprive him of anything, they adored their brother and placed him on a pedestal, far above any role he might have assumed. In the middle, between two strong sisters in front and three bringing up the rear, he was forced to shape an identity—when all the good roles had already been taken; the charmer, the designer, the worldly, the nurturer, and the maverick had all been cast. He might have achieved status as the jock of the family and was captivated by baseball and fishing. But neither sport held the potential to earn a living in the thirties, so he took the obvious route to the steel mills of the city. And became a spectator. Though enabling him to contribute a regular paycheck to family life, the job held little chance for advancement and no glamour but kept him at the house in the company of his sisters.

The only boy among five girls at the start of the twentieth century when males were revered as the carriers of the surname, Andrew's gender defined him and made it unnecessary for him to work at achieving distinction in other areas. There was an unspoken agreement that he was valued as the family's crown *jewel,* the solitary brother who remained flawless while the sisters constantly found fault in each other. Eleven years old when his father died, the young man was left without a role model, surrounded by a strong-willed mother and five dynamic sisters.

Though unlikely that a wife would have doted on him as these six did, the theory was never tested; Andrew never took a wife. A wife would have demanded fidelity in marriage as well as other things, while his mother and sisters required little of him. But his family devotion equaled theirs and was evident in the affection that he showered on the second generation. Among his sisters, Andrew was the carefree bachelor who vacationed, fished, and reveled in the new car every few years. Like his sister Rose, who followed him in age, he was content to live with only his personal possessions at the house. Finally, with neither children nor memorable accomplishments, he was simply a good man who left no tracks—exactly as his father had failed to do.

To be fair, and laying aside the obvious circumstances of Andrew's life—the only boy and the middle child—the fact is that boys never fared well among either Anna or Rosalie's children. Between the two immigrant sisters, there were twelve offsprings, four of whom were male. And only Andrew reached middle age. Of the *second* generation in both families, there were ten girls and two boys, and neither boy reached the age of thirty. Such facts elude logic but mysteriously weave their way through the story.

Kate is difficult to place, though she lived in the house for fifty years. People always assumed that she was one of the family, the sixth sister or favored cousin. But she had no blood ties. Kate simply came to live at the house because ... she had been invited. Marie invited Kate to join them when she first rented the house. Before the move, Kate, herself one of fourteen children of immigrant parents, had lived in a tenement adjacent to Anna and her family. The tenement, the same size as Anna's, was tight for the family of sixteen, so Marie made the offer. Kate would later say that with so many children in her family, when she left at age sixteen, no one knew she was gone when she came to live at the house! Her presence pushed the number at the house up to eight. Contrary to the family's view that they now dwelt in a mansion, space was precious, though not as prized as it had been in the tenements. None of them had been accustomed to the luxury of privacy so sharing a bedroom with only one person, Kate quietly slipped into place.

She soon learned the unspoken rules that governed the space—such decisions as which direction to head when entering the front door where a choice to retreat occurred immediately; ascending the staircase at the entrance, privacy could be found. But remaining on the entrance level promised interaction with others in any of four rooms, but it was the kitchen or sitting room that generally won out.

The popular sitting room had the only door that led down into the large basement where Kate often helped Marie with laundry. The basement sported unique, horizontal doors—doors on the ground which could not be easily torn from their hinges during a storm. The doors had been built to ensure safety against high winds from either hurricane or tornado, though no such disaster had ever been recorded in western Pennsylvania. Less was known about weather patterns in the early part of the twentieth century, so the builder had installed the hurricane doors as a precaution—or perhaps as an interesting accessory.

When Marie and Kate tackled the chore on Sunday nights, hanging clothes outside ceased as an option, though air-dried laundry was always a first choice. Even in the sixties the house never held a clothes dryer.

Grateful for her keep and soon to work for Marie at the new business, Kate questioned nothing of her new home. The accommodations met her needs, in excess. Content with the agreement, she never married but remained at the house until Marie's death. The rules of her life remained simple; the person who had invited her was gone, so Kate, too, left.

The remaining residents came in *through the back door*, either through marriage or as members of the second generation in the new country. And their stories are now mingled with those of the five sisters.

4

The Friscos

Leaving their homeland with a certainty that they would never return, Anna and her younger sister Rosalie had only each other as vestiges of the old country. Both in their twenties, the sisters uprooted and transplanted themselves into the soil of an unfamiliar land. They lived in adjoining cities, but with neither driving skill nor vehicle, the sisters found the miles between them daunting. They had no telephones; in those days, phones were found in only wealthy homes, about eight percent of the population.

Particularly in the early phase of the sisters' new marriages, when babies immediately began to arrive, each longed for the familiar contact of the other. Each was all the other had of their family of origin, and uneducated, the two could not even turn to letter writing to bridge the short distance between them. So during their first years in the new country, they remained isolated from each another, as well as the larger community of Pittsburgh. The booming steel city lay only a short distance away but remained foreign to them both.

Focused on their young families in the strange land, the two had no spare time. But were without complaint. Children were a cherished part of their dreams. From early childhood, young women of the early twentieth century of European peasant stock viewed their future roles as mothers as blessed. Motherhood was their assumed and coveted state and the image that Anna and Rosalie held before them. Marriage meant the wondrous gift of children and financial security—but not companionship. An arranged marriage, such as both sisters had, was not fraught with doubts about compatibility. Their dream of a better life in the new country lay rooted only in their optimism for the future lives of their children.

Rosalie had left the homeland earlier and at a younger age than her sister. More anxious to experience the world than the pious Anna, she arrived in the new country to marry the stranger Michael Frisco, and by the end of the nineteenth century when Anna's boat docked in New York Harbor, Rosalie had already experienced two pregnancies. But neither pregnancy nor childbirth had come easily to this daring sister. Only after several miscarriages and two stillbirths did Rosalie produce five living children.

Following the protocol of the day, she gave the firstborn her own name, Americanized to Rose. And Rose was followed in time by Michael, Helen, Johnny, and finally Mary.

After the babies stopped arriving, Anna and Rosalie managed to meet, especially on Church holidays when they could afford the cost of the public streetcar. Greeting each other like lost, beloved friends, the sisters sat alone together and talked in their native Slavonic for hours. Though all eleven children understood and spoke their mothers' language, English was now the native speech of this first generation born in the new country. Nor were they interested in the protracted conversations of their mothers—conversations about the old country, a place that meant little to them.

Being the children of immigrants, the children had nothing to connect them to the people and places of their parents' childhoods. Except for Aunt Rosalie and her children, Anna's family had no relatives, ancestors or knowledge of places where their parents had experienced youthful exploits. Without the old country as a backdrop, life was curious to them so the cousins grew close to one another, feeling fortunate during these family visits. At last they had relatives, blood connections, links in *their* native land.

While the mothers talked, the cousins entertained one another and soon formed tight bonds. Their ages coincided and in a natural way affected each child's choice of a playmate. Anne, the oldest of Anna's children, grew close to her cousin Rose, the oldest of Rosalie's children. Anna's middle child, also named Rose, became inseparable from Helen, who occupied the same position in Rosalie's family. Mary, the youngest of Rosalie's brood harmonized with Billie, the youngest of Anna's children. Even Marie and Maggie, of a different sex than their matching-age cousins Michael and Johnny, formed tight friendships with the two boys. And these unions held elements of divine providence, which went unnoted in the carefree days of childhood.

Overnight visits between the sisters and their young families generally came about at Rosalie's initiative. Just as she had lead the way to the new country, Rosalie charted most events, particularly after finances improved with her second marriage. When the father of her children, like Anna's husband, died before his time, Rosalie remarried—this time *into money*. Mr. Fez's finances could hardly be characterized as a fortune, but relative to their own abject poverty, Anna's children now viewed their aunt as *wealthy*. Their measuring stick for wealth could only be calibrated by their life experience.

After marrying James Fez when her youngest child was five, Rosalie provided better accommodations for visits than her impoverished sister could. When Anna arrived at her sister's with six children, thanks to Mr. Fez's generous chauffeuring, they were entertained royally, at least so it seemed to her and her brood. The food was of a quality that she could not have afforded at home, and the Fez house contained *real* toys, not the old pans, empty spools of thread and stocking dolls that Anna's children had at home. Because the fifteen-mile trip was difficult to manage, the family spent at least one night at Rosalie's before returning home, which allowed the children more time together.

Even in their adult years, all of Anna's children held glittering memories of these childhood trips. But, unlike these fond remembrances, eventual events in their aunt's family were bitterly harsh. The destiny of Rosalie's children held heartbreak. Mickey, carrying his father's name as the first boy, was a sensitive, brooding boy from the start, and teachers complained to Rosalie that his melancholy ways interfered with his schooling. By the time he was in his teens, his stepfather had been part of his life for three years, and the relationship proved troublesome for both husband and stepson. James Fez, a business man with no patience for his stepson's pensive ways, had only reproach to offer the boy. And the rare conversations between Mickey and his stepfather could only be construed as arguments.

"I don't know what I was thinking about when she asked me about the readings," responded Mickey to Fez's inquiry.

"And how do you plan to earn a living with your mind forever in the clouds?" came the second question without hesitation.

"I don't know. I don't think about those things."

Mickey's head was bowed, and he could barely be heard. But Fez knew the reply. His stepson had no drive and would never amount to anything.

So went Mickey's tortured school years. And then he fell in love. Love fit his dreamy nature—until she jilted him. The desertion proved more than the sensitive young man could bear, and in deep depression, he was committed to a mental institution, not uncommon treatment for the emotionally troubled in 1925. Helped along by his family's frequent visits, Mickey managed to survive institutional care for a number of years. But finally, at the age of thirty-six, he took his own life. Though both immigrant families mourned the untimely death, it was Marie, his complement in Anna's family, who never overcame the horrific event.

At first, Mickey's younger brother Johnny appeared luckier. He was outgoing and happy, sailing through high school without problem. Securing steady work that enabled him to marry, Johnny became the father of two healthy daughters and was about to become a father for the third time at age twenty-six. But dying suddenly of an aneurysm, he never met his youngest daughter. Maggie, the cousin with whom he had shared so many happy days of childhood, showered the three little girls with attention, often pondering Johnny's death and the message as it wove itself into her own destiny.

Rosalie's third child Helen was beautiful by all cultural standards, and by the time she was fourteen, beaus were constantly at the front door. Sensual as well as attractive, Helen found herself pregnant at the budding age of fifteen. Similar to mental illness then, illegitimate pregnancy was simply not permitted and dealt with in a manner so covert that it often led to disaster. Helen died in childbirth and was buried in a bridal gown—with her child in her arms. Looked on as a final gift, the gown symbolized the coveted wedding the deceased would never claim. Such was the tradition of the Russian Church in 1925, as well as a culture that defined marriage as the prime goal of all women.

Helen's premature death overwhelmed the teenage Rose of Anna's family. When told of the event, Rose at first could not speak. Then the words finally came.

"I ... I don't understand. Helen's *my* age. She wasn't sick." It was obvious that Rose was traumatized. And to ease the torment after viewing her cousin in the casket, she fashioned a rule that would serve as a life guide.

Only Rosalie's oldest and youngest children, Rose and Mary, reached old age, married and bore children along the way. But even this road was marred for Mary whose only child, a boy, died within a few days of birth. Complications of the difficult labor rendered Mary barren for the remainder of her life. Finally, only Rosalie's oldest daughter saw her five children reach adulthood, but even she was not free of calamity. Rosalie, who had sacrificed everything for a dream, seemed to be shadowed by blight.

Their cousins' tragedies affected Anna's children as they remained bound together at the house.

1917–1945

5

The Patriarch

Marie entered ninth grade in 1917 and feeling the spirit of the times, she eagerly looked forward to high school. Like Marie, America was growing. Admitting seven hundred thousand immigrants that year, the majority from central Europe like her parents, the new country was growing too fast and began to set quotas to reduce the size of its welcome mat. Still, the ensuing decade proved an optimistic time that encouraged beginnings. The League of Nations, the Veterans Administration, the American Legion, and the Nineteenth Amendment were all to come into being in the infamous twenties. In the decade, the stock market would reach dazzling heights, and the 102-story Empire State Building appeared as humanity's first brush mark against the sky.

But Marie never finished even ninth grade that year—the year her father died. She was fourteen, and though learning absorbed her limitless energy, she quickly ended her formal schooling, midst neither discussion nor second thought about what she would do. Already with far more education than her parents, she could read and write at an acceptable level, had some accounting skills, and knew a bit of history. And she had something that could not be acquired in school. Will.

Immediately stepping in to replace her father as head of the family, Marie knew that she could rely on her older sister to help with food and rent. But she had come to view Anne as lacking in what Marie valued—*elbow grease*—the effort and energy required for the future she envisioned for her mother and younger siblings, ages three through eleven. As Marie saw it, Anne's undue concern over appearance and in seeing the world would waylay her. Other than money for rent and food, she would not be able to depend on her older sister for help.

Though disappointed to leave school, Marie became energized by the goal created by her father's death. She would ensure that the family had food and shelter, the immediate necessities of survival. Though such goals were daunting for a fourteen-year-old, even then she had a bigger plan—to lift them out of the poverty she had known her entire life.

At the time of her father's death, the family lived in the country, miles from the city that would eventually provide them with the house. Without suburbs, the residential choices were clear: country or city; in-betweens were unknown. For people like Marie who had known the country only from a vantage point of destitution, cities were alluring contrasts that glittered in their minds. And the population of America at the time seemed to concur with her preference. With nearly half of the new country now living in cities, the trend was toward urban life. Marie longed to move to the city; rural life and poverty had become one to her, tied in a tight knot. Even later, when circumstances changed, she never adopted the attitude of the social class that looked to *country life* for retreat. Five years after her father's death, she and her sister Anne had earned enough to move the immigrant family to the city, where in the early twenties, both public transportation and well paying jobs flourished. And their choices increased tenfold.

They moved to the small city that would evermore be home and the eventual birthplace of the family's second generation.

Though unable in the beginning to afford anything but tenement life on First Street, Marie was elated by this change that her fighting instinct had inspired. She had left country life and, hopefully, poverty behind forever. As could be assumed from such simple things as street markings in the city, life would now be different for the family. Unlike country life where roads remained unpaved and unmarked, the streets of the wondrous city sported *names*—names that followed the lines of social class. The rows of identical tenements on First Street were part of the First Ward, a designation made by the city for schools and voting, and clearly the poorest section of the city, its slums. *Fifth* Avenue, the commercial heart of the city, was the dividing line even as railroad tracks are in fiction and occasionally in reality. Though her family resided now on *the wrong side of the tracks on*

First Street, Marie's dream was to someday move them to the hill section of the city, where the residences were clearly above the fray.

The monumental move had required Anne and Marie to work at menial tasks of packing and delivering items of all sorts—the kind of work that the untrained do. Later moving into domestic work like their mother, the sisters felt grateful to carry home a dollar between them each day, money that went toward food and shelter for the seven.

Assuming the paternal role, Marie often sacrificed her own dinner for the others. Wandering late in the evening to the black church in the same poor section where she lived, Marie was always welcomed with an offer of food. Though never admitting it even to herself, she was begging—from people who because of their race had been relegated to an even lower class of society than she. But they were kind, and she was hungry.

Finally at twenty-one, Marie was old enough for training in the city's local factory, known as a "sweatshops" for obvious reasons, where she would sew garments. Thrilled at this rise in the world, she quickly mastered the sewing machine and was able to turn out apparel at a rate that increased her salary to a dollar a day, doubling her previous wage. Satisfied with the boost, she was far from content; her dreams exceeded the pay increase. But the raise did allow her a few extra cents for her own pleasure, the local dance hall. The one luxury she allowed herself.

She loved dance of all kinds and quickly learned the energetic new step known as The Charleston. To do The Charleston, one hopped with turned-in knees and toes shifting weight from leg to leg with exuberant kicks and movement of hands and arms! The dance, whose exciting rhythm had been unknown until now among Caucasians, expressed the vibrating times that Marie felt within herself.

The salary hike also energized her dream of someday owning a business. Scouring the city for ideas on her long walks home from the factory, she pondered the kind of business she might one day own. and finally she arrived at a choice—food service. With real hunger pangs in her gut, her thoughts dwelt, for good reason, on food during the lonely walks. What grew from her own need evolved into an awareness of the times; restaurants were becoming more popular as the economy of the small city rocketed in the excesses of the twenties. Like the stock market, the service industry was on the rise. Eating out was now a choice for a certain class of people, and Marie's creative side recognized the financial potential of the new pastime. The insight took time to arrive; food on the table was a luxury for her family and going out to eat went beyond her worldview. But walking home from the factory hungry each night, certain that the people at the black church would again welcome her, Marie made a decision. Someday she would own a restaurant.

But the questions that followed such a resolution were more difficult to answer. How was such an endeavor possible? She had no experience running a business of any sort, and the chances of amassing a savings in her present circumstances looked dim. Every cent from the factory job went into the household—with one exception: the local dance hall. She refused to increase the nickel a week admittance price. Did this young woman, who had at age fifteen felt responsible for a family of seven, possess the grit to carry her this far? That remained the real question.

After working at the factory for three years, Marie secured a job that allowed her to begin saving. As a *girl Friday,* she began to work in Dr. Sunstein's office. Of course she had no formal medical training, but physicians were not yet specialized and still making house calls then. The office needs varied, and the good doctors themselves trained their own medical assistants. Marie had a wide variety of tasks. She kept the waiting room orderly; sterilizing and storing instruments in the large examining room, answering the phone, keeping the books, and the doctor's schedule, she was busy. Her job, like Dr. Sunstein's, was far from specialized. With a weekly salary now of $25, she began to put aside extra money in an old silk stocking. (Nylon was seven years in the future.)

Empowered by the stocking's visible growth, she became unstoppable in the quest she had begun at her father's death.

In addition to his new assistant's dedication and hard work, the good doctor also profited by the new patients she brought with her. He became Marie's *family* doctor, thereby holding a renowned position in the family for the next thirty years. With seven home births and two deaths behind them without medical assistance, the family knew how to tough it out when illness struck; when Dr. Sunstein entered their lives, everyone was healthy. But working for the doctor, Marie began to see medical care as important as food and shelter. Though such care was not as basic a need as the other two, it seemed part of her paternal duty to consider a doctor, who would develop a sense of the whole family and quickly come to their home if needed. Such a decision had nothing to do with health insurance. Except for the life insurance policies her mother had bought, the family had never considered insurance of any kind—and never would. In those days, even her brother at the steel mill had no such benefit as health insurance.

Mostly, Marie liked the social implication of a "family doctor". Having one placed them on the next rung of the social ladder. Though at that time they remained in the tenement on First Street, with their own doctor, they could now be considered "working class."

At first this bothered Anne, the oldest sister whose financial contributions to family life equaled Marie's.

"I think this is silly; who needs a family doctor? Why do *we*?" Though challenging her sister's decision, Anne never raised her voice, not even in anger.

"It's a good idea," Marie said. "Just take my word for it, like you did about the move into the city."

"But I don't get sick, and neither do you ... or anyone else in our family. The babies have stopped coming. We've gotten by this long without a family doctor! Without *any* doctor. I think you want this for show, Marie. You've always been a show-off."

"I know that we need to have a doctor in the wings. If we don't call him, and he charges us something to be available, it will come out of my paycheck. I swear."

"You care too much about what people think, Marie; what *class* the family's in. Just *act* classy ... stop that swearing you do too often. That's all that matters." In the end, Marie won the discussion, as the matter failed to hold her older sister's interest.

Encouraged by the shifts in her life, which included the growing silk stocking and an end to the begging, Marie's thoughts turned to practical matters: driving a car. She would need transportation if she were someday to own a business. Though walking home from work through the city had become second nature to her, the hike to the local dance hall—five miles one way—required too much of her time. On occasion, others who shared her excitement over dance offered her rides. But the fact that women drivers were a rare sight in 1925 galvanized her determined nature. And soon a driver's license became another goal.

At the time, budding drivers learned from seasoned ones and then passed the state-required test. Such things as learner's permits, driver's manuals, and driver's education were unknown in the twenties. With no manual to study, novices learned from the vantage point of the passenger seat, until they felt comfortable taking the wheel. Once Marie decided she needed a license, she convinced a friend who had driven her to the dance hall to help. Having his new student intently mark his actions—and pay for the gas—the young man set out to educate the beginner. But he was far from seasoned. Her teacher had spent most of his time behind the wheel on joyrides—a word that expressed the public's excitement over the automobile, which at the time had only been around for twenty-five years. Attempting to explain certain actions to Marie one day, at a speed more consistent with a joyride than lessons, her instructor was forced to make a sudden stop that threw his pupil against the windshield with a force that shattered the glass.

In the end, Marie got her license without further incident, but was left with a lifelong token of the experience; the last two fingers of her left hand remained forever folded towards the palm of her hand. The tendons in these fingers, which included her ring finger, had been severed by the broken glass and required immediate attention. Which she failed to get. Even with the newly acquired family physician, she refused to seek the help the injury required. Dr. Sunstein eventually looked at the fingers, but his assistance arrived too late to restore her left hand to its normal state.

As with many happenings in her life, Marie trivialized this with a remark typical of those with which she closed the discussion on many matters. "It will be fine."

"Why didn't you call me sooner?" the dismayed doctor asked.

But after a year, he knew his employee. She allowed no attention for what she classified as minor. Her goals, and the energy they required, outranked everything else.

Though delighted with the precious driver's license, Marie knew that she would have to postpone owning a car, even a jalopy. Even with her office job, a full stomach, and now a family doctor, she understood that some dreams had to remain in the elevated category of *someday*. And for the moment, things were good. This ability to rank her desires and delay those at the bottom of the list were strengths Marie had learned as a child. Early, she had discovered that by waiting for certain things, the possibility of greater results increased, all part of the self-discipline that she had learned through poverty and the Russian Church. Though Marie was a reluctant churchgoer, her mother had forced her to regularly attend Mass, as she had the others. So now, even with the new license, Marie put off any thoughts of either owning a car or increasing her nights at the dance hall and continued her three-mile walk between their tenement and the doctor's office each day.

But the walks accomplished more than transport. As she walked, Marie's dream took form, and she began to search for a space she might purchase with her stocking savings. Eventually, she stumbled upon the ideal location—a small newspaper stand. Aside from the selling price of three thousand dollars, an achievable amount for her banker—the silk stocking—the stand had potential. Well situated near one of the entrance/exits of the city's steel mill, the site fit the fast food image she carried in her thoughts. (In the twenties, the phrase *fast food* was unknown.)

Three of her siblings had increased their contributions to the household, enabling Marie to now save more, and ten years after her father's death, the stocking held the necessary payment. In 1927, she bought the newsstand that would become the business that had filled her thoughts for five years. Carrying the asking price in cash to the seller, she was overcome by a feeling that she had never experienced in her twenty-five years of life. Pure ecstasy.

Unhampered by her lack of business experience, Marie became inspired by a well of creative energy that overflowed with plans. She invented a simple menu for the enterprise: quality hamburgers made to order, French fries, coffee, soda pop, and penny candy. Her idea in 1927 to keep the menu small and basic was born in the predawn of the fast food era, thirty years ahead of Ray Kroc's idea to found McDonalds!

In the new business, there would be a few non-food items: tobacco, newspapers, magazines, and the popular comic books of the time. These items leftover from the newsstand from which her business evolved seemed suitable to the establishment. And punchboards soon beckoned to color the countertop. Quickly Marie recognized that her future customers, the blue-collar workers of the small city outside of Pittsburgh, sustained a gambling bent fueled by the hope of instant riches. Her business sense catered to their interest through the punchboard, which, unlike some forms of gambling, was legal. Such boards were profitable to small business owners and easily purchased at the local candy warehouse.

Generally eight-inch square, punchboards contained small holes, each with a tiny slip of paper hidden within. Players would buy a chance to punch out the paper where monetary amounts were printed, though the slips could also be blank. Having paid ten cents for one punch in the colorful board, the customer used a key similar to those attached to sardine cans to force out the paper sealed in one of the hundred possibilities. The player then collected from the owner. Such a lottery cost Marie $5 at the wholesaler and with total payouts of $15, had the potential for a $50 return. Several boards adorned the counter at all times.

Though never discussing the matter with others, Marie sensed that the culture shift of the twenties favored her endeavor. Breaking old bonds, women were testing their newfound wings. The metaphor became literal when Amelia Earhart flew across the Atlantic—the first woman to accomplish the feat, only a year behind Lindberg.

She now owned a small business of an ideal size for learning the trade. With four tiny tables where customers could *eat-in*, or if the occasion called for haste, *take-out*,—still other phrases unknown at the time. Though the square footage of the establishment was small, the haven offered patrons an opportunity to relax and dissolve their day-to-day realities through food, reading, and gambling. Milkshakes were added a year after opening as they seemed the only deficit in her scheme.

What Marie did not know about such an undertaking, she learned through mistakes and a willingness to work hard through long days. Not unusual for her to be on her feet for seventeen hours straight, she never stopped to give it much thought.

"I'll be fine," she said when the painful varicose veins appeared. Knowing they were a direct result of the unending hours on her feet, she had no intention of calling Dr. Sunstein. Her dream had nearly materialized, and two years later, she reached her goal. With a booming enterprise, she bought a used car. And rented the house.

The family left First Street forever. Having lived in cramped quarters their entire lives, her mother and siblings immediately saw the house as a palace. But their needs were modest. They had never known anything but outhouses—and the house had two toilets! Though three of Marie's siblings now had ample incomes, none considered residences of their own. Their security came from *family*; the uncertainty their parents had faced in the new land had created anxiety, although to admit such sentiment would have been just short of blasphemy for all six. Contributing to food and rent, the working sisters and brother continued to dwell together just as they had in the past, though now in a more spacious atmosphere. Marie insisted that her mother stop housecleaning in the homes of the wealthy, and her two youngest sisters were left with the luxury of completing high school, not a common accomplishment at the time.

The wondrous fulfillment of Marie's dream encouraged her to enlarge it. Nine years after leasing the house, she bought a *second* business. Her initial strategy had never included such a leap, but, as though by destiny, a large café adjacent to the hamburger stand became available, at just the right moment. When the owner of the establishment died suddenly of a heart attack, his stricken wife would not consider a tie to the business, which she believed had felled her husband before his time. The widow offered it for sale at one of those rare prices that requires little consideration by a potential buyer. Marie, who was literally next door when the tragedy occurred, recognized the bargain and quickly made an offer. Eleven years as a successful businesswoman had reinforced an inner confidence that she never really lacked.

Now she was ready to run *two* restaurants, keeping the original and calling it "the little store." The two businesses shared a wall, so she hired carpenters to cut through, making an enhanced menu available to those who rejected a leisurely dinner in her new restaurant. Customers could now have a full meal at the counter of "the little store" or take the food home. But enlarging the options at the little store did little to increase its gross. In fact, it never approached its past success, but Marie clutched sentimental ties to this, her first endeavor. And its gross proved unimportant.

Although the large tiled sign above the new restaurant—Leonard's Café—heralded the name of the previous owner and remained on all legal papers, Marie's new business became known popularly as *The Joint*. The Joint—an odd title that connoted a place of less class than the restaurant actually possessed. But unlike the little store, alcohol would be served here, and—though prohibition had been cancelled five years before—words such as *speakeasy* and *after-hours joint* remained, revealing mixed feelings about intoxicating beverages still held in the society. Used freely by her family in the beginning, the curious name soon caught on with patrons. *Joint* stuck, and without objection, Marie accepted the name that soon became indelibly written in the minds of her patrons. She welcomed the fact that serving alcohol and a variety of full-course dinners in this new space created a different atmosphere, a classier "joint" than the little store.

Though refusing alcohol herself, Marie could not overlook its monetary potential, especially in a culture that had begun to entertain itself through dining out.

In these busy times, she allowed herself one distraction. Just as she had once smuggled in the joys of the dance hall, she now found time for her new niece. Though not living at the house, as Marie had hoped at the child's birth, the little girl charmed her aunt from the beginning. Marie became the godmother, a role of honor and responsibility in the Russian Church. With the means now to buy the delightful toys and frilly clothes that she herself never had as a child, she gave the child every spare moment, as well as many she had to steal. When the little girl's parents made the move to another state, Marie left The Joint for the first time to make the eight-hour trip to their new residence.

ৡৡৡৡৡৡৡৡৡৡৡৡৡৡৡৡ

I have the honor of being this niece—the first of the second generation as well as the first child in the family delivered by Dr. Sunstein. Of course the delivery took place in the local hospital, but as a young child, I often went to his office where my aunt had once worked—and stuffed as much of her pay as she could afford into the silk stocking. The family had so much faith in the family doctor, the simple smell of the medicines mixed with the leather furniture in his office would comfort me today. Such was the message of trust I was given about this medicine man.

But my time with Mame came later than those days she spent working so hard to fill the silk stocking. By the time I came along, she had the money to introduce me to all the youthful thrills that she herself had missed. Daring, she knew what would fascinate children and joined in the fun, never defending herself with the common adult excuse, "I'm too old for that."

I found her choices wondrous and forever wanted to go with Aunt Mamie, as I called her. Living out the childhood that had never known such places, she never missed the fairs and circuses that came to the city and rode *all* the rides at the large amusement park with me. Kennywood Park, well known in its day, remains in the twenty-first century as a model for brazen thrills. Relaxed at least for her in these moments at Kennywood, Mame preferred the three deadly roller coasters for which the large park was famous: The Jack Rabbit, The Whip, and The Racer, each of which was named according to its specialty. The Jack Rabbit had the highest dips The Whip, the wickedest turns and The Racer, the greatest speed.

I anxiously awaited the time that I would finally be tall enough to ride The Racer, which was considered the least frightening of the treacherous trio. Finally, not quite of school age, I proudly boarded the two-seater car with my bold aunt beside me. She had no qualms about the endeavor, actually encouraging me as I marched to this milestone in my life. But I cannot recall much beyond the first dip when my terror made me grab her with such force that her brassiere snapped, exposing her breast, and our two sweaters flew from the car. Over the years, she and I often laughed over my initiation to the stomach-falling thrill of the rides she loved. And the incident failed to eliminate future rides for either of us.

ഇന്ദ്രഇന്ദ്രഇന്ദ്രഇന്ദ്രഇന്ദ്രഇന്ദ്രഇന്ദ്രഇന്ദ്രഇന്ദ്രഇന്ദ്ര

When Marie bought The Joint, she was thirty-five years old and appeared a spinster. Though she had eloped with Eddie seven years earlier. Reluctant to formally bring him into either the family or her business, she insisted on keeping the marriage secret. Even after the announcement was finally made to family and friends, Marie and Eddie lived separately, and he kept his job at the local steel mill. Her allegiance remained with her mother and siblings. Like most immigrants, "blood is thicker than water," was more than an intriguing adage; it was a fact of life. So from the beginning, Eddie took the back seat in her life. The two had met when he stopped by the little store on his way to the mill one day, and Marie took the time to chat with the attractive young man. Also a good dancer, Eddie soon realized that dancing dwelt in both their hearts. Though never formally meeting at the dance hall, each recognized the other the day he wandered into the little store for a quick lunch.

Aside from his good looks and dancing ability, Eddie had more than his share of a quality Marie lacked. With a quick wit, he could joke about the heartaches that accompany living. Taking life less seriously than she, Eddie was less driven. Though Marie saw this from the start, he made her laugh in ways she could not remember doing—ever.

Charming her in simple ways, he would ask in his lighthearted manner, "What would my Mamie like to do tonight?"

With his arm around her shoulder and eyes searching hers, he often posed the question. Though she had never desired to *belong* to anyone, his attention flattered her, and the thought of someone caring for *her* needs proved intoxicating. His flirtatious way took them through a romantic, though hectic, year-long courtship—hectic because even as they courted, Marie continued to work at making the little store thrive. And finally she consented to his marriage proposal.

From the beginning, she harbored no interest in an equal business partner. Succeeding so far with great independence, she was a woman who had raised herself from poverty in a classic bootstrap fashion. In 1930, when she married Eddie, Marie had a driver's license, a car, a business, and a comfortable living arrangement with her mother and siblings—an arrangement that she, the patriarch of the family had secured. Alone. For a woman of poor immigrant parents, it was an astonishing feat that she had accomplished through gut instinct—and a silk stocking. She had decided long ago that matters were in her hands, and though now flattered by the handsome man who asked to marry her, she never fully trusted either his business sense or his intentions. During the courtship, she overlooked Eddie's careless disregard for money and pondered his place in her business endeavor.

Hardly naive about her looks, Marie often compared herself to her four more attractive sisters and wondered if Eddie's attention was genuine. Though she could not be considered wealthy at this point in her life, she had more financial assets than he and had heard of men who were labeled *fortune hunters*. But the times frowned on spinsterhood, considering it a failing for women regardless of their other achievements. And *failure* hardly fit Marie. So she married the enchanting man who made her laugh as he expertly swirled her across the dance floor.

Contrary to the convention of the time, Marie remained the business-woman of the family while Eddie stood at a distance from the little store and dutifully took his shifts at the steel mill.

But The Joint changed matters. With a huge bar that accounted for fifty percent of the physical space and sixty percent of the gross, the new business forced Marie to adjust her thinking. Though Eddie, like Marie, abstained from alcohol in any form, she conceded the bar to the masculine domain. Undoubtedly, she would have managed the bar herself had she not married, but she now designated a piece of her world to him, opening a working space for her husband of eight years. The dining area of The Joint became her post, and Eddie entered the business by managing the bar. Concluding from the beginning that the size of her newest endeavor required two minds, she was far less sure of his.

The two were constantly busy. As a businessman, Eddie had entered a different world than the one he had known as a mill worker. He had much catching up to do while she designed the details of a menu for leisurely dining—a menu much different than the little store.

Once the marriage announcement was made, they finally lived together at the house but spent little time there—or anywhere else but The Joint. Not surprising that for a long time Marie never knew that her husband enjoyed cooking—as well as indulging in sweets—such a fact finally emerged, and his territory at The Joint expanded to include a part of the kitchen where he happily made his own version of vegetable soup on Sunday nights.

Of course, unlike the little store where Marie, and her younger sisters, took shifts and did the cooking along with many other chores, the new restaurant required permanent cooks. Though she and Eddie continued to fill in for a wide variety of jobs, she happily hired full-time employees. Within two years, The Joint had three full-time bartenders, three cooks, and five waitresses.

The new business did so well that Eddie proposed that the couple take an overdue honeymoon. After nine years of marriage, Eddie, using all his persuasive powers on his reluctant wife, finally won out. They traveled to the New York World's Fair of 1939. An easy drive, the extravaganza proved even more exciting than its billing. The facts about foreign countries and the innovations of the last decades transported Marie back to the school days that she had been forced to abort. For the first time she resented the sacrifices that had caused her to miss this official learning period. But she quickly overcame the feeling and entered the excitement of the moment with her spouse. She had never seen anything to compare to this event and was grateful to Eddie for his insistence on a trip that had nothing to do with business.

The next four years were busy, exciting ones for Marie. Though she still found relaxation difficult, things were, as she liked to say, *hunky-dory*—just fine in ordinary vernacular. She and Eddie lived at the house, and if it was a difficult arrangement for him, he never complained. The truth was that neither of them was there most of the time, arriving only to fall into bed each night at three o'clock in the morning after closing The Joint. Even though The Joint was closed on Sundays, its owners were there all day, seeing that things were clean and orderly for the upcoming week. Nine o'clock Monday morning, it would all begin again: one hundred hour, seven-day weeks for the couple. Both were so busy building the business, they failed to notice that neither mentioned dancing anymore; such moments were behind them forever.

Fortunately, the budding business thrilled them both.

Just as Marie began to feel comfortable sharing the responsibilities of the two businesses with her husband, America entered World War II, and Eddie was drafted. But unlike most wives at the time, unable to adjust to such a disruption in their lives, she understood how to manage—even *two* businesses—without a spouse. Even as the country made necessary changes, allowing women in factories to do what had always been men's work, Marie did what she had always done in the past, used her elbow grease. The bar side of The Joint, Eddie's domain, took some learning for her, but hiring two bartenders who were beyond the age limit of the draft, she also mastered the art of tending bar herself. Never bowing to feminine shyness, Marie held fast to what she knew needed to be done.

But in the end, Eddie's absence did trouble her in ways that had nothing to do with The Joint. She missed her husband. Stationed in France where the fighting was fierce, he had a chance of serious injury—at the least. Faced with the cold fact that she had taken him for granted all through the marriage, Marie planned on changes in the union on his return.

6

The Sophisticate

Rose's earliest memory was of walking along with her father at age seven. That wondrous age when children begin logical thinking.

Turning to her, he said, "You're my little princess."

As often happens with early memories, the image and his words became one of her lifetime guides. His simple statement meant something beyond a father's pride. And painted a picture of refinement for the little girl. At the age when children begin this process of reasoning, Rose was baffled by her father's words. Never having books of her own as a child, she learned at school that royalty lived in *palaces*, very different than the dwellings she had experienced in her short life. As her seven years had been spent in crowded dwellings, his words—meant as a compliment—haunted her. And she tried in vain to understand how life had somehow become so confused.

Her father died two years later, never to clarify his words. So Rose replayed the odd scene and remained puzzled about her destiny, even as an adult. Where did she fit into this family of immigrants, who occasionally used profanity and failed to exhibit anything which even approached royal behavior? Though brooding over her fate when her sisters raised their voices, sometimes swearing at each other, she held to her family allegiance—but the unanswered question remained.

The middle child in the family, she continued in school for six years after his death. Then at fifteen, just as her older siblings had done, she promptly quit to help with finances. Under her sister Marie's direction, the family moved to the city where Rose joined the work force. Like Marie, she was delighted to leave country life behind. "Country" meant lonely poverty to her too; one of the few issues she agreed upon with

Marie. The move also made it easier to find a better job in this small city, with its dazzling steel mills, on the verge of an economic boom. For a year, Rose worked at odd jobs until a friend mentioned that the burgeoning department stores in the nearby city of Pittsburgh were *hiring*.

The simple fact changed her life.

Rejecting the examples set by her three older siblings who without transportation of their own had secured local employment, Rose ruled out *walking distance* as a condition in her job hunt. Different than modern times, "walking distance" then was defined as five miles, and Pittsburgh exceeded even this number, huge by today's standards. The metropolis that lay beyond a reasonable walk offered Rose exactly what she had long sought, an identity separate from her family. The chance for a sophisticated image. And public transportation between the two cities proved simple. So she followed her friend's casual remark and was quickly hired as part-time help in one of Pittsburgh's largest department stores.

Within a year, the store managers recognized her potential and offered her a full-time job that included benefits, something even her older sisters lacked in their work. Attractive—and as well-dressed as her finances allowed—Rose communicated style and grace to customers. She forced the supervisor to take note of her commitment by never missing work, for any reason. Ecstatic over the full-time job, she fondly recalled the day the proposal was made as, "The happiest of my life."

Ironically, the same year also delivered tragedy for Rose—as though the gods required a balance between the good and bad in life. Her beloved cousin Helen died just as the two girls turned sixteen. Though Rose clung to the excitement of her new job throughout the funeral, even this joy could not lighten Helen's sudden death. Gazing at Helen in bridal regalia in her casket, a Church custom for unmarried women, Rose became hysterical. The bizarre nature of the scene was enhanced by the fact that Helen also held her dead child, and it proved too much for the sixteen-year-old viewing the remains. Slapping her to restore emotional control, Anna later chided her daughter for questioning, through her outburst, God's judgment in Helen's death.

Rose never again displayed such emotion, arriving that day with a tenet that remained with her for life. *Change occurs more quickly than humans can absorb so it's best not to pursue it.... and to travel lightly in this life.* At Helen's death, she vowed to hold tightly to the important pieces of her life. And not to acquire new ones.

The reason for such a profound decision at so young an age was not without precedent for Rose. Helen's death proved the *third* abrupt turn that she had experienced in her short life. When she was four years old, her young brother, closest to her in age and only two at the time, unexpectedly died from the ravages of a high fever as Rose and her mother attempted to reduce his body temperature with a cool bath. The family had no medical help and such a death was not uncommon among the poor. Two years later, their small dwelling caught fire and burned to the ground in less than an hour as Rose, alone and horrified, helplessly watched from a distance. Now with Helen's death added to the other terrifying events, she convinced herself of the fragile nature of life. At age sixteen, she would make her life as fixed as possible.... and play it safe.

The gift of the job in the big city dazzled her. Pittsburgh, more cultured than her own city, offered a chance to display the refinement that she had always felt inside herself—perhaps begun when her father called her his princess so many years ago. And the commute proved simple. With neither driver's license nor car, she depended on public transportation—streetcars in the beginning. Later a commuter train came into being, and as the more elegant of the two modes, it became her immediate choice. While the streetcar ride was bumpy, hot in the summer, long with multiple stops, and a bit dusty, the train was clean, fast, and air-conditioned, and the roundtrip took only an hour of her day. Of course the cost between the two reflected the differences, but Rose absorbed the extra cost without a second thought. Her sisters found this a wasteful choice and criticized her for her lack of thrift.

Billie began the discussion. "So the streetcar takes longer. Just get up earlier."

Anne, in her shocked manner, added her own brand of humor. "A difference of fifty cents a day between the train and the streetcar adds up. Rose, that's three dollars a week you'd be saving! I like convenience too, but $156 worth of it a year?"

But their disapproval had no effect. Rose quickly learned that *professional* people rode the train while a different class frequented the streetcars. For the first time, social class came into focus for her. Knowing that her family stood low on the social ladder, she saw only two ways to climb into a higher class—education or money. Money could come through a marriage, particularly for women, or through work. In a different time, she would likely have considered more education, but the new country was now deep in the Great Depression. And, as a member of a first generation of poor immigrants, Rose could not allow herself to hope for an education. Like her older siblings, she had quit school at sixteen to help with family finances. Working hard, the four had raised themselves above survival, and nest eggs had become important to them all.

"Save for the rainy day" was a family message. The family had known many such days. And their vulnerability at the loss of the breadwinner would not be repeated if they carefully put money aside for the future.

Aunt Rosalie, Rose's namesake, had followed the trend of the times and with her second husband, had married into money. Though she had been Rose's role model from the beginning, Rosalie's repeated pregnancies in both marriages and Helen's horrible death, convinced Rose to postpone the marriage part of her aunt's path ... at least for the time being. Money to guarantee both security and social class, she concluded, could be acquired through her own hard work. And she now held a job that she adored. Determined that in time her job would weave magic, she became even more attached to it.

In the twenties, most women were married by the time they reached twenty. Slightly beyond this cultural landmark now, Rose was not searching for a wealthy partner. Unmarried, her older sisters were doing fine. Anne had recently earned a license from a local trade school, and Marie, with an office job, planned to someday own a restaurant. But their career decisions held little allure for the third sister. Looking forward to the day she could afford to have others wait on *her*, Rose found her job as a sales-woman in a large city consistent with the image she held of herself. Rather than *serving* others, she was a clothes *consultant*.

In her mind, the job offered Rose the chance to develop a refinement that felt natural to her. And the daily commute allowed her both worlds: the classiness of the large city and the security of family. Her older siblings were working to support their mother while the two youngest sisters remained in school, and Rose followed suit with no plans to break these patterns that defined the bonds of blood. With an instinct so natural to immigrants, Anna had instilled family devotion in her children.

Though determined to live all family messages, which prescribed behavior in a subtle way, Rose would do it in her style.

When she assumed her cherished job, large department stores had just launched their fifty-year run of popularity in America; their heyday had begun. Her store had eighty different departments, and as a full-time employee, she moved for two years from one section to the other in the large building. Throughout the transitions, Marie encouraged her sister to become more aggressive and seek the elevated title of "buyer".

"You've worked at that store for nearly three years. You must have a sense of every department now. Let them know which department interests you and take charge! As the buyer of a department, you'll have *standing.*" Marie's counsel was anything but new to Rose.

"I'm not in a big hurry," she said. "I don't rush all the time like you."

"I don't understand how you can take orders from people who are less able than you."

As Marie's voice began to rise, Rose frowned. Conversations between the two forever reached an impasse.

Though Rose would have welcomed a higher salary, her competitive spirit was more about style. When finally offered the job of buyer, so esteemed by her sister, she turned it down. She disliked the idea of clerks working under her. Her princess image was a personal one and failed to include directing others, which would surely come with the title of Store Buyer. And that would mean change.

Even without the elevated title that her sister argued would place her in a higher work and social category, Rose felt connected to the store. Considering the department store's size, she was a small cog in the machinery; one of five hundred full-time employees, plus the many extras added at Christmas and through the summer. But she saw herself as an intimate part of a system. The owner of the store was a public relations genius who made himself known to his employees, often wandering through the store calling each of the hundreds of workers by their first names. Understanding the advantage of personnel who felt closely linked to the enterprise, he often invited entire departments to his elaborate city apartment to meet his family. Not some distant CEO, the man was accessible, and Rose felt part of an extended family.

After working throughout the large store for several years, she alighted on what proved her ideal department. This department was different than the Women's Housedresses, where she had turned down the title of buyer. (Housedresses, printed cotton dresses no longer in style, were popular in the days when women did not wear jeans and required something other than their Sunday best for housework duties.) Such apparel hardly fit Rose's style, and influenced her refusal to take on the responsibility encouraged by Marie. After twelve years in the store, she became a permanent salesperson in the Women's Suits and Coats department. Not only did this fit her formal taste in clothes, it offered commission on all sales. Her income soared, and even Marie admitted that her sister's choices were far from dire.

Wanting the security of savings as well as the class that money could buy, Rose regularly placed her extra cash in a special investment account that the store endorsed. Through no fault of her employer, the stock market crash that set the stage for the thirties wiped out her small savings, proving again to Rose that unexpected events shake life beyond human limits. But eventually she found the ultimate safety for her investments: U. S. Savings Bonds. What was safer than the new country?

The year of the infamous crash had a positive side for her. Marie leased the house, and in it, Rose at last found her castle. But even before this move to the special space, she had had no plans to leave family. That would have been a quantum leap in which she had no interest. Though she and her sister Marie disagreed on most matters, Rose found the move delightful and, though, like her working sisters, Rose had only Sundays off, she quickly volunteered to regularly cook dinner when they all returned from Sunday Mass. The gesture gave Anna a day away from the kitchen.

Unions and work laws that later demanded five-day, forty-hour weeks for employees, had yet to form. Sundays in the teachings of the Bible as well as the commercial world in the thirties were not *business as usual* days. Most Christian churches insisted that as God had rested on this the seventh day of creation, humans must follow suit. Sundays were days of rest.

Life at the house, as well as in society at large, reflected such a dictum. Blue laws demanded that businesses close, and around the house, Anna allowed no housework of any kind. Even mending a garment, still a common act, was frowned upon before sundown on the Sabbath. Only tasks of survival, such as cooking and washing the consequent dishes, were permitted. But Rose enjoyed cooking for the family and attending Mass, so such rules mattered little to her. Unlike her older sisters who had permission from their mother to ready their businesses for the week ahead, she never missed the Sunday service. And she became known for her Sunday dinner specialties, savored by those who indulged.

Rose followed her mother's model; Anna's cooking was all from memory, so Rose created her own dishes, based on her recall. No cookbook ever entered the house, but this never slowed the new Sunday cook. Everything was "from scratch" as she labored for hours over stuffed cabbages and her own version of potato salad. She sautéed chicken in butter and then baked it while mixing horseradish with freshly mashed beets.

But still unsure of her place in this lively group, Rose failed to join the others as they sat down, delighted with her house specials.

Though she cooked and shared responsibilities around the house, she remained content with the one room that she called her own. Part of a family, Rose was also a tenant in the house that Marie had leased. After several years and commuting six days a week to Pittsburgh, she showed no sign of moving to a place of her own. But her bedroom showed no inkling of her presence, no favored pictures, photographs, or even jewelry and make-up to adorn the dresser. Nothing that revealed the character of the room's sole occupant. Reluctant to overflow into her environment in material ways, Rose feared the chance that life might again suddenly shift under her.

Now a solid member of the store's coat department, she designated from her paycheck a fixed amount for savings but also afforded herself personal luxuries. Instead of making breakfast before leaving the house and packing a lunch for the workday, as her sisters advised, she ate a freshly baked pecan roll at a delightful coffee shop *intown*. Rose forever referred to Pittsburgh in this way, which by her tone of voice clearly placed it in a classier category than the small city where she lived. And breakfast was followed by a late lunch or, on the one day of the week that the store kept evening hours, dinner. On these days, she left the store and walked to a stylish cafeteria that offered enticing vegetables cooked to perfection, the only temptation that briefly led her away from her workplace.

She did all her personal shopping inside the department store. Boasting everything under one roof, the store housed three restaurants and a variety of services that enabled her to have her hair stylishly coifed while her long nails were manicured, twice a month. Such extravagance her sisters found tantalizing—but wasteful. Her workplace carried everything from the tailored clothes that had become her fashion to pharmacy items. And there was an exclusive bakery and a gourmet food department where she sometimes picked up delectables to bring home: unusual items not found there in the past. The commonplace foods and house supplies, she left to her more domesticated sisters.

Between the department store and the house, Rose felt secure. In these spaces the unexpected would not shake her life again.

Only vacations allowed an exception to her rule to avoid change. With her large commissioned sales, she could now afford a *vacation*, something she had often heard discussed on her train commute. Though her oldest sister, Anne, traveled, *vacationing* was different for Rose. Rose's intent was relaxation and entertainment rather than education. So her annual vacations became another first among the family. Though these forays meant change for her, they were brief respites rather than permanent alterations to her life, thus permitted. Her trips were to the same resort in the same city. And with an annual paid leave from the department store, she had surplus cash with which to vacation each summer. Traveling with a small group of female friends, she vacationed on the boardwalk of Atlantic City, a space sufficiently popular to be immortalized in song: *On the boardwalk of Atlantic City, life will be peaches and cream.* Seven hours by train from the house, Atlantic City in the thirties was *the* vacationland of the East, if not of the entire country. And Rose looked forward each year to her time at the famous seaside city.

During one of these weeks away from the house, she met a man who interested her. As an attractive young woman, Rose had had other beaus but had never taken them as seriously as she took her job. Forever determined not to abandon her ideals, she had searched for the *right* suitor. But one summer on vacation in a space that was all fun and relaxation, she let down her defenses, and suddenly, there was Jim. And romance. He was well versed in the ways of the world and displayed a refinement that appealed to Rose. When she returned to the house and job that year, Jim, with his own car and obvious means, appeared in Pittsburgh to court her with dinners, movies, and occasional live theater. The train commute became less a part of her schedule that fall, as he often drove her to or from work. Seeming to appear suddenly out of nowhere, he had charmed her with his madcap but mature manner. Even her job slipped slightly in priority, though the highs of romance never caused her to miss work.

The exciting period forced Rose to consider breaking the promise she had made to herself at Helen's funeral: travel lightly in this life.

That marriage would prove a major shift, she never doubted, but she now mused over possibilities and outcomes. How would Jim adapt to a family that never quite fit *her*? At a time that saw few working wives, what would become of her beloved job? Could she leave the house? Her family? Rose knew that with his independent nature, he would never entertain thoughts of living at the house, even for a brief period. Besides, there was no room for him there.

Still, her feelings were strong enough that after a year-long courtship, she allowed herself to enter into a mutual plan with her suitor. Adoring her times with him, she wanted them to continue; this point she could not deny. So the two agreed on a date and time when they would run off together and become husband and wife. Like her sisters, she would elope. Despite her insistence on a style that underlined good breeding above all else, Rose had no thoughts of a glamorous wedding. She had been raised without possessions and shared with her sisters a practical bent that dismissed wedding finery as garish, momentary shows.

But in the final moments of indecision, Rose did not carry out her side of the plan. She did not meet Jim at the appointed spot. Warnings from the past surfaced, and questions arose that, in the end she answered by herself—questions reinforced by her old cautions.

"Was he the right one? How did he feel about children, her work, the Russian Church?"

Some of the questions might have been answered by the potential groom. Had she asked. Nor had she disclosed the rendezvous to any of her sisters, who might have offered ideas that would have helped her to adapt to a new life. Her sisters, with the exception of Maggie, had always found fault in her choices. Rose simply talked herself out of the marriage.

After failing to meet Jim that winter afternoon, she never heard from him again. Without reproach for her decision, she simply dropped him from her conscious thoughts—a means that worked well for her. Her entire life, she had refused to mournfully abide in either the past or the future. Though she could bring back fragments of the family's past in the form of captivating stories better than any of her sisters, she never featured Jim in any of these colorful tales. In future family talks at the house, everyone tried to understand the affair and imagined reasons for his sudden departure from her life, hoping Rose would fill in the missing pieces. The sisters tried every angle, even hinting that Jim might have been a gangster that Rose had been forced to abandon. But even as the tale was retold and embellished as repeated stories often are, Rose never commented. She simply smiled, and her life went on in the usual way: the job, the commute, the house, and Atlantic City. Without Jim.

From the beginning, Rose took the meaning of *namesake* literally. Hers had been Aunt Rosalie, and she modeled well her aunt's grace and classy demeanor. In her psyche, Rose yearned to be a benevolent aunt, as she had known. Knowing that the title of aunt had nothing to do with her own actions, she merely had to wait for one of her siblings to produce an offspring! But the hope to be known as *"Aunt* Rose" existed in her mind long before the blessed events, which would bestow the coveted title. When she did at last become an aunt, Rose often cared for her nieces in the evenings, giving the parents time to socialize—in any manner they chose.

She saw that her nieces were bathed and properly tucked in, and even got into bed with them to read delightful stories for as long as their squeals persisted. The *Prince Valiant* comic strip was a favorite Sunday event for both aunt and nieces. Reading stories and novels of every kind had been a part of her own entertainment in the past, so now sharing this love with the next generation delighted her even more. When she arrived at the house after work, she shared weekly radio programs with the little girls—those intriguing stories that dominated radio in the beginning. But this pastime never equaled their aunt reading to them, though listening to the programs *with* her came in a close second. As they grew, Rose bought the girls special outfits while on break at work, forever careful not to spoil them. Instead, she placed the money that she could have afforded to spend into savings bonds—for the education she never had.

Now in her thirties, Rose's life felt right to her. She had a job that she loved, family at the house, two nieces and had had one opportunity to marry. The title of spinster did not cloud her life. Her identity as a well-mannered, classy woman was well established at both work and the house, though the residents often admonished her tastes when she chose expensive wine over beer, beef Wellington over round steak, and Parliament cigarettes over Camels. Still, no one denied her contribution to the family in either affection or money. After all, she still played poker with them in the kitchen and never suggested that they play bridge.

When her mother died, Rose had no trouble concealing her grief, as Anna herself had impressed upon her at age sixteen. Only the enormous spray of red roses from her employer finally broke her resolve. Holding this gift of sympathy from the store, which had become her second home, she sobbed—but only for a brief moment. For the remainder of the wake and through the funeral, she displayed little emotion.

Watching her sister Marie at the burial Mass, Rose mused to herself. "Mother would have been outraged at such behavior; Marie needs to get hold of herself."

7

The Looker

From the time she was twelve years old, Anne had held the title of the "looker" of the family. Modern days would likely label her "a perfect ten," but that would be deceptive. Definitions change with the times. In the twenties, a title such as "looker" implied physical beauty, and skeletal bodies held no appeal; certainly, they were not sexy. Sexy women in those times were well-proportioned and pleasantly plump. As was Anne. Even the siren of the fifties, Marilyn Monroe, wore a size 12 dress. In a family of five females, "looker" was a coveted label, and the designation went uncontested by all of the sisters, including Anne herself. In her typical manner, she embraced the title with neither false modesty nor conceit, accepting the tag as—just the way things were.

"If you can't beat 'em, join 'em" she would advise, accepting even the hurdles of life casually. Of course the "joining 'em" dictum proved much easier when the odds were in her favor. But odds never influenced Anne. She relied on luck and her own common sense.

As the oldest in a large family of immigrants, she had recognized early that her survival hinged on how she interpreted matters. Regardless of the situation, she always found the glass half full. Sixteen when her father died, she accepted that a high school diploma would not be hers and quickly found a silver lining around the foreboding cloud that hovered above her, the oldest in a stricken family. Quickly adjusting her sights, Anne began to look forward to learning the ways of the world. Rather than through schooling, she would learn firsthand. She saw so many mysteries embedded in life and decided to experience as many as she could. Though her interest was not that of a scientist wildly searching for the keys to the universe. She coveted the excitement of experiences rather than explanations.

Working at odd jobs in the beginning, Anne allowed the workforce to become her teacher. After the family's move to the city, she found a job sewing garments at the local factory. Even knowing that factories were called *sweat*shops, she viewed the art of sewing as another life adventure and came to accept the humdrum days. Her practical nature even drove her to purchase one of the outdated machines—for future use.

Though venturesome, Anne was sensible. After three years in the factory, the routine and long hours prompted her to quit. Such an impulsive move was considered madness for an uneducated young woman with no visible prospects. (In the twenties, it would have been redundant to speak of prospects and marriage in the same breath; other than marriage what other kind of prospect was there for a woman?) Her casual attitude convinced others that her decisions were hasty, but such was not the case with Anne, especially when it came to money. She saw herself as having dependents, though, technically, she had none.

When she left her first full-time job at the factory, Anne had a plan. Long before the termination, she had decided to attend cosmetology school, hoping to eventually manage her own beauty business. Though an elusive goal for someone without savings, professional training as a beautician had become her burning ambition.

Before severing relations with the factory, Anne connected with a local modeling agency and modeled part-time for the tuition to a nearby trade school. Magazine illustrators were still searching for new models to sketch, though photography had been around for a century. Their drawings accompanied articles just as photographs do today. And her brief foray into modeling, a mere year, could not have come at a more opportune time for an attractive woman in need of funds.

The heyday of such famed illustrators as Howard Chandler Christy and Charles Dana Gibson, the times were marked by hundreds of their memorable sketches of young women, which have passed the test of time; the famous Gibson Girl as well as females in uniform for the armed services recruiting posters of World War I appeared then and are still known today. Though Anne had no opportunity to connect with the famed New

York illustrators, there were lesser known artists in her small city. And her goal was to finance schooling, not to build a modeling career.

Thrilled at her ability to earn enough for school and help her mother by merely posing, Anne quickly earned tuition, went to school, and obtained a beautician's license, all before the age of twenty-five. Though these early years were stressful, Anne was never frustrated, at least no one ever knew it if she was. Her life appeared easy—and exciting. Even with her schedule of work and school, there were social dates from all over the county, and she quickly added *men* to her list of fascinating world mysteries.

"I like to keep my beaus guessing about whether or not I will give them a tumble," she often said with a smile that quickly engaged her listener.

Speaking in a soft voice, she implied no sex, though her words appeared to hold such reference. Such an allusion to sex by a woman even in the Roaring Twenties would have been in poor taste and not worthy of the refinement Anne presented. For her, the word "tumble" meant that a female had strong feelings for a certain man, and that he *might* become exclusive in her life, increasing his changes for her hand in marriage. Sex before the bonds of matrimony was frowned upon by the culture, not simply the church. Though the rule relaxed in the case of men.

For a number of years, Anne had many dates but offered few tumbles. The men who were lucky enough to be exclusive in her life soon learned that she had no immediate interest in marriage, different than the intentions of most women at the time.

Just as her practical side guided her at her father's death, Anne understood that a marriage and the children that would likely follow, would limit her experiences in the world. As the firstborn, she had watched her mother's struggles with a new baby delivered at home every other year, usually without the assistance of even a midwife. And though Anne cherished her relationship with her favorite cousin, already with two children, and eventually served as godmother to all five of Rose's children, she rejected this pattern of an early pledge to married life and children. At this stage in her life, culturally defined at age twenty-five as *latent* maidenhood, Anne sought the thrills of courting—without expectations of any kind.

The truth is that Anne, while enjoying both the courtships and the men she found so available, never had much confidence in the opposite sex. Though she found men interesting and funny, even wise on occasion, when it came to trust, she decided early that women needed to depend on themselves. But knowing that talk of such things would be too heavy in social conversation, she kept such beliefs to herself. Had she verbalized this mistrust even to her female friends, she would have surrendered a bit of the humor that was now central to her personality. Confining her comments of men mostly to their appearance, Anne played it safe. A man was either "handsome," "cute as a button," "good looking," or "funny,"—or she kept her thoughts to herself.

The first man in her life, her father, died when Anne was sixteen, so she had the opportunity to know him longer, and at a more mature age, than her siblings. But this history bestowed no stories that revealed Alex's traits. Remaining loyal, fearing that his premature death would smother his memory, Anne often brought his name into family discussions.

"He looked like our brother and was very handsome," she replied when her sisters asked her to describe their father. They had been too young to remember him, and box cameras still belonged to another social class at the beginning of the twentieth century. There were no memories of the man sealed in a picture.

Anne, as the oldest, had been her mother's confidante and knew that her parents' arranged marriage had not been what her mother had anticipated. Alex had been described to Anna as a "rich man who owned land in Russia." Land ownership, an undeniable asset at the time, magnified her mother's hopes for an easier life than the one she had left in the old country. And when his possession had proven of little value in the family's everyday life, Anne made a lifelong decision to depend only on herself.

And what better way than owning a business to make such a resolution good? As with her sister Marie, being her own employer moved Anne's life. Given the poverty of their youth, as well as the stories they heard from an early age of the peasant life their mother had endured—Anna's oldest daughters searched for something that would be permanently their own. After working as a beautician for three years and witnessing her power,

Anne proudly opened her own shop, moving herself from blue collar worker into the middle class.

Simply known as Anne's Beauty Shop, her business was located on the top floor of the tallest building in the city, which had become home to the family. On the tenth floor, Anne had a bird's-eye view of the city's main business hub. The panorama from the two large windows of her shop was not the world she had dreamed of someday seeing, but still, it proved an admirable step for this, the oldest of the first generation of penniless immigrants born in America.

Determined to work for herself, Anne had the immediate expense of equipping the space. Fortunately, her modeling forays enabled her to get a loan, but the cash proved too small to pay an assistant to aid in the endless tasks. The space, merely six hundred square feet, had been divided into three rooms that led in a direct line to the back of the shop. Customers entered a waiting room complete with phone and appointment book. This room also held the portable nail lab, which could be wheeled from dryer to dryer; those who chose the service enjoyed the convenience of having their nails fixed in synchrony with their hairstyling. The middle room sported an oddly shaped sink designed for professional hair-washing and two dryers. Unless the hair was unusually long, a vanishing hairstyle, the *set* hair was dry in thirty minutes.

The last room, at the back of the shop, was the largest and most exciting of the three. With the only windows in the shop, it offered customers a spectacular view of the city. In this the finishing room, where customers prepared to re-enter the world with a new look, Anne combed and styled their hair in a large leather chair.

The versatile chair swiveled in any direction, and its back, when needed, dropped parallel to the floor for eyebrow plucking, a procedure that often made customers think they were back in the dentist chair! Though painful, this shaping of eyebrows had become a popular service. Eyes, too, were receiving new attention, and, without pain, eye*lashes* were curled with a special tool and then touched with a bit of Vaseline to produce an alluring shimmer—helpful when lashes were flirtatiously batted.

Also performed in the leather chair, in its upright position, were "finger waves," the trendy hair set of the era. A finger wave was exactly what the name implied; waves made in short hair with the stylist's fingers and then held in place with metal clamps while the hair dried.

Across from the large leather chair was a permanent wave machine. The most fascinating piece of equipment in the shop, the machine had been invented just a year earlier. Instead of permanently curling the hair with chemicals, as happens today when customers request a "perm", the machine curled the hair with excessive heat. Measuring five feet in height, the device had metal clamps swinging from electrical wires, which attached to curlers in the hair during the perming process. The foreboding picture of customers attached to the machine by electric wires resembled penal executions—in the electric chair. A consolation to users of the wave-machine was the fact that the chair itself had no connection to an electric current; only the machine above them and the hair were attached to electrical outlets. But its toll on human hair, as well as the looks of the contraption, made it extinct by the forties, and by that time, Anne was no longer performing such services.

The time was 1928; the "Roaring Twenties" when women were ready for just about anything, including the tag "flapper" that encouraged them to "make whoopee." Changes in appearance were necessary; ladies were beginning to "let down their hair," in more ways than one. The journey from the past had led women from long tresses, which were once braided or styled around lofty constructions of wire to be made into back-of-the neck buns of the nineteenth century. Either way, the cultural message had then dictated uncut hair. But after World War I came the startling short bob. Women now had the right to vote, and such permission affected hair-styles—in the form of short, feathered hair.

When Anne opened her shop, women were just beginning to seek hair-dressers to help them alter their looks. Sometimes, they chose to have their hair permanently curled—or shockingly *tinted*. Tinted hair, after several shampoos, returned to its natural color. Like women across the country,

Anne's clientele was not yet clamoring for permanent color; women were still testing the water in those days, and lasting changes remained for the future, as did blow-drying, highlighting, streaking, and teasing hair—for a changed look.

And hair was not the only change in female appearance when Anne opened her shop. Nails, shaped and painted in a variety of colors, had cuticles softened and even cut. Women's hands became sensual and not simply for "woman's work." Now accepted by a higher social class, cosmetics no longer produced "painted ladies," once assumed to be brothel workers.

The time was right. And Anne was flooded with customers.

But even with such success, she had no plans to leave her mother and siblings and strike out on her own. Though the signs of the times all pointed to a new freedom for women, the attitude that females left the nest only at marriage prevailed. The Constitutional amendment that gave women the right to vote had not changed this aged custom. Anne, never mindful of cultural restrictions, remained with her family—because it was home.

By now, her sister Marie had leased the large dwelling soon to be known as "the house." And Anne found her one bedroom ample, even sharing it with Kate proved no sacrifice. Anne had lived her entire life with five siblings in spaces only three times the size of her new bedroom. The house was a luxury to her.

Like her sisters, she gave no thought to the walk up the steep hill after she closed her shop in the evening, though she often had a beau waiting to drive her anywhere she wanted to go. Anne had been too busy with the beauty business, obtaining a license as a professional hairdresser, and then managing her enterprise, to concern herself with driving a car. All the necessary places in her life, including the house, were within a square mile. She could easily walk. After quitting high school, she did a great deal of walking, and now most of her beaus had cars. Men as escorts made sense to Anne, and she classified driving as a definite masculine activity.

Even the Russian Church proved an easy jaunt. Though Anne, like the others, begged her mother for an occasional reprieve from Sunday Mass. The blue laws, which prohibited businesses from opening on the Sabbath, were still in effect, so only Andrew, who worked shifts at the mill on Sundays, was allowed to miss church. But their mother made no such exception for her three oldest daughters. Anna's reasoning was simple: anyone with Sunday off would attend church. In the Russian Church, no priest could serve communion more than once a day. So there was no possibility for the working sisters to attend Mass later in the day. In the evenings, a vespers service was offered, but this did not include communion and was quickly rejected as an alternative to Anna.

Sunday was their only day off, the sisters argued. Eventually, Anne and Marie convinced Anna that their new businesses, though not open on the holy day, required their attention on this one non-customer day of the week. And reluctantly, Anna allowed the two oldest to occasionally skip Mass, recognizing how hard they were working to make their mark in the new country. To Anne, the best piety was to enjoy life, but her mother would not accept such a sentiment, so Anne kept such thoughts to herself. Still, such disputes did not prompt anyone to break family bonds by leaving. Marie had leased the house, and the four oldest siblings paid the expenses—but the rules were Anna's.

Still, to Anne, their differences were small. She had life at her fingertips.

Anne's Beauty Shop was well established when she met Tom. And within a year, she knew that she would "give him a tumble." This time felt different from the others. Though she was now thirty-two, the alarming title, "spinster" stirred no rush to marry. In the few tumbles she had had, there had been little intention of marriage. Two of her four sisters were married now, but neither had announced her union. Anne suspected that they were secretly married as they sported longtime partners, but such disclosures would not influence her decision to remain single. She happily returned Tom's attention and excluded all other men, but the obligations of marriage continued to trouble her

Instead of settling down to marital bliss, she and Tom began to travel. Even though women were enjoying freedoms unknown to them in the past, the times did not accept such travel arrangements between the sexes—without the visible wedding ring. If there was gossip, Anne ignored it, blatantly discarding custom as she had always done. Though disappointed at her refusals to his many proposals, Tom came to accept the unusual arrangement; he would travel with the woman of his dreams, and quite simply, he adored her. Anne was "the egg in Tom's beer."

"What do you want, *egg* in your beer?" he would often ask. The question suggested the same prospect as "What do you want, *icing* on your cake?" But Tom, not much of a cake eater, relished a cold beer and found this question more appropriate to his taste. Both adages imply that extra touch that makes the good even better, though a bit too much to hope.

For the next ten years, the couple made many trips together. Their journeys never extended beyond a week, as Anne had her shop to run, and Tom did shifts at the local steel mill. Given the time restraints and Tom as the sole driver, the couple visited only those points of interest within a one day's driving radius of their city. But with New York City within that range, they had many choices; this was the height of the Broadway musical where the music of Irving Berlin and George Gershwin could be heard for the first time. They could have broadened their horizons with the newest form of transportation. But neither one had ever flown. Anne's love of adventure had its limits when it came to sky travel.

"There's nothing to see up there. I can see clouds anytime," she said, cleverly covering her obvious fear when the convenience of flying was suggested. She *liked* the car, and with a good-natured companion, Anne was doing what she had often dreamed.

Atlantic City deserved repeated visits. And the wondrous World's Fair in Chicago, followed six years later by the equally impressive exposition in New York City, enchanted them. Neither Anne nor Tom had seen anything like these extravaganzas of progress. At the Chicago World's Fair, Anne stood speechless in front of the newly patented incubators designed for premature babies. Live babies in incubators were smaller than any human she had ever seen. Parents who had agreed to the exhibition received free use of the new life-giving machines. Such displays left Anne speechless, feeling that she had now seen everything. But even these wonders were quickly trumped when she viewed the Dionne quintuplets exhibited in a fenced play yard. This exhibition was sponsored by the Canadian government—the province of Ontario having taken them from their parents when they were four months old. Like Anne, much of the world stood stunned by such spectacles. Humans were now producing *litters*, and at the same time, keeping them alive at earlier stages of life!

After one of their excursions, Anne and Tom arrived back in the city they both called home to announce that this trip had been different. They had gotten married. The simple announcement surprised no one at the house. For years, everyone had accepted Tom as her lifelong companion. Though faithfully abiding by the family tradition of elopement, she chose not to keep the marriage a secret as her sisters had done. Willing to keep some family traditions, Anne also lived by her own ideals.

Many of her departures from family messages came from her identity with her aunt. But even here, she drew lines. Had she sought Rosalie's opinion on her marriage, which Anne did not, her aunt undoubtedly would have encouraged the kind of elaborate wedding her own children had had. But such an expensive celebration would not have fit Anne's thrifty nature. Spending money on an adventure whose memory lasts longer than a day was her way.

After the elopement, she made a second decision consistent with this practical side. Having amassed a nice nest egg, Anne decided to buy a house. This decision seemed to imply that she and Tom would follow custom and *settle down* to married life. But Anne's business sense took precedence over convention—most things took priority over convention for Anne. And she viewed real estate as a sound investment for her money. Of course, when the couple announced their marriage, Marie immediately encouraged Tom to move into the house.

"Of course there's room for both of you," Marie said casually.

"I've shared a bedroom with Kate all these years. There's no room," Anne pointed out.

"Why would you say that? We'll do something to *make* room. Maybe you and Tom can rent the space where the Taylors live. Their daughter is twelve now; I could ask them if they plan to renew the lease." Marie insisted and undoubtedly would have found space for another resident. But Anne declined.

Would Anne become a *house*wife? Her four sisters pondered the startling question. But even with a place of her own and the title of wife, Anne had no intention of either surrendering her freedom—or separating from the pack. Becoming a *wife* had been a difficult decision that had taken her ten years to make, and to now preface the word wife with "house" was more than she had planned. "Housewife" carried expectations, which she had no intention of accepting. Still, recognizing Tom's need for an official celebration of their union, she temporarily recanted and agreed to host a housewarming in their new home. And the event proved the only foray she ever made into the role of hostess. Though the party proved a success, entertaining in Anne's book was another of the housewife duties that she rejected. She had no interest in "guests"—by her definition, those without blood connection. She preferred to explore new haunts with friends rather than play hostess in her home. But family was an exception and fell into a special category; she welcomed them into her home at any time.

It was 1944 when the couple began their married life together. Engaged in a world war, the second in less than thirty years, America excused Tom from the draft. When he was twenty years old, there had been an accident in the steel mill that had left him without a right thumb; a thumb on the dominant hand is necessary for firing a gun, so he received an immediate 4-F classification.

Though now officially living together, the two knew each other well from their travels, and the marriage vows did not change their work lives. Life under one roof was new, but they themselves were no longer young. So the question that lingered between them became that of *starting a family*. Though the same age, only Anne's forty-two years raised doubts about such an event.

8

The Romantic

Too young to understand the money crisis caused by her father's death, Maggie was one of the three kids at home when her mother and older siblings joined the workforce. When Rose also quit school to find work, Maggie was left to play big sister to the youngest, though only three years older than the little girl. Still, she took on the job that fell to her as seriously as did her older siblings who, along with their mother, were generating income. Though the two young sisters shared the housework, cooking, shopping, and, finally, schoolwork, Maggie as the oldest played the parent, carefully clasping her sister's hand on the long walks to the store and church on the country roads that surrounded their dwelling. While Maggie, who was only twelve, fretted over what she might do to make their living space homey for the arrival of the working members of the family, her kid sister climbed trees, happy that her daily tasks were complete. Maggie took her duties to heart but never felt up to the huge task, which would forever bestow on her a loving but cautious nature.

In good weather she found time to join her young sister and frolic in the wondrous river that lay less than a mile from their dwelling. The two learned to swim together, and most of their friends were mutual ones, creating bonds that would last a lifetime.

Maggie's reward for her early work at home was the distinction of being the first in the family to finish high school—an achievement she viewed as a privilege. Her older siblings, seen as role models in most families, had been school dropouts, but however family legacies become etched in their members' psyches, the benefits of education were evident to all Anna's children. Even to the four who had aborted theirs. High school was as far as any of them could have dreamed at the time, and Maggie understood the importance of completing the twelve years. Hoping that her success would bring joy to her mother and pay tribute to the sacrifices of the others in the family's struggle for livelihood, she sought a diploma. And received one with honors.

The year of her graduation, the family moved into the house and a ready-made job awaited Maggie at the little store. Her turn to join the workforce had arrived. This post, different than the caretaking that she had assumed in the past, would earn her real money. Less than twenty-five percent of Americans were high school graduates at the time, so the age of eighteen was late to become a worker. And her job training had not come from her general education in high school. Now she would be faced with strangers rather than the family members she knew and loved. Maggie's only training had come through osmosis as she listened to the trials and tribulations of her working siblings. Seeing them begin work as early as fourteen, and now comparing her accomplishments to theirs, she questioned her skills.

Though reluctant to confront Marie, Maggie made her feelings known. "I'm scared of being behind the counter by myself. When you need to be somewhere else, I'll be alone. I know how you are, always flitting someplace in a big hurry."

"I'm not afraid of anything and neither are you," Marie said. "I wouldn't have offered you the job if I didn't think that you could do it. Guys younger than you work at the mill … around blast furnaces! You'll just be slinging hamburgers and smiling nicely at hungry people. That's not hard."

Knowing it was her turn to become a wage earner, Maggie accepted her big sister's argument.

Maggie's presence in the little store ten hours a day sparked Marie's hope for making her enterprise a *family business*. Anne and Rose had dimmed that dream by choosing other work, but Marie now turned her sights on Maggie and speculated that with this sister, things might be different.

With a variety of customers making demands on her each day, a trial by fire as she felt in the beginning, Maggie soon found that the job came naturally to her. Genuinely enjoying the patrons, she listened intently to their orders—as well as their troubles. Forever enchanted by people, she overcame her fears and found herself in her element. Early in life, she had developed a quality that her siblings had found no time to explore. Outgoing and sensitive to others' needs, she rejected surface feelings and continually searched for life's deeper symbols. Out of necessity, the family had focused on survival and failed to understand this peculiar bent in Maggie. Often the family accused her of being melancholy and "too attracted to the dark side of life." But Maggie was quick to point out that life indeed *included* a dark side, as they should well know, having witnessed the short lives of three of their beloved cousins.

Of the three tragic deaths in her Aunt Rosalie's family, Johnny's death from an aneurism at age twenty-six, proved most difficult for Maggie; she had been close to him in both years and temperament. Johnny left behind three daughters whom Maggie often visited, doing what she could to help the girls and his widow establish a home life after their sudden loss. She adored children, so her time with them delivered mutual joy, and the visits quickly confirmed her siblings' predictions; Maggie was destined to be the mother of the second generation in the new country.

Unlike her older sisters, Maggie harbored no interest in either travel or vacationing. Instead, she had pastimes that required no journey that would take her far from home. Movies, in their infancy, were at the top of her list. With the appearance of the talkies in the late twenties, even controversial themes were explored on the Big Screen; released in 1936, *Showboat*, depicted love between the black and white races, though mixed marriage was illegal in the new country until 1942.

Combining family with her love of movies, Maggie suggested that the five sisters meet every Thursday night to see whatever movie happened to be playing at the Memorial Theater. Any movie title would have been fine for these weekly gathering of the sisters in this exciting time for the new form of entertainment. Once a movie left town, there was no hope of seeing it again; a popular movie could be released a second time but not often.

Their city had two theaters, but The Memorial was the most glamorous. Richly decorated, it modeled the typical movie theater of the thirties, sporting a large stage and lavish curtains, both relics of the vaudeville days of the previous decade. It became the meeting spot of an exciting tradition for four of the sisters, who found themselves forgoing other activities in order to enjoy each other's company—by Maggie's design.

ଓଃଓଃଓଃଓଃଓଃଓଃଓଃଓଃଓଃଓଃ

As a teenager, I went to many movies with Aunt Marg, who originated the sisters' movie-night-out. By then, the Thursday night ritual had ended, so it was only the two of us who walked to the theater from the house.

But I have an earlier memory of the night I was once included in the custom she had designed. Thrilled at my invitation, I was too young to care that the rule of exclusivity agreed on by the sisters was broken just for me, then the sole representative of the second generation. The nature of the movie, *The Wizard of Oz*, likely influenced my invitation. Nor did I know that this was the bumper year of all time for motion pictures; as the year that delivered, *Gone With the Wind*, *The Wizard of Oz*, *Frankenstein*, *Wuthering Heights*, and *Mr. Smith Goes to Washington*, 1939 made Academy Award decisions unusually difficult. Today, these classics are all listed in "The Hundred Best Movies of All Time", meaning that out of eighty-two years of awards, '39 delivered *five* of the best movies of all time! Some years failed to make the list with even one film!

I tried to use my influence as her godchild to convince Mame to come with us, but she merely repeated that movies were a waste of time. Still, she welcomed us at The Joint after the show and promised, as amends, to take me to the candy warehouse the following day.

Because *The Wizard of Oz* was a bit longer than most and started earlier, I remember the time concern as we waited for Annie to finish combing out her last customer, who left with her nails a bit wet. And then there was Ro's train that, though generally on time, was nothing you could set your watch by.

Watching Dorothy come to life in the body of Judy Garland was a wondrous event, and in the company of the four sisters on their special night even then felt mysterious to me. Between my mother and three aunts, there was later talk of *Gone with the Wind* and *Wuthering Heights*. But to these movies, I was not invited, though I later gleaned their plots from discussions I overheard in the sitting room. Discussion about the passion between Heathcliff and Katherine before the world found them, and the greater sex appeal between Scarlett's loves, Ashley and Rhett, lasted for months.

ෲෲෲෲෲෲෲෲෲෲෲෲෲෲෲ

In addition to motion pictures, Maggie enjoyed window-shopping. As she was less interested in buying than observing the shoppers, the sport required no cash, so her lack of money mattered little. Though she often used the phrase "window-shopping" to describe the diversion, *people-watching* is a more apt name for her pastime. Today's enclosed malls with their benches, water fountains, and various shoppers would have nicely satisfied her interest, but these future market places were not even shadows when Maggie began her hobby in the thirties.

Window displays were competitive even among the smallest of stores then. Potential buyers milled about in front of every store on Fifth Avenue, and the shoppers made their decisions about whether or not to enter by the wares exhibited behind the glass.

Invisible among the shoppers, Maggie enjoyed the displays and made her mental notes on human behavior.

Though courted by the same young man for several years, by the standard of the day Maggie was approaching spinsterhood—at age twenty-five. But that conclusion came only from an observer ignorant of the messages of her family. Following the family's tradition of elopement and sustained secrecy, she had married five years earlier. Like her sisters, she recognized that an announcement of the union would force painful decisions about living arrangements. Also, to broach the subject beforehand might hurt her mother, who had no money for a wedding. So, like her sisters, she tactfully eloped.

Such an action of course, invited rumor. Pregnancy presented an embarrassing reason to disclose a marriage. But such did not occur, and no defense was needed for their secret years of marriage—years when Maggie lived at the house without her spouse. But her time with Johnny's daughters awakened a longing in her for children and forced her to finally announce the union—to the relief of the bridegroom of five years. The proclamation, and her husband's insistence brought about a move to their own apartment a half-mile from the house.

The distance was negligible, but Marie worried over the action. Was her sister about to embark on motherhood? Would this upset her hope of a family owned business? Though Maggie had always been viewed as the likely mother of the second generation, Marie had reassigned that role to her youngest sister who had already given birth.

Marie's blueprint for the family—guessed at in only the broadest of terms by all the residents of the house was never open to their input and possible veto. As in most families, assumptions were made and subtly implied, and Marie, in her paternal role, practical by necessity, envisioned only *one* Demeter in the family. Watching her mother give birth at home so often, she knew by experience what the cautionary adage, one more mouth to feed, meant. So, Marie had recast Maggie into the family business.

But Marie's power in such intimate matters as children proved small. Maggie loved her job at the little store and was reluctant to leave. Making the move to an apartment as seemed important to her husband, she decided to quit only when she became pregnant. Time passed, but the momentous occasion did not occur. With the acquisition of The Joint, Maggie even had a choice of working environments. Choosing the newer establishment, she found that she enjoyed the formal waitressing even more than tending the counter at the little store. Attractive, svelte, and with shapely legs that ideally fit the short skirts and high heels of the times, she proved the picture-perfect waitress. Add to this a personality that delivered personal attention and genuine interest in the patrons and the grumbling on her days off was predictable.

Walter met his bride-to-be, just as Maggie turned eighteen. And the attraction proved immediate and mutual. Her good looks and gentle nature had attracted boys in high school, but only making mental notes for future reference of the different types of masculine attention, Maggie put her energy into her studies. Interested in all human behavior, she decided to take these notes to the dating lab for testing—later, after high school. And such was to Walter's benefit. By the time they met, high school was behind her, and he had something that the schoolboys lacked: a maturity that one year of training and three years of working at a job delivers. *And* he wore a dashing blue uniform. Until now, all the adult men in Maggie's life had worked at the local steel mill, so Walter stood out.

His work, clearly defined by the uniform, made him distinct, the ideal protector, Maggie reasoned. As a policeman, he made their city a safer place. The sudden death of her father followed by responsibilities too great for her years had frightened her, and she welcomed now the assurance of her suitor's career, forever proclaimed by his work clothes. The fact that he proved as sensitive as she, clinched the attraction.

Trivial to her during the wonderment of courtship was the fact that Walter's work provided him with more than intrigue and wages. The police force of men in the small city afforded him a natural social group, making Maggie's eventual return to the house, first for her ailing mother and then for the sake of the other residents, easier for both of them. Having accepted her nature and his place in the equation of her life, Walter found that he enjoyed his bachelor-like existence as he played cards, went to ball games, and frequented the horse races in the adjoining states—all with his fellow cops. Happy when his wife of five years announced their marriage and agreed to their own apartment, he found no fault when she continued to work for her sister. Maggie proved a loving, attractive companion, a good cook, and a fastidious housekeeper who even ironed his socks!

At first, when they moved to the apartment, Walter lost track of his social group at work, and the couple found themselves exploring together Maggie's fascination with motion pictures; talkies were only a decade old at the time. But the forties brought the Second World War and a disruption in the young couple's life together—in the form of a draft notice. Walter remained stationed in the states, so she flew to visit him on two occasions.

With little interest in travel for its own sake, Maggie had never flown, but anxious about her husband, she decided to discover for herself how he was being cared for so many miles from home. In addition to the attention she gave her soldier-husband, the trips enabled her to pursue her intense interest in people. She viewed the changes in lifestyles and attitudes among those who, though sharing the same country, lived very different lives than the one Maggie knew, and her interest in people grew.

Safe and sound, Walter returned to their apartment, hoping that at last they would start the family the two had desired for so long. But it was not pregnancy that changed the trajectory of Maggie's life. When Anna was diagnosed with a terminal illness, there was no question who among the sisters would serve as caretaker. Maggie had starred in such a role at a young age. Returning to the house, she stayed at her mother's side when the diagnosis was delivered and later at the deathbed—and administered all the insulin shots in-between. Without either hesitation or reflection, she saw her mother through the final months, and such commitment required no reflection. Her mother needed her, and the others welcomed Maggie back to the house. Not only did she nurse her mother, she again nurtured her siblings, cooking and organizing for this group with their disparate schedules. But she juggled her jobs, caring for her apartment as well as the house and its residents. In her free moments, Maggie substituted for sick and vacationing waitresses at The Joint.

Rather than the imagined changes that separations bring, the couple's life at the apartment fell back into old patterns. Walter's camaraderie with fellow cops grew stronger—and finally became vital to him. He found himself opting for time "with the boys," and the fellowship that he found there replaced his need for family.

Choosing to remain for a time at the house after her mother's death, Maggie continued to care for the others, who were now truly motherless. Though a temporary arrangement, they loved it and encouraged Maggie to again make the house her permanent home—with her husband, of course. Too overcome by grief to consider such a change, she postponed the decision.

Maggie longed to find her mother's spirit, to preserve the powerful energy that would sustain her for the remainder of her life. Helping her to heal after the death, the braid which she had made from hairs saved from Anna's old hairbrush could always be found close by. Faithfully recording from memory her mother's ethnic recipes, Maggie also became a devout churchgoer, attending Mass on special holidays as well as Sundays. She and her youngest sister—the two "kids at home" when the others had joined the workforce—always attended Church with their mother. And as Anna's preference had been to attend Mass as often as possible, church participation came most naturally to her youngest daughters. Maggie felt that tradition and proper values could only be found there and hoped to encourage her siblings in a strong devotion to the faith, as a tribute to their mother's life.

Such religious leanings flew in the face of the Darwinian ideas that lay behind the Scopes Trial. Though it had taken place twenty years earlier, it had not lost the sting that the media had granted it. A high school biology teacher, John Scopes, had strayed from the Genesis version of the Bible and taught evolution from Darwin's book. Though the defendant lost the famous trial and was fined one hundred dollars for his *crime*, the question lingered in the culture; had the well researched theory of Charles Darwin eliminated the possibility of a Higher Being? Was faith such as Maggie's fruitless? Obsolete?

Maggie, seeing less of her husband these days, began working extra hours at The Joint. And eventually the inevitable occurred.

She noted the flirtations of one of the customers, directed at her.

Her fascination with the police uniform continued, so it's not surprising that another blue coat captured her attention. The engaging fact was the man's name. Love. Love Haskins and Maggie began a friendship that slipped from innocent flirtation to intense conversation. Though hardly the trajectory of such things, this was her nature: to plumb the depths of existence with another mind. Though Walter was sensitive and cared deeply for his wife, he lacked Love's ability to listen and respond to her probing questions. Finding people and their stories intensely fascinating, Maggie enjoyed the long dialogues with Love who matched her in interests and conversation. And was single and very attracted to her.

In the past, the attention she received from others had to do with the expert care she bestowed on them. Now she devoured Love's attention. Forever meeting the needs of those around her, Maggie found something different in this relationship. Love sat listening to *her*, responding and offering a sounding board for her many thoughts of life and the people who filled it. The discussions happened after her shift at The Joint and were innocent—and condoned by her husband. Knowing Love well from the police force and not a jealous man by nature, Walter viewed his coworker as a friend of the family. As did Maggie's siblings.

Love attended Anna's wake and funeral, and present in the aftermath, he proved vital to Maggie in her grief. He repeatedly drove her to the cemetery and took a sincere interest when she fretted over an appropriate headstone. A large plot meant to someday hold all the residents just as the house had done in life, the space needed flowers and shrubs: Maggie's constant attention. Love became her support system in this period of grief and healing. Their discussions now had to do with death and an afterlife and were often enhanced by melancholy tunes from the jukebox at The Joint; ballads such as "The Tennessee Waltz" and "Those Faraway Places" were popular at the time and carried the two friends to other realities. Never concealed, the rendezvous relieved Walter of his duty as listener. And he felt fortunate.

9

The Rebel

Attention matters to everyone, but the youngest of a large family struggles to find fresh ways to capture it. And Billie was no exception when she looked to stand out in this dynamic group of sisters. The repeated story of the premature plans for her name gave her an edge in her quest for an identity. The role of *boy* had rightfully been taken by her only brother, but content with the acclaim given him for his gender, Andrew had nothing to prove and showed little aggression even in play as a young child. So Billie, fulfilling her intended name of William, became the combative tomboy of the family, who reveled in her nicknames of *daredevil* and *spitfire*—giving her sister Maggie anxious moments in her early childhood. Billie found challenges in nearly every foray into her world.

Welcoming dares of all sorts, she kept all her sisters guessing as to her next action. Learning to swim at age five because another child defied her to jump into the river at a depth of twelve feet, she spent a perilous childhood, which included physical fights with both friend and foe. Some skirmishes became so intense that her older sisters, Maggie in most cases, were forced to come to her aid as their kid sister took on multiple foes, often larger than she. Resolute, Billie likely would have reached adulthood without defense. But her sisters had their doubts. The fact that she survived childhood relatively unscathed only increased her determination to meet any venture that life offered. She had no intention of following a stereotype.

"Who decided what girls can't do?" she asked.

Her nature matched the climate of the twenties. Women were on the march and won the right to vote in America the same year she entered first grade, so she never heard President Wilson as he argued against the Woman's Suffrage Movement.

"Women lack the ability to reason as soundly as men," the Commander in Chief thundered. But even as she came to understand his fighting words, Billie never showed an interest in the Women's Movement.

Even as an adult, when the cause caught its second wind in the sixties, producing the drive for ratification of the Equal Rights Amendment to the Constitution, she showed little interest. It was a fight she chose not to enter—an unusual twist, given her personality. Attractive and feminine in all aspects except her gait, which was too lively and determined for a *graceful* woman, she saw the authority of men as undeniable. Her name provided all the power she needed in the patriarchal society into which had been born. Unconsciously, she knew that the equality that women demanded would deflate the unusual gift of her name.

Entering high school the same year that the legendary Babe Ruth hammered out his sixty home runs in one season, a record that remained for thirty-four years, Billie soon embraced the sport of baseball. Though professional female sports were nonexistent at the time, and she never seriously played, she followed the game as men often do. The Pirates, as the home team, received the bulk of her fervor, but she also tracked the American League and the fight for the pennant each fall. Baseball was all-American, just as she thought of herself.

Her confident nature aided her mother even before she became a high school graduate. Illiterate, Anna found herself anxious over paper matters in the new country and looked to her youngest daughter to act as a go-between, a link for the immigrant mother to the outside world. A shield that kept her safe. By law, Anna had to regularly connect with the Federal Immigration Bureau, and Billie easily filled out the necessary forms that clarified her mother's presence in the new country. Knowing that her daughter could not be coerced and had the intelligence to resolve difficult situations, Anna turned over household bills and general annoyances to her.

Like her sister, Billie finished high school with a great deal of pride. And her joy is evident in the remaining photographs of the event. The box camera, in common use for over forty years when she graduated in the thirties, reached her social class just in time for the graduation ceremony, enabling her to capture the excitement in a way unheard of in the past. By the time she began to pose and snap pictures, human subjects were not as stoic and contrived as they had been in snapshots earlier in the century. Though subjects still posed, smiles, for some reason previously forbidden, appeared in photographs of the thirties. A period she cherished, high school was preserved by the pictures that she tucked away to remain safe for the rest of her life. And these snapshots of herself in cap and gown, the ceremony and her classmates, were rare mementos and required special care.

Less than forty miles from where Billie once stowed her cherished pictures, a collection of eleven million photographic negatives is now stored below ground at Iron Mountain, Pennsylvania. The national archive reflects the new country throughout the entire twentieth century. Preserved at temperatures below zero, the negatives will last forever in the controlled conditions. While time took its toll on Billie's cherished pictures. Fading, they finally left her with only blurs of a carefree youth—that vanished too quickly for the energetic spirit.

As do commencement speakers, Billie's heralded life's possibilities for the graduates eagerly sitting in front of him. What the orator failed to mention was the economic collapse within the new country in 1932. The Great Depression had caused the national unemployment rate to soar to twenty-five percent, dimming the hope of immediate work for this graduating class. But the little store had not significantly suffered, so Billie, like Maggie, had a job awaiting her. Like the other members of the family, she possessed a fierce work ethic and began her job three days after the graduation exercises.

With lower prices to accommodate the jobless workers of the city, Marie's business was doing well after five years. The production of the steel mills remained good and only slightly below previous levels. Other businesses in the city, dependent on the mills, did better than the national average. As Billie joined the workforce, she realized that her sister had raised the social level of the family when she rented the house three years earlier, and now Marie *employed* two sisters.... when millions were out of work. The awe she felt for Marie only grew as she assumed her first job at the little store. Compared to the country, their entire city faired well in the years of the Great Depression.

Seeking employment, citizens from surrounding towns flowed into the booming city. And among the new arrivals was Robert, a handsome, outgoing bachelor. Contrary to ordinary first attractions between the sexes, looks were not the entire draw for Billie. Robert possessed the perfect credentials for a young woman eager to embrace life's challenges. Though admiring young men had surrounded her through high school, in Robert she found the one quality high school beaus had lacked. Seven years her senior, he was less available, and the question circulating among her friends was, "Who will land this catch?"

Robert had a reputation that preceded him, so Billie knew of him before the fateful day of their meeting. In the neighboring city where he had spent his youth, he was known as the most eligible bachelor. And he soon developed a similar legend in his new location. After spending time in college, he left middle class parents and a string of disappointed girlfriends and arrived in Billie's city to work at the county airport. For the young woman who had spent her youth defying the odds, his marriage proposal became her challenge.

Unknown to Billie, his offer would be easy to attain. From the beginning, he was smitten with her; the old saying "Opposites attract" never appeared as apt as in their case. An only child, Robert also had two maiden aunts and had grown up surrounded by four doting adults. While Billie as the seventh child of immigrants had disappointed her family at birth—by being a girl. When she brought Robert to the house for the first time, she introduced him to spontaneous activity on a level that he had never known. The house, so filled with life, mesmerized him. The residents were coming and going at all hours, and food, talk, and card games erupted at odd times. Accustomed to precisely timed, planned meals and activities, Robert wanted to be part of the excitement that had nurtured this lively young woman at his side. Though people yelling out in the kitchen's cut-throat poker game did create a few questions that briefly daunted the bachelor. To Robert, this game of poker appeared all about unruly raises and calls and contrasted with the studied bids in the bridge game that he understood well.

Still, his doubts quickly vanished in the wake of romance.

She said *yes,* and the couple quietly followed family tradition by elop-ing. But this form of nuptials, so common in Billie's world, proved offen-sive to her new in-laws, who had long envisioned a large, elite wedding for their only child—a ceremony aligned with the family's social standing, where they could flaunt their pride and joy. But following the etiquette of the day, weddings fell in the woman's domain, so the parents and aunts blamed the bride for their disappointment. Robert—just as he had always been in their eyes—was innocent in the blunder.

For his family, such furtive nuptials placed the couple in a lower social class. To them, marriage was about display, not secrecy. Though they had met Billie before the marriage, details of her background unfolded now against the backdrop of the missing wedding. In their eyes, Robert's wife was a first generation of immigrant parents and lacked roots and social ties of any sort. So from the very beginning, the elopement launched Billie on the wrong foot, a position that even over time she felt helpless to change.

It might be said that the marriage simply got *off to a poor start*; the union stumbled as it left the starting gate. But such a launch only served to highlight the many differences between the bride and groom.

At the house, Robert was welcomed by the residents, and he charmed them all just as he had his wife. The dashing college man from another city, this public relations manager at the county airport who had no con-nection with the local mills, smiled and joked in the friendliest of ways. The family looked on him as worldly, and even years later, all referred to Billie's partner as "the perfect host and gentleman."

Billie's close cousin Mary married a short time after the elopement. Mary, the youngest of Aunt Rosalie's children, had been like a sister to Billie, until recently when serious male relationships had fully occupied both young women. Now she invited the new couple to be part of her elaborate nuptials, which included six attendants. So Billie shared in her cousin's joy and happily attended the affair with her new husband at her side. But the dazzling event convinced her that bypassing such a short, costly display had been right, regardless of her in-laws' objections.

The cousins continued down similar paths for the next two years, and when both young women found themselves expecting babies within five days of one another, no one was surprised; their lives had forever paralleled each other's. The babies were born only a day apart, but here the similarities abruptly ended. Mary's little boy lingered only a week and then succumbed to damage incurred during a difficult labor, while Billie's daughter proved hale and hearty. The tragedy caused her to hold her baby a bit tighter, during the standard two-week hospital stay at the time.

Unsure during the pregnancy how her nature would adjust to the restrictions of motherhood, Billie found herself curbing old impulses as she adapted to a role that reduced her freedom. She took on the insistent job of breast-feeding, a practice that she had learned from her mother. Nursing all her children out of necessity, Anna had passed on the benefits of this the oldest of traditions. As the first of her generation to become a mother, Billie faithfully followed suit. Bottle-feeding was just beginning to emerge as an acceptable alternative and the preferred choice of the time. And Billie's in-laws grasped the opportunity to shake their heads in disapproval at the practice. Reminding their daughter-in-law that wet nurses, always of a lower class, had been used for such necessities in the past, they dryly pointed out that the new feeding bottles eliminated such duties—among a certain group of people.

The birth changed other things. Robert soon insisted on a residence away from the house. He had agreed to stay there, but his fascination with the unusual living arrangement had proved short-lived. As a permanent resident, he had come to feel the energy at the house crushing and invasive, different than it had felt in his besotted days as an observer. Beyond walking distance of the family nest, the couple's new apartment shocked her siblings. Forced to remind themselves of this sister's rebellious nature, they realized that the youngest was the only sister to marry a man from out of town and—the first of the family to bear a child.

"Just our Billie," they repeated among themselves to clarify the situation, at least in their own minds as they accepted the new living arrangement

Earlier, Billie had vowed to live an *exciting* life, regardless of where such a promise led. But the birth of her child only strengthened her ties to the house. And though the couple's apartment was within the city limits, the reality that her quest for the exotic had paired her with a man who worked for a national airline exposed anxieties, which the courtship had veiled. For the first time, she admitted to herself that moving anywhere in the world was a possibility now.

Five years after the marriage, her fears materialized. Robert's transfer to the state of Michigan, followed three years later by a transfer to Virginia, had her reeling. In Michigan, she had made an effort to meet young parents like herself, people with whom she and her husband could share a social life as well as the tribulations of parenting. But the second move, though placing her closer to the house, proved too much, even for this, the rebel of the family.

More than the distance and three moves in their eight years of marriage troubled Billie. She found herself pregnant for the second time, and Robert's job required that he travel for weeks on end, leaving her in unfamiliar surroundings with one child, soon to be two, and no car. Thoughts of the active life of the house with her siblings and mother, where she needed no car or anything else, haunted her; even the security of the Church was missing in this new location. The Church, within walking distance of the house, was now absent, and she recognized, perhaps for the first time, the place it had held in her life.

Billie found herself homesick and wanting to be nurtured. There were letters she wrote to Maggie who answered with the same caring support that she offered in person. And though her other siblings failed to write, they called and made occasional visits.

Feeling fortunate that she could connect with Dr. Sunstein by phone, she had him to discuss the pregnancy and her young daughter's health. Regardless of the miles between them, he remained Billie's doctor for all medical needs. Though her second daughter's birth occurred when the couple lived in Virginia, the birth certificate records her place of birth as—Pennsylvania. Traveling to the house a month before the due date, Billie assured herself that Dr. Sunstein would be the attending physician, just as he had been with the first. Though the good doctor still made house calls in the forties, he did not cross state boundaries to offer such services!

Both deliveries were made with mutual trust between doctor and determined patient—without the aid of either Lamaze or anesthesia. Even without Dr. Sunstein's counsel, Billie would not have considered a painkiller of any kind while in the throes of labor. She proclaimed childbirth among the most natural of acts for the human female, forever contrasting labor with the "unnatural" practice of dental work, which required an anesthetic. In the three years that followed her second daughter's birth, Billie recaptured a bit of her old nature and, though lonely, dutifully cared for her young children in a place that felt foreign to her.

When Anna became bedridden, Billie yearned to be with her mother during the final days, and as travel in Robert's job reduced his time at home, she turned to her sisters for help. Neither she nor her sisters found the request heavy. A blood-is-thicker-than-water attitude prevailed, so all favors between them were casual, mutually understood agreements. With her oldest child now in school and the second one in the midst of the terrible twos, Billie made the decision to leave them in their own home. The practical arrangement allowed her to stay at the house for two-week periods.

Rose and Anne, the two who could more easily get away for a week at a time, quickly answered their sister's appeal. Rose, on vacation from work, came first, and four months later, Anne, her own boss, arrived to stay with the little girls. Though they came with the best of intentions, neither sister had the credentials to undertake what had only appeared a simple endeavor. Both understood hard work but had been too busy over the last fifteen years to learn the details of running a household alone, especially with two young children, ages eight and two. Accustomed to life at the house, where what one resident failed to do another did without comment, the two followed the only family system they knew.

But never knowing their aunts as authority figures, the nieces did what might have been expected—they tested the limits of the new situation and requested special foods and odd games their mother would never have accepted.

"I only eat Campbell's Chicken Noodle Soup for lunch." Anne was soon informed by the oldest.

Though having seen the bright red, white, and gold labels on grocery shelves, Anne had never served soup from a *can*; condensed versions could not compete with her mother's wondrous soups, and knowing little of the condensed varieties, she failed to add the required can of water in preparation.

"You make it better than my mother," her delighted niece squealed, reveling in the salty taste of her favorite dish. Life had definitely changed.

When Rose came she innocently agreed on a rainy, indoor play day, to a new request.

"May we roller skate in the attic? It's so much better than the concrete in the basement. Pleeease? The floor in the attic is wooden just like the roller skating rink. It will be so much fun!"

Bringing friends to join in the skating party in the attic, her niece knew that such a thing as skating in the attic had never been allowed. And Rose suffered from the only migraine of her life. The hectic visits for the two aunts bestowed lasting memories, even for Billie who returned each time to a disjointed household. Even her two-year-old had learned some surprising new tactics in her absence. But her sisters' trials enabled Billie to spend time with their dying mother, where memories of the days when she was a permanent resident of the house returned. After the second trip, the home she shared with Robert felt lonelier than ever.

After ten years, the marriage faced its fatal flaws and ended. Robert claimed that separation from the house was impossible for his wife while she argued that his self-centered nature left no room for a wife and two children who needed his attention. Although his attention had in fact wandered beyond his job, Robert did not ask for the divorce. Knowing for some time that things were not good between them, he took the simple path—and found a girlfriend. Billie could not overcome the shame of the infidelity. On learning of his betrayal, she immediately initiated divorce proceedings.

"It's a huge step. Are you sure about such this?" Marie cautiously asked.

Marie would have likely flown to Virginia and seen to the details of Billie's move herself but feared that her sister had only acted on an angry impulse.

"He's been seeing another woman. Of course I'm sure."

"Perhaps it's too soon to consider divorce. You and Bob fashioned that home together. You have two children that belong to both of you; take some time," counseled Rose

Billie listened to their thoughts. "I don't know," she said with hesitation.

"You know that this may be about his parents," Maggie said. "You've never gotten along. Have you talked with them?"

"No! Why would I talk to them? They'll just defend him; they always do."

"I've always liked Bob," Anne came in with a feeling, not a question. "Anytime I've visited, he's been so friendly. The perfect host. I think you two can work this out."

Only one question remained in the minds of her siblings. Was there a chance that the couple would reunite if she remained in her present home? But the moves to different states had separated Billie from the anchors of her life—the house, her family, and the Church. Her in-law's rejection, followed by her husband's infidelity had further damaged a self-image that had once been strong. All events had exacted a toll on her bold nature, and she struggled now to regain her determined spirit. In the end, she chose the divorce.

Nineteen forty-five, the year that saw the end of World War II, brought several closings in her life. She became a divorcee, motherless, and a single parent all in the same year. And just as her life changed, the social climate in the country shifted. The soldiers returned from *the great war* and both the American birth and marriage rates soared; so dramatic was the rise, it caused the new generation of babies to forever carry their own title through history: the Baby Boomers. In this climate focused on family life, Billie found herself living miles from the house, alone, and with two young daughters to raise.

Ironically, but unknown to her, after the war, divorces in the country peaked as dramatically as the marriages. While the soldiers were away winning the peace, American women had gone to work in record numbers, suggesting that perhaps a woman's place was *not* necessarily in the home. This was the sentiment personified in the poster featuring the fictional Rosie the Riveter, which had encouraged six million women to join the workforce during the war. Women going into the workplace changed the marriage bond that had formerly relied on wives to keep house. Had she known about the rising divorce rate, Billie might have felt less alone in her role as a single mother, but such statistics were not public then.

Divorce ended the Church's sacrament of marriage, and no one at the house had ever considered such an act. The family interpreted Billie's action as still another act of defiance. Her easiest decision that bright fall day would have been to call the movers and return to the house after the courts had granted the divorce. Though her sisters had advised against a rush to end the marriage, Billie knew she would still be warmly welcomed home.

Following the divorce, there was much to consider in the debate Billie waged with herself. Her mother was gone and that would change the dynamics at the house. Without Anna's motherly presence, and now with two children, would she feel as she had a decade ago? Life for her was different now. She often appealed to oracles to help her through such labyrinths of life. So now she looked to her dreams and other intuitive signals for guidance, and Anna's death shortly after the divorce seemed like such an omen; Billie decided that a return to the house at this moment would be wrong. Disrupting her daughters' lives after two losses, their father and grandmother, would be too much. Besides, she needed to prove to herself as well as to Robert that she could survive apart from the house. Hoping to shatter his argument that her affinity to both the space and the lifestyle had destroyed their marriage, Billie decided to stay where she was—for the time being.

From a practical side, the decision was flawed. Her annual income, now alimony and child support, fell well below the national average of $3,000. She knew that she had a full-time job awaiting her at The Joint, and with tips, the decreased cost of living at the house, and the elimination of train trips from her present home, her income would increase. With six months left on her lease, Billie had half a year to ponder the decision.

She could continue her train trips to the house and work at The Joint when possible, and the train, leaving her within a mile of the house, was convenient. So like her movie heroine Scarlett O'Hara, she decided to "think about it tomorrow" and postponed a final decision.

ॐॐॐॐॐॐॐॐॐॐॐॐॐॐॐॐॐॐ

So when I was nine, Mother made the tentative decision to remain nearly three hundred miles from the house. As the older of the two children hustled onto the train, I anticipated every trip with excitement. The returns also carried their own anticipation, that tingle which arises regardless of the thrill of the flight. On occasion, I felt sad when we left our home, but it wasn't a dreadful price to pay for such extraordinary journeys.

But undoubtedly, the decision to move or stay was the challenge of my mother's life.

1945–1963

10

The Gambler

Anne and Tom's new home stood on the same side of the same hill as the house. Only a cobblestone alleyway separated the two structures. Different than the concrete streets that surrounded the homes in the area, the alley curiously linked Anne to the house as though the city had planned the connection well in advance. A minute's walk separated the two homes. (Only the friendly recognition of neighbors increased the time.) Proximity to the house was Anne's first priority; if needed, her house would catch the overflow. A gambler at heart, she never ruled out possibilities. Though from the beginning Anne's search for a home had been about location, she had never expected such convenience. After her rural beginnings, easy walks to the house and the commercial section of the city were her priorities. And as the house was less than a mile walk from the business district, her search proved easy.

With its sharp incline, the hill on which both houses sat, required a bit of energy especially on the uphill return home. It may have been a deterrent for Anne who searched for simplicity; but the city had many such hills, and accustomed to walking, she took the terrain in her stride. The city was a mock workout for life with its ups and downs, she reasoned.

Tom, bowing to his wife's decision, said little about her choice. He accepted her contrary attitude to "woman's work" but still viewed a home as a woman's domain. And Anne had paid for their home herself. There was no mortgage, and her choice made his daily walk to the steel mill easy. Like her choice to travel in lieu of marriage, the purchase suited her needs and so satisfied him.

Size distinguished their new home from the house. Though both were frame structures and of the same vintage, theirs was smaller and sat on a tiny lot, which placed them within five feet of their neighbors; unlike the house, theirs was *sandwiched* in place. But similar to the house, a previous owner had partitioned off a section to use as a rental. Alterations in both structures undoubtedly had taken place during the Great Depression when homes, like survival, were stretched as far as possible. Instead of a single-family home, as this one was intended, it could now shelter two separate households.

The entire second story of her home was an apartment with a private side entrance, and these rooms were the original bedrooms and bath. The apartment upset the initial configuration meant to be taken as a whole. When one entered the front door on the ground level, it was necessary to walk through bedrooms in order to access either kitchen or makeshift bath. And there was no dining area. All meals had to be taken in the kitchen, ruling out guests. But enjoying the convenience of one floor, Anne decided to ignore the second floor; there were only two of them, and they hardly needed two floors.

Except for odd modifications necessary during the conversion to a two-family dwelling, nothing had been done to modernize the structure since its erection over fifty years earlier. And Anne saw no reason to remodel now. Within walking distance of the significant things of her life—the house, the commercial section of the city, the Church, and Tom's work—her new home had a favorable location, if not a modern style. As a dividend, a mom and pop store sat close by and provided the couple with handy shopping. The small family business stocked the latest comic books and frozen delights, which excited her nieces when they visited. And to Anne, these were the important things.

Not a fervent shopper, she bought some furniture and linens and stocked the kitchen with minimal dishware. Absolute necessities. Living at the house for the last sixteen years, she had never had use for household articles, and there had been no bridal shower to help with such items. Her purchases, like her decorating, proved minimal; marriage had not changed her values; material possessions were low on her priority list, so her home remained spartan. She would not pay rent, owned a home close to the house and in a convenient location—and had no mortgage; these were the things that mattered. Never finding it necessary to assume airs or follow convention, Anne was not about to begin any novel practices.

Early in the relationship and long before their marriage, she and Tom had arrived at a mutual understanding around finances. All of their trips would be Dutch treat leaving neither of them with what Anne saw as tiresome obligations. In this same spirit of equality, when they officially became man and wife, she used her savings to buy their new home. And then proposed that Tom be the sole wage earner in the future. He agreed, and to everyone's surprise, Anne sold her beauty business—and retired.

Announcing that she had worked six-day work weeks for the last twenty-seven years, she ended the statement with three final words, "Enough is enough."

Such phrases as "silver bullet" and "early retirement" were not part of the cultural lexicon when Anne retired at age forty-three. Retirement age was then commonly accepted as seventy-five, even though this figure exceeded the average life span at the time. And Anne's Galician ancestors, with their unending struggle to survive, harbored no hope of a retired segment of life. But she gave no weight to a *suitable* age for leaving the workforce. Quietly dismissing such directives as she had in the past, Anne did what felt right to her and assumed that others would do likewise. For selling a prosperous business when she was hale and hardy, she offered no explanation. She openly disliked both housework and entertaining and had neither children nor grandchildren, all of which could easily have served as defense for such an action. Rejecting the standard options for women of her time, she unwittingly blazed trails for the feminists.

Still, her retirement made the possibility of children more real to onlookers; occasionally women had what was known then as a "change of life baby." Though no evidence or formal announcement of such an event issued forth, rumors flew among residents of the house. But speculation soon died. Pregnancy had not prompted her to sell her business.

But what *would* now consume her time? Like a fog, the issue hung in the air, vague but obvious. The question haunted others, but Anne had already answered it for herself. She wanted freedom to do whatever felt right to her at the moment—an impossible hope when a work schedule had to be followed. Even for the self-employed, as Anne had been, spontaneity was difficult. As the oldest of a large family of poor immigrants, she had become a worker when her siblings began to arrive, helping her mother and those younger than she. And she was ready now to do what did not *have* to be done. And such decisions, *she* would author!

Defending her actions, in retirement or anything else, ran counter to her personality. When she addressed the question of time on her hands, she would offer only a metaphor.

"The really tasty things in life also make us fat," she began and then followed with examples of her favorite dishes, buttered pasta, and deep-fried chicken. This usually blocked more discussion of retirement, but if the questioner persisted, Anne expanded the observation.

"Things that make us happy often carry a price."

She knew that her decision to sell the thriving business was financially foolish. But her need for freedom remained and was greater than her thrifty nature—freedom would make her happy. Accepting the price as she accepted the fat in the foods she loved, Anne was satisfied with her decision.

She now had the luxury of time and security but no personal income. Having no customers waiting for her each day or the financial woes of helpless siblings to consider, Anne enjoyed a leisurely breakfast over the morning papers. And the remainder of the day was hers for whatever she chose, at her own pace. Tom, as was the custom in the steel mills, carried his lunch and generally worked from six in the morning to three in the afternoon. An early dinner became her only responsibility in her daily routine, and she happily accepted it. Pleasantly surprised at her culinary skills, Tom delighted in the meals. Never part of his long attraction to her, the delicious dinners proved a dividend.

Those fortunate enough to eat her meals were always amazed, because it was unclear where she had acquired such talents. Never one to collect recipes or examine cookbooks, Anne had filed mental notes about food as she attended to the needs of her customers; the friendly conversations had taught her to cook! But unlike most skills that prove a source of pride to their owners, this one she had kept a secret. Cooking had come naturally to her, but she had no desire to be known as a chef. Such a tag could lead to that of *housewife*.

Just as Anne was becoming comfortable in the new role, her mother's death shook her world. But, unlike Marie and Maggie, she did not require the same extended period of grieving. Her strong identification with Aunt Rosalie had not diverted the love she held for her mother, but her calm spirit allowed little overt sadness during the wake and funeral. If Anne suffered a grieving period, no one knew. She concealed any strong feelings that might contradict the happy persona she presented to the world, and the technique worked for her. Truthfully content most of the time, she simply did not allow for *un*happiness.

Having earned the title with her own efforts, Anne now accepted herself as a "lady of leisure." She welcomed the luxury of now loafing, a word she used with pride, not shame. Her home belonged to her, not the bank, and she had a devoted husband with a secure job, who relished his role as her companion. Considering her roots, such a life was amazing. But she had patiently worked towards this place for a long time.

Her free time allowed for "firsts" in her life, simple symbols of leisure that had been denied her in the past. Such things as a pet and a flower-vegetable garden in the back of the property now became possible. When she had moved to the house at age twenty-eight, Anne had owned a canary, a whimsical gift from a smitten beau, but the bird had died because she had forgotten to cover the cage one cool night. Its death had secretly bothered her, and she vowed to someday own a pet—when she could do a better job. And the time was now, and the pet came in the form of a Siamese cat.

Another pastime in these early days of retirement was walking "downstreet." Downstreet was the term used for the commercial part of the city by those who lived in the surrounding residential section. At the bottom of the hills, lay the stores—thus the origin of *down*street. And downstreet,

Anne's frequent destination, required preparation. Though she had traveled there daily when her beauty shop lay in the hub of the city, this was different.

Now she could meander, a term she prized. Leisurely strolling downstreet after a casual morning at home was another first for her, and contrary to other formalities she had rejected in the past, she enjoyed preening before such forays. Going downstreet proved a serious endeavor that required particularly women to look their best. Including preparation time, a journey downstreet took the better part of a day. As she had hoped, these would be simple trips, leisurely and without a specific purpose. Even the walks, as she chatted with neighbors and ran into old acquaintances, excited Anne. Finally reaching the commercial section, she examined new items in store windows but purchased little. If she picked up something for dinner, that was good, but if not, leftovers tasted fine, too. Such casualness had been her hope.

ભ્ર ભ્ર ભ્ર ભ્ર ભ્ર ભ્ર ભ્ર ભ્ર ભ્ર ભ્ર ભ્ર ભ્ર ભ્ર ભ્ર ભ્ર ભ્ર ભ્ર ભ્ર

Another excursion for Annie in these early years of retirement was a leisurely trip to the large city of Pittsburgh—*intown,* as her sister liked to call the robust Steel City. I called her Annie in these years—somehow dropping the "e"and *adding the "ie"* made it less formal to me. Without the need to buy supplies for her business, she could now pursue her real love—experiencing life. Though at the time, I never thought deeply about it, I know now that such experience cannot be purchased.

On one such outing, she took me, her ten year old niece, to the city's public morgue—and it became one of those happenings of my youth that I never forgot—or repeated. Even at such a tender age, dead bodies were neither foreign nor frightening to me. I had often viewed them during wakes and funerals in the Church. Though a morgue lacked the religious overtones of my previous encounters. I adored my times with her; she never seemed burdened with worries. When I was with her, she was always in the moment. But even her high spirits failed to lift mine in the morgue that day. She was fascinated with this place where the city held its unclaimed bodies and found no gloom in her discovery that it was open to the public. Actually, Annie found little darkness anywhere. She simply shared a hidden sliver of life with me that day, interpreting it as a significant part of my education.

CRCRCRCRCRCRCRCRCRCRCRCRCRCRCRCR

The only snag in Anne's easygoing life these days was her thrift, which she carried from her early days when she watched the babies arrive in an impoverished home. Old values were harder to shed than her beauty business had been. Without a personal income, she felt a need now to see the savings from the sale of her shop grow. The stock market, though frightening to the novice, mesmerized her. Reasoning that if *she* no longer worked her *money* must, she explored investing. Several trials with stocks increased her confidence, and Anne decided to expand her pilots into the market.

Her attention drifted to the vacant floor of her home. After four years of marriage, she had accepted the fact that motherhood would not be her destiny. So expanding their living quarters to the upper level of their home made no sense. Instead, she soon found tenants to occupy the space, and the separate entrance made it convenient for both families. She found that being a landlord was uncomplicated and profitable. And by investing the additional income, she also set aside money for future trips. Enjoying life remained her priority.

With an income to accompany her freedom, Anne discovered another missing element in her life. A driver's license, proof of a skill that she had never missed during her working years, suddenly became important. Freedom begat freedom. In the days of her shop, convenient transportation could have eliminated many demands on her time, so this desire to drive now seemed odd. But Anne noticed the rising number of female drivers and identified a missing element in her life—which might enhance her adventures.

Willing to drive his wife short distances on his days off, especially the ten mile trip to her cousin Rose's where he felt welcome, Tom was surprised at Anne's desire to drive herself, at this point in life. But she longed for time alone with her cousin. Knowing there was little to occupy Tom while the two women caught up on each other's lives, in ways that women do, she envisioned visits during his work time. Over the years, the small bar that Rose and her husband owned as well as their family of five left little time for such socializing. And there were other jaunts that Anne would surely find; she was now ready to become a driver.

In his steadfast devotion, Tom struggled nobly for two years to teach her. But his efforts proved futile. Though she desired the skill, it appeared that her learning window for driving a car had truly closed.

"You're just too old," Marie chided. "It's something you must do early in life, when you can take more risks."

The comment, a reflection of the rivalry Marie had forever carried, proved correct. Sitting in the passenger seat for so many years, Anne was too tense when confronted with the steering wheel, accelerator, clutch, brake—and traffic. And she failed to pass the drivers' test even after several attempts.

Though disappointed, she took the failure in her usual stride, concluding, "It wasn't meant to be anything but a page torn from my book."

Anne's book of life would also lack the pages on motherhood, but she did not dwell on such debits. She defined life by its victories rather than its disappointments and failed to allow one to dilute the other. Forgetting the license and relying on Tom to drive as she had in the past, she found instead other pastimes. Though small by others' standards, her interests were luxuries to her. Rediscovering the missing elements of an impoverished youth and a hectic work life, she sculpted for herself an exciting retirement.

She listened to serial radio programs, read newspapers in a new way, and completed the crossword puzzle between breakfast and lunch. She devoured magazines that had once lined the waiting room of her shop but that had been off-limits to her. Less interested in novels than her younger sisters, she often spoke of *Lost Horizons* and *Wuthering Heights*. These two books were mysterious enough to capture her attention. Only the imaginations of these authors exceeded the excitement she could find in real life; she refused to be diverted by the figments of another's imagination. And the popular non-fiction of the day, books such as *Silent Spring*, *The Feminine Mystique*, and *The High Cost of Dying*, she found depressing. Like the fight for the rights of women in the twenties, Anne preferred to *live* her values rather than join the causes.

Trips in this, the second phase of Anne's life, were different than those preceding her marriage. Now she traded in the old role of starstruck tourist and combined travel with her longtime fascination—gambling. With her investments and tenants, these days money felt less tight, though such a sport as gambling begged clarification in light of her thrifty nature. She resolved the contradiction in one simple sentence.

"I'm just *lucky*," she often proclaimed as she reached into the grass for a four leaf clover that she then pressed into a book. Admittedly, four and five leaf clovers did seem unusually profuse in her presence.

In case the claim faltered, Anne possessed a variety of tricks that evoked her luck: knocking on a deck of cards before they were dealt, walking around her chair before an important throw of the dice, blowing on a ticket to make it a winner, and lightly scratching her right hand with the left when she needed an even greater dose of luck. This variety of charms presented her with options; different situations called for different talismans.

On one vacation, she and Tom traveled to the shores of Maryland where slot machines flourished. Gambling had not yet flooded their old haunt in Atlantic City, so they were forced to *fly* to Las Vegas—a new experience for both of them. The state of Nevada was a bit farther than Tom wanted to venture as the sole driver. Actually, the entire trip took a bit of convincing for him. Not feeling as lucky as his wife, he simply went along for the ride. Because he enjoyed her company. He may have resisted more strongly had she lost large sums of money, but forever putting her luck to the test, Anne usually came out ahead.

Though Atlantic City, as it later blossomed with casinos in the eighties, would have been more convenient than Las Vegas, Anne welcomed the opportunity to experience the original City of Sin. "What happens in Las Vegas stays in Las Vegas" remains the city's motto today, and this libertine attitude appealed to her curiosity.

Marriages, divorces, and classy brothels, as well as gambling, have grown in Las Vegas since their visits in the late fifties. Both marriage and divorce are easy in the city that uses its dubious reputation as golden publicity. Garish wedding chapels decorate street corners, helped along by a twenty-four hour waiting period for a marriage license. A wide variety of risqué burlesque is available nightly, along with exotic foods served in anything from all you can eat buffets to elegant dining.

Even then, it seemed to Anne that anything was available anytime in this, the nation's sin city. Her practical side prohibited participation in anything but gambling, though she liked being in the audience of such debauchery.

Closer for the couple, the state of Maryland with legalized gambling introduced Anne not only to the one-arm bandits known innocently as slot machines, but also to horse races. The variety served to broaden her fascination with the sport of gambling. As she had hoped, the freedom of retirement endowed her with wonders beyond her expectations. But the casinos held little interest for Tom, so he found new foods, cold beers, and unusual sights to interest him. The long drives too, often on interesting two lane roads, brought out the "barbershopper" in him. He loved to sing in the car, and the times provided him with a repertoire of songs. Songs such as, "The Girl Who Married Dear Old Dad," "Daisy," "She'll Be Coming 'Round the Mountain," "Home on the Range," "Side by Side," and "Lydia Pinkham," enlivened his trips, especially when Anne joined in the harmony.

But Anne's enchantment with gambling did not require travel; it also bloomed at home. Her favorite card game, poker, was available nightly in private homes around her city, where she either knew the host or was invited because of her rumored love for the game. In her early years at the house, she had turned down dates in order to play the game in the kitchen with the family. Poker turned them all, even Marie, into expert card sharks!

When Anne played poker in the kitchen of the house, the game held little stature in society hardly on a par with bridge or canasta. At the time, the choice of games defined social class as clearly as residence, dress, and food. But poker's engaging qualities caused its comeback in the twenty-first century, and the residents would be delighted to know that today *their* game is no longer a cowpoke activity.

Anne also played the numbers each day. When she had first moved to the city thirty years before, she had begun the sport, and her winnings had helped to fund her tuition to beauty school. Frequently winning encouraged her to increase her bets and endowed her with the label, *Lucky*. To play the numbers, players chose a three digit number and then bet some form of it; if the choice of a number was 786 and the wager was for the maximum amount, the number that hit (won) that day had to be exactly 786. But for a smaller purse, such combinations as 687 or 876 would be winners as *boxed* numbers of the original choice. As many three digit numbers as personal finances allowed could be played, and one number hit each day. (The numbers, an interesting game that carried its own allure, required a jargon of its own.)

How such an activity found its way into this small city in western Pennsylvania where gambling is still illegal remains mysterious—and likely linked to organized crime. But hope of winning large sums with little effort made it a popular sport in Anne's day, and players gave little thought to its origins or legality. The gradual release of the digits throughout the day titillated bettors. At two in the afternoon, the first digit was made known; by three, the second was publicized, and by four, the number had *hit*. The practice proved so popular that by late afternoon, on every street corner, one could hear, "Is the number out?" An enticing sport, playing the numbers dangled the chance to be a winner in front of anyone who wanted to take part—everyday except Sunday. Because of the blue laws, no number came out on Sundays.

Anne, not as amenable about vacation destinations as her husband, did appreciate his willingness to follow her fascination with gambling. In return, she frequently joined him in one of *his* favorite haunts: The Loyal Order of Moose. A service organization with lodges and chapters throughout the world, the club served as a social setting for Tom. Enjoying a cold beer and a rigorous game of pool, he often met his buddies, as well as new friends at The Moose Club, where, in addition to pool, there were always a variety of games in progress. All games, whether cards, Ping-Pong or shuffleboard, were played only for social reasons and to hone members' skills. There were no overt wagers. So Anne's time at the Moose Club was honest companionship with her husband. And knowing that he relished the friendly atmosphere, she happily shared the time. Still a bit slanted to her side, their social time modeled a give-and-take marriage that served both partners.

Church attendance proved the one thing that Anne failed to increase with her new freedom. Though the vacuum created by retirement sometimes brings a dramatic rise in church interest, this was not the case with her. She attended Mass but never with the commitment of her younger sisters. Even accepting her mother's faith and the Church's positive power in shaping all their lives, she saw no reason to attend *every* Sunday morning. God knew she was a good person through her determination to enjoy the life she had been given—even when she missed Mass.

Thus the *retirement* phase of Anne's life proceeded according to plan. Though her activities were far from earth-shattering pursuits, the mysteries of life that had tantalized her in the past now opened and were embellished by her unusual relationship with money. Never having been driven to make her way up the social ladder through material goods, she liked to see her nest egg grow because it increased her freedom, and this choice nicely included a bit of gambling and travel. Funds from her winnings as well as from the rental property allowed her to become an active investor that completed the cycle.

She had created an idyllic life for this the third phase. But lately, a persistent worry that she had kept tucked away in a low level of consciousness, had begun to weigh on her. For a time, she felt that Marie's determined nature would rescue her from what appeared an impending danger. But Anne had begun to wonder if confrontation, a difficult action for her, might now be necessary.

11

The Architect

Marie ran The Joint without Eddie's help for the three years he served in the army, and business had been good. Though the two atomic bombs that America dropped to end the fighting drew critics, bells of every sort rang across the land to proclaim victory. The local mill sounded its whistle for an hour on the official V-days, and though citizens were familiar with the sound that daily signaled the end of shifts, an *hour's* shrill signal left no question that dramatic events had occurred. Joy enveloped the new country, supported by the hope of future peace that came with the birth of the United Nations. A tenfold increase in business at The Joint came with the closing celebrations.

But a painful conclusion occurred later that year for Marie. Her mother's life ended, and the event upset her life in a shocking way—for this the stalwart of the family.

"It'll be okay, honey. You know how sick she was," Eddie pleaded.

"Mama! Mama!" she screamed as she grasped the body, fully intending to pull it from the open casket.

Life and limb intact, Eddie had safely returned from the war and was at her side at the funeral Mass. Though his quiet presence helped, Marie's emotions overwhelmed her. The somber ritual of family members filing by the casket to bid their farewells completed the Mass, moments before the casket cover was brought down for the last time.

"She can't breathe! She can't breathe! Don't close it," she again cried as the top of the casket came down.

Had Eddie and the priest not restrained her, she would have pulled the casket from its wheeled stand. The depth of Marie's grief, seen in her loss of control, stunned onlookers. Created by the emotional force of her pain, the scene could have been catastrophic. Sitting in the pew a short distance from her sister, Rose—whom her mother had slapped when she lost her composure at her cousin Helen's funeral—could now feel her mother's disapproval of the dramatic scene.

Until now, the level-headed businesswoman who had, on her own, accumulated a small fortune, had been strong for the family by keeping her emotions in check. Though Anna's death visibly shook all her children, the others had accepted her terminal illness and prepared for the inevitable. But the death released in Marie the one feeling that she had managed to quell her entire life. Fear. The family might not have survived, at least not at their present standard, had she gotten cold feet at their father's death. The fact is that Marie *had* taken the reigns—and succeeded. Another sibling might have risen to the occasion, but personal drive and dreams change when one family dynamic shifts. When variables change, all bets are off on future outcomes.

Now as the faithful pallbearers carried the body from the church, a fear once buried by Marie's past resolve overtook her. That winter day, the powerful head of the family staggered for the first time.

For the following months, Marie struggled with a loss of purpose. Taking on the patriarchal role of wage earner, she had carried the resolve of her mother's dream—hope for a better life in the new country. Like Anna and most immigrants at the time, Marie had had no time for introspection and simply did what needed to be done. Just as her older sister Anne had modeled herself after Aunt Rosalie, Marie identified with their mother; Anna had been this daughter's heroine and accounted for much of the drive that had pushed Marie to work her way into the middle class—with neither money nor education. Striving to fulfill her mother's dream, she was now empty inside—allowing for the return of old ghosts.

Open caskets were common at the time of Anna's death and a critical part of the burial rites of the Church. Significant to the grieving process, closure and good-bye came through viewing the body before it was committed to the ground. Though Marie had often seen bodies at wakes, the sight of her lifeless mother suddenly unveiled her own mortality. If Anna could die, so could her daughter, and Marie faced for the first time the certainty of her own death. And death for her had become strangely entangled in the fate of her cousin Mickey.

When Mickey died of his own hand in the asylum fifteen years before, she had hidden her shock as well as her fear. As a child, she had paired off with Mickey as had her siblings with their cousins of matching age. And seeing the similarities of the other pairs, Marie secretly concluded that she and Mickey, who shared the position of second born in each family, had common instincts, though she was lost as to what they might be. With very different natures, the two saw little of each other as adults, but Marie's early deduction that they had something in common lingered. Outgoing and aggressive as an adult, while Mickey had been depressed and finally institutionalized, she had held to the notion that the two shared some vague quality, just as the other pairings had. Though not consciously present in her daily life, the thought huddled in her unconscious.

Marie, newly married and the owner of a small but successful business, had taken the tragedy of the suicide with little reaction. Saying nothing, she dutifully sent an appropriate floral arrangement and attended both the wake and funeral. But in later conversations, it was obvious that the matter weighed on her. Sensitive to the pain of his self-inflicted demise, she never said anything to hurt the grieving family, but occasionally at the house, her attempts to deal with it all became obvious.

Saying such things as, "That's as crazy as Mickey Frisco," Marie accidentally made clear to the others that she harbored deep anxieties. Such flip comments issued forth long before Anna's death, when Marie was still in control of her fears.

Billie, sensing her sister's anxieties, tried to shrink them with comments such as, "Mickey was very troubled, Marie. That's why he never even held a job! Surely you're not comparing the two of you simply because you played together as kids?"

Rose supported Billie in the plea, but as her words never had much affect on Marie, she soon fell silent.

Anna's funeral forced mortality on Marie, confounding her with irrational thoughts. In the past, she had felt the power to change matters, usually by ignoring what seemed trivial to her. But such was no longer true. Could Mickey's premature death somehow be a warning of *her* demise? Would she someday die in an asylum of her own hand? Was her life, so planned until now, spiraling out of control with the death of her beloved mother?

Still, Marie had proven herself a remarkable survivor, and such fortitude cannot vanish into thin air. Surely remnants of that strength were available to her now. Reminding herself of the thriving business and the house that sheltered the family, which now included the second generation, Marie reasoned that she needed a new dream that would help her regain her bearings.

Less than a year after her mother's death, she bought the house.

It was a simple transaction, unhampered by radon and mold inspection, appraisals, pre-approved loans, or an amortization chart to clarify monthly payments and penalties. With a notary present, she merely met the owner, signed papers, and handed over his asking price of six thousand dollars—in cash. Having faithfully paid him rent for the last seventeen years, Marie knew the man, and red tape at the time was minimal. Both of these longtime inhabitants of the city appreciated the business sense of the other, and the entire transaction, making the house hers, took less than ten minutes.

Seeming to shake off the fears that overtook her at her mother's funeral, Marie had a new purpose. A new goal. The plan to buy the house included a lavish renovation scheme that had quickly formed in her creative mind. No fleeting thoughts of a *new* house for her and Eddie in what had become the classy suburbs of their city clouded her scheme. Even with her mother gone, she harbored no plans to disrupt the nest she had worked so hard to build. Besides, the new suburbia only reminded her of the country life that she had escaped.

The house, a wooden structure sixty years old, had been well sanded by the heavy dust from the local steel mills. Now Marie planned to modernize it. She admitted from the start that this renovation, especially the decorative bit, would never have been part of Anna's vision. Her mother—frugal and practical—would have considered such a plan extravagant and encouraged instead that the money be put aside for rainy days, especially now with a new generation in the wings. But she reasoned that her mother never knew the potential of her businesses, so Marie pressed on with a dream that was now only her own.

The house had been partitioned by the original owner to duplex style during the Depression, so tenants were still living there and came with Marie's purchase. But she had plans for this smaller space; after buying the house, she invited her sister Maggie to buy the previously rented area. Though frequently at the house, Maggie was reluctant to relinquish her apartment and make a financial commitment of this magnitude. But Marie's logic prevailed.

"Why pay rent on the apartment, when you can buy something that will belong to you? It will be an investment," Marie argued.

"I'm not sure that Walter would be happy there."

"Why not? Eddie and your brother live here. They have no complaints. The location is convenient to the police barracks and downtown. And I bring tasty food from The Joint. In the long run, it would be cheaper for you."

"But if our family increases.... I don't know, Marie. We don't have that kind of cash."

Marie quickly agreed to monthly payments, which were similar to their apartment rent; she would make the transition as simple as possible. Maggie hesitated but finally yielded to the strong argument and bought the partitioned section of the house for the sum of $2,000, a fair price for one third of the structure.

Buoyed by these developments, Marie's spirits rose, and for the first time in her life, she became a shopper. Clothes had never been a priority; her previous shopping had been confined to the businesses, kids' apparel and toys for her two young nieces. Now she began to explore furniture stores, and bought linens and housewares of all sorts. In the past, securing a simple toaster, viewed as a lifetime purchase, was monumental for any member of the family, but Marie searched now for quality—and distinction.

The time she now had available to devote to a shopping excursion had increased. The business at The Joint continued to flourish, and she had become more comfortable with Eddie's management skills. On occasion, she still complained that he had "no business sense" and found it difficult to be gone in the late evenings when the receipts were tallied, feeling that these told the real story of the restaurant's success.

Still, the new goal became her priority.

This energetic period of renovation even served to bring Rose and Marie, the sisters whose relationship appeared most contrary, a bit closer. Though hardly in agreement with her sister for the need for such elaborate remodeling, Rose offered the use of her store discount, available only to family members, and faithfully watched for new furniture pieces as they arrived in the store. Reluctantly, Rose even surveyed competitive department stores for the elusive items on Marie's list, so most of the new furniture came from Pittsburgh. Marie made weekly excursions there, though her city was booming, as seen in a growing population: new stores and classy suburbs, where the doctors of the city lived on Pill Hill!

The large city of Pittsburgh that except for Rose, Marie and the rest of the family had merely skimmed on occasion now delighted Marie. Appreciating for the first time her sister's awe of Pittsburgh, Marie found it amazingly close. Her short jaunts offered more choices as well as opportunities to sample the restaurants of a metropolis. Comparing them to The Joint, she was smart enough to recognize that the clientele in Pittsburgh differed from the workers who enjoyed The Joint's home-cooking, and she made few changes as a result of her forays. Her focus remained clear: the renewal of the house, which she now owned.

She hired painters and carpenters to replace windows, remove partitions and such old-fashioned touches as the French doors that separated the living and dining rooms. The kitchen took on the style of the fifties—chrome, plastic, and red and white tile. Though some spaces were opened to restore the original integrity of the house none of the renovations included Maggie's side. Marie was happy that her sister had agreed to the move and had no intention of now overstepping her bounds, an act that would have been consistent with her dramatic personality. Life now flowed freely through the entire structure, and the remaining partitions created a proper separation between the spaces owned by each sister and gave the small family some privacy. Still, the divide was more imaginary than real; Maggie often cooked in Marie's now modern kitchen—as others seldom did. And all residents entered and left by the same door.

Marie purchased furnishings of high quality, designed for casual living. With the exception of two rooms. The large living and dining rooms, she decorated with ornate furniture that set them apart from the rest of the house. These rooms were replete with crystal chandeliers, long velvet draperies, leather and marble topped tables, linen wallpaper, period furniture, statuettes, and expensive china. Marie obviously intended that these two rooms be used for refined entertaining, rather than general living.

Though outgoing and friendly, Marie had never shown an interest in entertaining of any sort, so as the two rooms reached completion, the riddle grew. Other than dance halls, where she went to dance not to meet people, she had socialized little her entire life. She had been too busy working towards her goal to be hampered by a social life.

Rose finally asked the question that haunted all the family. "Why are these rooms so lavish? I don't understand. What's the purpose?"

"I'm a businesswoman. Remember?" Marie curtly answered. "I haven't forgotten The Joint in all of this!"

Always a bit frustrated by her sister, Rose replied, "What do the living and dining rooms of your own *home* have to do with The Joint?"

"I plan to invite my patrons, the special ones who have been faithful customers, to the house on holidays."

"I never heard of such a thing! Business owners don't make guests of their customers; they send them a free drink occasionally … or tell them that a meal is on the house. Marie for goodness sake, what are you thinking?"

The two often had such disagreements, and as usual, Marie heard little of the last exchange. In the splendor of the rooms, she would entertain groups to acknowledge their patronage.

Though an interesting business ploy, the idea proved short-lived. After several such events, Marie found this display of gratitude awkward. *On the house* need not mean *at* the house, she soon concluded. Her customers, who were all drinkers, consumed free alcohol at the gatherings in the garish rooms, and Marie became bored with their progressive gibberish during the occasions. The house was about family, so thereafter she expressed appreciation by giving summer picnics at spacious local parks where unlimited food and drink were provided for all invited guests. In the new setting, she was not forced to listen to anyone for any length of time and could mingle—and move on.

So the living and dining rooms stood idle. The other family members had shown little interest in her project from the start. Such elaborate furnishings were not required to fit the mold of the mansion they carried in their psyches. At work most of the time, as was Marie herself, the others desired only a comfortable place at the end of their workday to *flop* and bask in the company of family. And now they missed the old ambience, especially in the living and dining rooms. Except for Rose's comments, no one overtly criticized Marie's efforts, but like Rose, they lacked enthusiasm, causing her to reassess the final product. Her previous goal had been so clear; family survival had been sought and delivered in spades.

Now the inventive patriarch questioned her new goal. If customers were not to be entertained in the new space that she had created, and the residents did not value it, why *had* she taken on the project? She struggled to release her searching questions, and finally merely took pleasure in the fact that she now lived in a lovely home that was made warmer by family. Buying the house had brought Maggie back into the fold, and perhaps now her sister Billie would reconsider. With no thought of growing *a personal* group of friends to entertain, Marie still had her nieces to share birthdays and Church holidays in the ornate dining room. The girls adored her choice of a Christmas tree each year, an unknown tradition when Marie was a tenant in the space. When it came time to buy the annual tree, the children squealed when she insisted on the tallest tree in the lot, one that fit nicely beneath the high ceiling of the lonely living room.

Marie found herself drawn more than ever to the children. Their carefree ways helped to erase, though temporarily, the anxiety of her mother's death. And devoted to them, she even shared in their difficult times. Not satisfied to merely hold her niece's hand through a frightening medical test needed because of a curious heart flutter, Marie had the identical procedure done simultaneously on herself. The act reassured the little girl that the test was benign, and both patients came through with a clean bill of health.

Six years after her mother's death, the remodeling project and the brief experiment in entertainment had passed. And the childhoods of her nieces, too short for the adult onlookers who loved them, were closing. Marie had accomplished another goal, but the results this time felt vacant to her. Without a sense of direction, shaken and unable to quell her old fears about death and destiny, she found herself unable to sleep at night. For the first time, she began to leave the business before closing in hopes of relaxing and falling into a natural sleep, a luxury which she had never afforded herself. In an attempt to help his wife, Eddie brought into their bedroom the new gadget known as television.

She watched any educational show she could find in the hours before dawn, her most difficult times. The shows filled some of the need she had abandoned at age fourteen when she quit high school. Learning things fascinated her, and the programs, which ended with *The Jack Parr Show*, took her up to three in the morning when Eddie arrived at the house after closing the business alone. Even his sleeping presence calmed her restless spirit and allowed for sleep.

In addition to the loss of purpose, Marie was now going through menopause. The two happenings may have been related, a synchronicity that was difficult to unravel—or perhaps merely bad luck. Doctors suspected a link between depression and menopause at the time, but even sisters did not talk of "the change" among themselves. So Marie sought Dr. Sunstein's advice and faithfully followed his recommendation of a hysterectomy. The doctor, a child of the times, advised, "Get the change over quickly, in one quick sweep of the scalpel."

But the surgery made no difference in Marie's emotions, so the good doctor encouraged a specialist. She had known of no one except her cousin who had frequented these new doctors known as psychiatrists.

"Mickey Frisco had such a doctor, and what did it do for him?" she asked Dr. Sunstein.

"Just try it. I think it's a good idea." he replied.

In Marie's mind, no one knew more than the family doctor, so she paid a visit to a psychiatrist intown. None were available in her small city. But the therapy proved short-lived; she made one visit and never returned. Having briefly examined what medical science could do for her, her old determination surfaced. She would do this alone, just as she had in the past.

This time the focus would be on her.

She began to attend Sunday Mass. Too busy building her business, she had been only an occasional churchgoer. In fact, she attended twice a year on the high holidays. Trying hard now to understand the devotion that had filled her mother's life, she fought to experience again the strength of this woman whom she had loved so deeply. Until now, her life had been too hectic to develop a routine necessary for such commitment. But now her survival was at stake, and she understood survival well. Her businesses were closed on Sundays, so it was not an impossible task, making her wonder why she had stopped attending in the first place. Discovering a caring among the congregation in the local Russian Church, she remembered the people in the black church of her youth. And realized for the first time that her hunger had been quelled not only by the food but also by their generosity.

Though she questioned such Church practices as confession and communion, the regular attendance proved effective. Her sleep patterns improved, and her depression began to lift. With her own power revived,

Marie thought of a second curative act. Walks. In addition to church attendance, she began long walks, miles and miles around the city each day. Exercise was not heralded for health reasons in the fifties, but in thinking back to her youth, she recalled the walks between home and work. Thirty years ago during these walks, she had planned her life. Though those were out of necessity, she recognized the benefits that went beyond transport. At a different vantage point in her life now, she hoped that such a practice would again help her.

It was the summer of 1952. The two personal changes had lessened the insomnia, and as nothing succeeds like success, she decided on a third change. Tanning. Lying in the sun was second nature to many women in these days; the dangers to the skin and the need for protection against ultraviolet rays, the UUAs and UUBs, were as yet unknown. (Although the southern belles with their parasols avoided the sun even then.) Far too quiet and pointless an activity for Marie in the past, tanning was an activity she had often overheard, especially from her sisters who *worked* at their suntans. She had decided to test some her sisters' behavior. Unlike her sister Anne, Marie had never allowed time for preening. And the quest to obtain a bronze was certainly a form of this pastime.

So Marie obtained her first tan that summer, and her customers began to compliment her on her looks. In the past, she had received comments on her business sense but not on her appearance. And the praise inspired her to further embellish her image. She began to buy expensive clothes. With two exclusive shops in her own city, one specializing in shoes and the other in women's stylish clothes, trips to Pittsburgh proved unnecessary this time. The owners of the classy establishments immediately recognized potential in Marie's patronage and personally helped her. Knowing that they were dealing with one of the richest women in the city, the owners assured that all dealings were on a first name basis.

All of her new clothes had matching accessories, shoes, and jewelry. Only her purse was not part of the scheme; it never matched anything. Carrying a similar, black leather purse her entire life, she had limits to the accessory piece of her outfit. The practical handbag, a substitute for the briefcase not yet toted by career women, seemed to hold the core of her businesses and was always visible.

Though sacrificing time she could have devoted to The Joint, the pastimes worked—she was now sleeping at night. Until now, such leisure had been unknown to her. Conquering the insomnia had been her goal this time, but the leisure activities had had other dividends; she noted that the new routine even changed her relationship with her four sisters. Trying on some of *their* diversions, she found that she could more easily join in their conversations and even share in a movie from time to time. Perhaps the renovation of the house had failed because it had been about changing *thing*s. While walking, tanning, and church attendance were about personal changes in her life.

For as long as she could remember, Marie had felt the need to stay ahead of the pack. Playing out the father's protective role, she had scouted ahead for danger that might affect the family. Like a shepherd, she had remained outside the herd. And she now felt part of things—and more relaxed. Perhaps success has different constructs.

After two years of her own therapy, Marie appeared rested and happy. She no longer suffered insomnia. But plateaus never lasted for the patriarch. Life forever nudged her on, and now, feeling good, she sought another goal. Her search began anew. Revived by her new practices, she was blind to their necessity in her life. In a casual decision, she relinquished all three, and within a year, found herself sleepless again. Though the condition reared its head in the dark of night, her stress dwelt in the fears she tried to submerge during the daylight hours.

જીભ્જીભ્જીભ્જીભ્જીભ્જીભ્જીભ્જીભ્જીભ્જીભ્જી

Occasionally, Mame invited me into her bedroom on a sleepless night. A brief discussion about school and the new things I was learning there seemed to waylay her fears, finally easing the way for sleep. I was young and carefree and had no trouble falling back to sleep when I returned to my bed, though Ro forever chided her sister for interrupting my sleep; in the house little went unnoticed. I enjoyed our late night conversations—conversations that would not have happened in the light of her busy days. Though not a frequent happening, the talks found us chatting for at least an hour at these times. She relished details of my classes, asking questions at every juncture. As our talks reached a logical end, I would stay awhile to watch the end of a talk show with her.

Calling me into her room as before, Mame surprised me one night. Approaching the time for me to begin college, I had been accepted at a state school and assumed that she would sponsor me, but the specifics of the money matters had never crossed my young mind. She placed her black purse on her lap; I had seen her carry what seemed to me the same purse my whole life. But now she extracted seven one hundred dollar bills, and in the simplest of ways, handed them to me for my first year at school. And then the two of us proceeded with the talks that had engrossed us during such rendezvous of the past. Late in August for the next three years, she carried out the casual ritual that funded my college education—in her bedroom in the wee hours of the night.

CRCRCRCRCRCRCRCRCRCRCRCRCRCRCRCRCRCR

Eddie, who had previously consoled his wife, had grown tired of her nightly insomnia, and late night television had lost its original success. Coming home after closing The Joint to find a sleepless wife, when he himself was exhausted, he offered another remedy: a sedative that a pharmacist friend had prescribed.

With the proper name, a description of the potion that he offered her could have been found in any medical directory. Phenobarbital—a barbiturate that interferes with nerve impulses and whose effect lasts up to sixteen hours—is highly addictive.

12

The Connector

For months after her mother's burial, Maggie grieved long hours at the graveside and worried over the headstone and flowers.

"It's only here that I find peace" she said when her sisters questioned her actions. This was the sister they had long accused of undue melancholy.

Often visiting her mother's grave, Maggie walked the short distance from the house to the cemetery. Walter knew from the start that it was not within him to help her through the difficult period, so he outsourced the job to Love. Love went with her to the grave site and provided the listening ear she needed in these soulful days. Though grateful for the attention, she never allowed things to move beyond a deep friendship. So Walter's instinct to trust his friend, as well as his wife, proved correct. Though she harbored deep feelings for their mutual friend, Maggie loved her husband—and recognized temptation when it so clearly presented itself. Her vow of fidelity, taken years before, won out.

A year after Anna's death, Maggie returned to life with Walter in their apartment. Though she had never abandoned the dwelling, always keeping it clean and orderly even as she did the house, Walter felt a permanency this time; emotionally, his wife had returned. The couple sensed their lives reverting to the days when they first leased the space. But unlike Anne, Maggie found little contentment in freedom. Hearing from Marie that one of her waitresses had suddenly quit, she considered a full-time position. The job would provide the security that had forever eluded her, and two full-time salaries would raise their standard of living and perhaps include the possibility of their own home.

But just as she was about to give Marie a nod, Maggie's health became a variable in the decision.

Convinced that some mysterious malady had seized her body, she failed to consider the obvious. Though the signs were quite normal. Only Billie, who had experienced firsthand the same condition on two occasions, arrived at the correct conclusion. Both Maggie and Walter scoffed at her notion; the two had been married for eighteen years! But when Dr. Sunstein made his diagnosis, all doubts vanished. At the house, the good doctor's words were always the last ones, and after he spoke, no one looked for second opinions. The stork's shocking journey had begun.

The future parents beamed, and Maggie's joy infused her surroundings. Though she had overcome the grief of Anna's death, there had remained a void in her life, apparent to those who loved her. She had mothered them all—Walter, her nieces, her cousin Johnny's orphaned daughters, and the needy patrons at The Joint. But a child of her own had always been her deepest desire: the most cherished but most fanciful of her dreams.

A first pregnancy at age thirty-eight and during the heat of summer proved long and difficult. Hearing the benefits of exercise during pregnancy, she often walked from her apartment to the house. Conveniently, Anne's was the half-way mark for Maggie, and after reaching it, she had the small, family-owned store next door that provided a cooling treat, her favorite *vanilla* popsicles. Once there, Maggie either stopped to visit with Anne or walked the short alley to the house where she could enjoy the front porch shaded by the large oak in the front yard, a comfort unavailable at her apartment.

As protracted as the pregnancy seemed, labor and delivery felt even longer for this older first-time mother. After many hours, a breech birth, surely a cesarean section in a different time and place, succeeded naturally under Dr. Sunstein's supervision. Though never leaving his post through the long hours, he kept his concerns to himself during the labor and delivery, but later told Maggie that it had been a close call for both mother and child and cautioned her against a second child.

"Appreciate this healthy, baby girl and ask for nothing more," he counseled the ecstatic mother. Overjoyed parents welcomed the infant, who also had a happy clan at the house eager to hold the first baby in the family in seven years.

Already firm from the shared experiences of their youth, the bond between Maggie and Billie grew stronger after the birth. Of the five sisters, only these two had experienced labor and childbirth, both choosing to bypass anesthetic during either phase and also following their mother's example of breast-feeding through the first years of life. These two would parent the second generation in the new country.

Just as Walter began to search for a home for his family, Marie invited the couple to purchase a portion of the house. Though the decision to become permanent residents proved difficult for the new parents, Marie argued the financial health of the arrangement. And within three months of the blessed event, Maggie and Walter packed up their apartment and moved back to the house, never to move again.

Even as they packed, Maggie looked at her sleeping infant and promised herself that only she and Walter would do the parenting. Knowing that she would enjoy the familiar ambience of the house, Maggie had a new life to consider and feared that the family would pamper her new daughter. Would the little girl learn the boundaries of life in this unusual setting? Would parental restrictions cause domestic discord? Such unanswerable questions plagued the new mother.

Still, Maggie moved with her family into the house, and found that even with the new dynamic of a young child, traffic flowed easily within its walls. Most of the partitions from the previous tenants remained so her section was clearly defined and provided them some independence from the others. The secondary entrance that the tenants had once used was soon forgotten. Maggie began to cook in the remodeled kitchen on Marie's side, and soon both sections merged. The statistics: eight full-time residents, three others for one-third of the year, and Anne and Tom who lived so close that their presence was never interpreted as company. In all, thirteen residents resided in the compound.

Living at the house now as a parent and interested as always in people, Maggie saw more clearly what she had always known but never admitted to herself. Her four sisters divided naturally into two camps; Marie and Billie were similar in personality and like their mother, while Anne and Rose displayed qualities of Aunt Rosalie. And Maggie belonged in neither camp. Though she shared passions with Marie and Billie, which allowed her to forsake appearance from time to time, she also possessed the reserved demeanor of the other two sisters. Less like any *one* sister, Maggie was a bit like all of them, the unique collective. Trusted by all as the most objective of the five, she had definite attitudes of her own. She understood both groups and served as a bridge, a link between the two sides when disagreements arose. Unconsciously, she had played this role in the past and, residing at the house now, found that she better understood her unique place in the family.

Maggie's concerns about the move failed to unfold. Sensing her determination to raise the child by her own rules, the others did not indulge the little girl. Marie, who had witnessed Maggie's warm nature as a waitress, became the only culprit but soon found that as a mother, Maggie remained firm in her decisions. Whatever was bought or done for the little girl required her mother's approval. And though willing to share the joy of her daughter, she refused to make the rearing of her child an open affair, where such things as bed and mealtimes were arbitrary. She had waited too long for this gift.

The surprising effect of the move for Maggie was Walter's fading presence. Because of his excitement over his daughter's birth, she had expected his active support in parenting. But such reasoning proved faulty; Walter seldom appeared at mealtimes, even when his shifts on the police force permitted. Showing no interest in tasks in the male column of family duties, he would suggest that Maggie call someone, when she tried to involve him. Though he worked a variety of shifts at the police station, sleeping through the days for the night vigils, it became obvious to Maggie that his free time was spent with his fellow cops. The practice, hardly unique for the times, took priority. Still, faithfully turning over his pay-check to his wife, Walter supported his family, and Maggie eventually became too busy with motherhood to object to his absence. Though not always visible, he remained available when she needed him and that was not to be taken lightly by someone who had lost a father at age six—and taken charge of a large household six years later.

Maggie found motherhood everything she had ever hoped, and she rel-ished every moment of the demanding job. Trailing her toddler through the first wobbly steps around the broad expanse of the house, she was exhausted at the end of the day but happier than ever before. The two sets of steps leading to the second floor needed to be watched. And in the large rooms that Marie had decorated so lavishly, the expensive furniture and china needed to be guarded from the tiny feet and curious hands.

When the little girl was four, Maggie took her to her cousin Johnny's, whose early death had increased Maggie's allegiance to his three daughters. The girls, now teenagers, took delight in the child and immediately volun-teered their services to baby-sit. Knowing the three since their births, she was touched by their offers of, "*Any* time." Still, she hesitated to leave her child, except occasionally with the residents of the house. Her protective nature that sprang from the early responsibilities of her youth had grown with age; she was, after all, nearly a generation older than the average first-time mother of her day.

When her daughter's steps led to the schoolhouse door, Maggie faced a frightening new stage of parenthood. How could she leave her in the care of *strangers*? Especially one with sixteen other youngsters in their care? Never having denied the label of protective parent, she had witnessed a bad fall when her daughter was three, and it had increased her fears. Freak-ish, the incident required stitches in the little girl's tongue, and though, in the end, no permanent damage was done, the accident increased her anxi-eties and made school, Maggie's first step away from her child, loom large.

The prospect of a solitary walk to and from school for the six-year-old stood out among her misgivings.

But what had Maggie to fear? Signs of safety filled the air in the fifties, a time when the new country emphasized the ideal family. World War II had shifted cultural messages to security, and for its thirty-fourth president, the nation elected in a landslide a decorated war hero. Elvis introduced the country to a lively beat with gospel overtones known as rock and roll, and Marilyn became a new kind of sex symbol, more kittenish than those who had previously worn the mantle. The country was safe and sound as the school doors opened for the new first grader.

School buses in the cities were rare then, especially for short distances. In good weather. Maggie would accompany her daughter on the half-mile walk, but in foul weather the trek was difficult.... for an adult. (With different outlooks than adults, children view hikes in rain and snow as exciting or unremarkable ... but never threatening.) But unwilling to leave anything to chance, she decided to learn to drive.

Until now, walking had answered all of Maggie's needs. She had never envied the freedom of her two sisters who had driver's licenses in their twenties. But as a mother, her worldview changed. Observing more women in the driver's seat these days and noting that even her sister Anne had become a student of this male skill, she asked Walter to teach her to drive. As always, he quickly agreed and made himself available at any non-work hour of her choice. The lessons began. Though her anxieties were as great as Anne's, Maggie's goal made her a more determined student. She *would* drive her daughter to school. And after six months of lessons, she became a licensed driver. But as it had one goal, the license proved of limited use. In the future, her times behind the wheel were confined to a small radius around their city.

Though easing Maggie's worries, the license failed to help the little girl gain the independence she would eventually need. Fearful that something might happen to her cherished child, Maggie found even such childhood skills as balancing on a two-wheel bicycle foreboding. Chauffeuring her daughter had quelled a mother's fear, but growing children forever find additional worries for their innocent parents. And their ventures increase in risk as they grow in awareness. Motherhood stirred the insecurities that had plagued Maggie since the days when she was forced to assume responsibilities that belonged to those much older than she.

Though busy with mothering, Maggie had not forgotten the vow made at Anna's death—to help preserve her mother's spirit by strengthening family ties to the Russian Church. Discovering the sacred holidays sprinkled throughout the year, which were distinct from the familiar Sunday Mass, Maggie now attended services during the week. Rather than deter her Sunday attendance, the job of mothering increased it as she learned that her spiritual participation delivered other dividends. Never in a hurry, as her sisters often were after the Sunday service, Maggie relished the details of the lives of other church members. Exchanging thoughts with other mothers in the same pivotal stages of parenting.

CRCRCRCRCRCRCRCRCRCRCRCRCRCRCRCR

I never called her Maggie. Somehow this recasting of the name Margaret never fit this aunt who focused on feelings and home. I called her Aunt Marg. She always seemed to understand, without asking, my needs, especially during the complex teen years. Just as she bridged the differences between her sisters, she became my link to adulthood.

When I longed to wear high heels, at least the hint of a heel on my otherwise flat, childlike shoe, she sensed my desire, without words passing between us. Heels were as important a rite of passage to females in those days as the move from knickers to full length pants had been to males a decade or two earlier. Even a small heel on my shoe would indicate that I sat at the portal of womanhood. And Aunt Marg saw that I was ready for some sort of initiation at age thirteen, even though my mother found my steps towards womanhood difficult. Aunt Marg convinced Mother, as only she could, that my desire was natural and that I was not growing up too fast, a common concern about girlhood at the time. I finally got the shoes with the tiny heel that my aunt and I chose. And I remember them well even today: black suede with a bit of red leather in the right place. The heel had only a hint of what would someday be a spike. And thrilled, I had Aunt Marg to thank.

Then there was the bathing suit. With Mother's permission, the summer I turned thirteen, Aunt Marg and I went shopping for a bathing suit. The arrangement worked well; she adored shopping expeditions while my mother dreaded them. Aunt Marg would take my sister and me while Mother worked at The Joint.

Even as a new mother, her devotion to us never wavered. As I tried on suit after suit, I realized that her counsel was inspired by her values, most likely always the case. Approving of the solid, navy blue suit that revealed for the first time the waist of a young woman, rather than the sack-like ones that I had worn until then, she cautioned against the colorful suits with low cut bust lines and high cut legs. As with the shoes, she was willing to go with the more grown-up look, but the potential for attention in the sexier suits exceeded her boundaries.

For many years, I viewed the incident as my protective aunt uneasy with her niece attracting older males. Men whose intentions may not have been within the emotional range of a thirteen-year-old. But with the benefit of time, I see it as something bigger—about family. Aunt Marg saw that the flashy suit (which I didn't buy that day) would have made me stand out. In her thinking, if any member of the family stood out, for any reason, the positions of others in the group would be altered in some way. To Aunt Marg, equality among family members created harmony. And it had become her job to keep it all in balance.

CRCRCRCRCRCRCRCRCRCRCRCRCRCRCRCRCRCR

After the move, Walter realized that too many years had passed to now redo himself as a family man. Delighted with the prospects of fatherhood, after the initial shock of his wife's pregnancy, he forced his thoughts back to plans for a family life. After the birth, he had planned to talk to realtors about a home that he might afford on his cop's salary. (He preferred the informal word to any other on the list of unlimited synonyms for policeman.) But even as he began his research, Maggie was being drawn back to the house by an invisible force that he failed to understand, spending nearly all of the last three months of her pregnancy there. If he objected to the return, would it make him appear unmanly? It would mean an expression of feeling culturally forbidden to men of the time. Was he fearful of what came first in his wife's life? Her ties to the house simply implied devotion. Or so he consoled himself.

When they moved into the house with their infant, Walter felt like a minor player in his new home. Though awkwardly putting in an appearance for an occasional dinner, he always had something that prompted him to leave after the meal. He enjoyed the open-ended social life with his fellow cops, and his wife now had all the help she needed. She faithfully set a place for him at meals when he wasn't scheduled to work and kept his clothes and surroundings spotless. But he remained on the periphery, failing to find a place other than his own bed that was comfortable for him. Still, the desire to somehow fit into this unusual life that his wife had chosen weighed heavily on his sensitive nature. But as a man of the fifties, he could not have verbalized such anxieties to anyone, even his friends. Even he was unclear about the emotions that kept him away from his home.

Around this time, Walter began to chew snuff. The manly habit reduced his stress. Just as some turn to cigarettes, as well as other self-medicating forms for their uneasy moments, he found the finely shredded tobacco wedged between his bottom lip and teeth a soothing presence. Men at the time who indulged in the activity referred to the practice as "chewing" snuff, but the tobacco simply remained in place in the mouth while the natural saliva carried flavor and nicotine into the body; little *chewing* was involved. When the flavor and nicotine began to fade, it was replaced with another pinch from the snuff box. Though no longer called *snuff* and sold under the brand name of Skoal—among others—in the twenty-first century, the practice, likely older than cigarette smoking, still has its adherents.

Walter had observed the custom among his fellow cops who found cig-arettes awkward at difficult moments on the job. Advised that snuff had a calming affect for those tense work shifts, he had resisted the habit until now. But at his most difficult shift, when he became a full-time resident of the house as well as a father, he turned to the habit, which would remain with him for the rest of his life. The habit seemed to clear his thinking.

After living at the house for three years, Walter found a niche for him-self—in his own backyard. Behind the house sat a large garage. Though a part of the property, it was not used for either cars or storage. In some of his early dreams of family life, he had pictured a workshop attached to his home, so the space now intrigued him. Though never learning handyman skills from his father, he was excited by this chance at somehow becoming a *man* of the family. At least in appearance.

Drawn to the space, Walter saw the garage as a definite part of the house but vacant and filled with promise. After some thought, he ruled against an ordinary workshop for home repair. Eddie's growing variety of friends at the Joint generally took care of such tasks at the house. The garage, ignored by the others, seemed somehow the opening Walter sought; it only required a purpose that suited him.

After talking with his close friends on the police force, he decided on a commercial repair shop. Though not versed in such work, he knew that television had become the popular home entertainment, making the times right for a TV repair business. Still in their infancy, the new gadgets had tubes in their inner workings that burned out and required trained people to replace them. Walter reasoned that with a bit of research, identifying and replacing the faulty tubes would be simple. And as a dividend, the business would increase his income. Maggie often worried over finances, so he felt that he had come upon the perfect hobby. There would be more money—and the endeavor would grant him a role at the house.

The setup took time, but Walter's excitement was palpable. Maggie sensed his desire to be around the house more often and was delighted with the venture. The culture at the time clearly differentiated between men and women's work, and she accepted that child rearing remained in the female column. Requiring a purpose, even in the time spent with his fellow cops, Walter disliked idleness and had at last found a role—at the house. Knowing that this new role, which he had sculpted for himself, did not contribute directly to the life there, he observed that the other two males of the household donated little of *their* free time to the upkeep of the property. Andrew cut the grass or shoveled snow when his shifts at the mill allowed; and Eddie, forever busy at The Joint, sent out one of his friends when serious repair required attention.

The shop would be Walter's second job and tied to his deeper hope of becoming a real member of the household.

He worked hard to transform the pipedream into a reality. His long-time job on the police force provided many contacts for initial repairs and also fellow cops who wanted to make a few bucks on the side. Though Walter quickly learned a bit about the workings of television sets, he needed an expert and hired two full-time employees. With little overhead, the enterprise did well, and eventually he won a prize through a television promotion for outstanding customer service.

A sponsor of the annual Miss America Beauty Pageant in Atlantic City, the promoter sent him two tickets to the celebrated event. Though he had no interest in the spectacle, Walter proudly turned over the prize to Maggie, who faithfully watched the televised extravaganza each fall. Maggie invited Anne, the only sister free at the time, to join her. Delighted at the prospects of seeing the show live, she would also be accompanied by the family traveler. Anne had visited the famous city many times and promised to act as guide.

Rather than resenting her lack of travel at middle age, Maggie held to the solemn vows of her first job, when she was forced to take over the household. As then, she chose now not to wander far from home. Journeys of any kind removed her from what she considered the sacred duty of the home fire. The homebody of the family, she preferred the pleasures of a smoothly run house to those of travel.

But the event was a mere four days, and the sparkle of the world famous city on the shores of the Atlantic Ocean now excited her. The anticipation of seeing the entries in the Pageant could be felt throughout Convention Hall, and when the two sisters were not in their first class seats, they walked the Steel Pier that daringly jutted out into the endless ocean. Anne, having experienced the sights many times, delighted now in her sister's excitement—and also in having all meals prepared and rooms cleaned with no bill to accompany such luxury. Such was Anne's definition of convenience.

The pageant, which began in 1921 with an emphasis on bathing suits, was formalized and finally televised for the first time in the fifties, when the focus then turned to evening gowns. But by the early sixties when the sisters attended, protests from the woman's movement brought more changes; scholarship and eventually social action were attached to the list of attributes for the ideal American woman. Was a woman's worth measured by her body or her brains? Could it, as the pageant now claimed, be both? Perhaps all attributes needed recognition, reasoned the sisters as they watched the live competition.

The famous master of ceremonies for the popular event was Bert Parks. Synonymous with the role he had played for years was the Miss America Song, which he sang directly to the winner as she made her way down the runway, out into the heart of the crowd at the large convention hall. "There she is, Miss America ... your ideal," he crooned to Miss North Carolina as she made the famous walk down the runway that year. And even those who had no connection with the winner's state fought tears or simply allowed them to flow. And Maggie and Anne were no exception.

The contest was an all-American event, and the two in their late-night talks in the hotel room now considered the ideal American woman—offstage, who was she?

"I think Miss Idaho's answers to the personal questions made a lot of sense," Maggie began.

"But Miss California had more poise and was really talented. Women need to be able to care for themselves these days," Anne offered the belief that she had long held.

Both agreed that the competition's emphasis on looks and body dimensions strayed far from the values of their mother's peasant background. But for the sisters, the ideals of their mother had changed; their lives in the new country were different than hers. The sisters themselves were now conscious of their appearance in public. Both preened before leaving home for any reason. Anne had spent years at beauty work and knew its impact on women and the culture in general. And Maggie, having waitressed, knew well the effect of her appearance on customers at The Joint. But perhaps the focus ought to shift to brains and action for American women, they mused. The family's second generation was three females and college was a given for them—at least in the minds of the sisters. The topic endowed them with much to consider in this unusual time they shared.

The unfamiliar surroundings encouraged the two to go deeper into their feelings—of family. Though it would have been simple to connect with Anne on any day at home, the new setting rejected routine. And Anne and Maggie found themselves in an intense discussion about their sister Marie, the sister whose age placed her between them. Maggie wanted to engage Anne, the oldest in the family, in what had become the family secret—the health of the family patriarch. Maggie forced onto the table that evening a conversation that Anne would not have initiated.

Both knew that Marie suffered from insomnia and had once conquered it with her own cure. Though inspiring in the beginning, her solution finally failed as a permanent one. Now the sleeplessness had returned, and Eddie was supplying her with something that kept her unsteady on her feet, unsure of herself, for several hours after waking each day. Happy that Maggie had now broached what had been unspoken in the family—the elephant in the middle of the living room—Anne listened as Maggie described what she had witnessed.

"She's usually up and dressing for work around two in the afternoon. That's when I begin to hear stirrings upstairs."

"Well, sleep has been difficult for her for years. She probably doesn't fall asleep until the early dawn, close to six," countered Anne.

"But when she comes down the steps clutching the banister, barely able to walk, it terrifies me, and regardless of where I am in the house, I run to the staircase. I don't let her see my panic and find something that will distract matters; I compliment her on her new outfit, or ask about The Joint. But I live in fear for the rest of the day. We need to confront her and Eddie about this! What is going on?"

"I'm not sure how they would react to…. accusations. Marie is an adult and makes her own decisions; she's made *family* decisions for a very long time! And since her business seems to be going well, those judgments seem sound. I don't like making waves; we'd be interfering in their marriage. You know, I've always said—peace at any price."

"But now the price is our sister's health," Maggie replied, frustrated with her sister's old standby. She too wanted family harmony, but this cost was too high.

Though they came to no agreement that September day, the discussion eased Maggie's burden. Having released the cat from the bag, she returned to the house refreshed by the talk…. and the exciting excursion.

The Atlantic City treat proved so successful that Maggie made four other trips in the next eight years but not as a tourist. Her succeeding journeys had to do with family, so that wondrous sights were merely a dividend. Making one trip to help in preparation of her niece's graduation, Maggie later traveled to help another niece care for her newborn, the firstborn of the third generation in the new country. And there were the two trips with her sister Rose to offer extra hands in packing, as the families of the second generation began their life journeys. By coincidence, one trip also included a sightseeing tour of the nation's capital, where the spellbound group caught a glimpse of the President four months before his assassination, providing ample data for future conversations in the sitting room of the house.

This era in Maggie's life eliminated one element of her past. After moving back into the house, she never again waitressed at The Joint. Even after her daughter became self-sufficient, she refused to substitute when unexpected illnesses felled regular waitresses. Though she had once enjoyed the job, she chose to funnel her energies elsewhere these days.

And for reasons unknown at the time, this decision protected her from future pain.

13

The Aunt

Rose was thrilled now to have her brother safely home from the war. Though the two shared only rare chats, they had the tacit closeness of residents without partners. (Living at the house since the beginning, Kate though single was not *blood*, and this distinction created a separate category for her.) Like her sisters, Rose adored her brother and never criticized him. To cement their connection, she named him beneficiary of her nest egg—appropriately, U. S. Savings Bonds. Since the collapse of the department store's savings plan during the Depression, Rose preferred the security of the federal government. Surely, there was nothing safer than the government of the new country. A common practice during the war, regular deductions had been made from her bi-monthly paychecks. Painlessly, her bonds had begun to grow.

Andrew's name as beneficiary on her savings also reflected the times. Rose harbored concerns about his future at the mill; would steel production remain in their city? Having been drafted, he was promised his job on return, but the U.S. steel industry was showing signs of change. Labor had organized at the local plant, an action her own workplace had avoided. Union membership in America had risen to sixteen times what it had been at the turn of the century. And steel workers across the new country had begun to win benefits, but the strikes had closed American plants for extended periods, thereby opening the country's doors to steel imports. Rose sensed that something was off balance in the economic system and worried that her brother would soon be jobless, a frightening thought for those who had lived through tough times.

Unknown to Rose at the time, the decline of the U.S. steel industry had begun.

Still, comforted by his return, Rose knew that she now had an ally in her objection to Marie's renovation project, which appeared endless. Often witnessing disagreements between his sisters, Andrew made a point not to take sides. Like Rose, he found the changes needless but as a man, easy to ignore. But his presence strengthened Rose in her resistance to the elaborate plan. She had been impressed at Marie's ability to purchase the house but found the remodeling effort, especially in the two large rooms, senseless. And dramatic changes troubled her. In time, she relented and aided her sister by searching for items *intown*, enjoying the rare praise she received from Marie. But material items meant little to Rose, and none of her sister's arguments altered that fact.

Forced to admit that the project delivered one positive result, Rose delighted in the fact that Maggie was again a permanent resident. The enticing noises of a toddler resounded throughout the house these days. This third member of the second generation delivered joy to all. And to none more than Rose. Her lifelong desire to be the kind of aunt that *she* had known as a child now had a third opportunity to play out with the delightful child. This niece, different than the other two who were part-time residents, brought with her the context of childhood. With toys, highchairs, cribs, schoolbooks, homework, report cards, playmates, pets, and finally, cosmetics, cars, and boys, she changed the atmosphere—something the remodeling could not do. And Rose's opposition to the physical changes at the house was easily deflated by the little girl.

Taking her for long walks in the stroller, Rose became familiar with the neighborhood that she had lived in for twenty years. Because she had vacationed during her free time and gotten her exercise through walking up and down the hill for the commute, she had never meandered around the surrounding streets. In winter, it was too dark when she returned from work, but in the summer, she walked for miles, to the toddler's delight. Nor was her time with the youngster confined to the outdoors. Sitting and playing games, Rose reveled in the squeals of joy, innately understanding this role of aunt that she had chosen.

And daily at the center of a large department store in the heart of a robust city, she had access to the newest fashions in children's clothes. Though continually defending her purchases with, "I don't know much about kids," she showered the little girl with the loveliest of outfits.

For Rose, times were good, *hunky-dory* as Marie would have said. (Rose never allowed herself such slang and often corrected her sister.) Even the train commute to Pittsburgh remained a wonder to her. The ride placed her with an interesting group of people during her nonwork hours and proved a social time that she welcomed. A natural forerunner to today's happy hour, the ride allowed neither food nor alcohol, only cigarettes and conversation. If she felt unfriendly on some days, she picked up the morning paper on the walk from the house—or the evening one on her return—and read during the commute. The act offended no one; each of the commuters chose a similar escape on occasion.

In the fifties, spinsters often remained with their families of origin, so her choice to stay at the house was not unusual. Though secure in such an arrangement, she had built a second life—a work life—that temporarily separated her. Returning home each day was as important to her as the city half of her life, but except for the stories she occasionally told of her work days, the two halves never touched. Entertaining even coworkers who lived close by the house was out of the question for her.

Though her life seemed routine, she was happy in the arrangement. Contentment could be felt in her demeanor, which was neither whiny nor moody. Though often disagreeing with Marie, now technically her landlord, Rose found pleasure in every detail of her life, even in the daily walk to and from the train, though the half-mile jaunt home meant she had an uncompromising hill at the end of a long workday. The trek, difficult on mornings when she proceeded down an ice covered hill, only energized her spirits.

In her hours at the house, she shared in chores and in her spare time, happily read. The princess, as her father had once called her, continued to devour fairy tales, though now in the form of popular novels. Rose demanded in her books what she called "a good story." The author's technique was far less significant than plot, and when books failed to establish a strong storyline, she simply read until—it put her to sleep; she found purpose even in the books she labeled boring. Constantly exchanging paperbacks—hardcover was not a luxury she afforded herself—she forever had a variety of books in her bedroom. And these remained the only evidence of her presence in the house. Her bedroom, though referred to by everyone as Rose's room, contained only her clothes, and even those were concealed in bureau drawers and dark closets.

Had she suddenly packed and left, only her physical absence would have been felt. Nothing throughout the large house belonged to her.

Just as she made no material marks, Rose's income remained obscure. Choosing to remain in the coat department as a commissioned salesperson, she could boast a notable salary these days but never chose to discuss figures; such a disclosure would have felt unrefined, inconsistent with the image she presented. Without such information, Marie's argument that Rose had not risen to the management level continued.

"It's time to move ahead. You've been in retail for thirty years; why are you still taking orders from other people?" insisted Marie.

"I like what I do."

From another vantage point, Billie said, "I don't care what your title is, but maybe you could be a bit more thrifty. Eat breakfast at home; take your lunch."

Annoyed, Rose replied, "I don't ask anyone for anything. What's all this about?"

Her salary more than met her needs, and self-sufficient, she contributed to life at the house, spent what she wanted on herself and gifts for her nieces and laid away a serious amount in savings.

After her affair with Jim, Rose allowed dating to fade from her life but continued to vacation with close friends in Atlantic City. But as time passed, social events, with the exception of her vacation, began to wither. Working in Pittsburgh six days a week, attending Sunday Mass, and cooking dinner on her one day off seemed to satisfy her. She enjoyed her nieces and books in her free time; what else was there?

In the midst of this contentment, a tidal wave washed in to alter her world. As she walked to the train one ordinary day, the sun seemed especially bright, and her thoughts settled on the beauty of the spring morning. As she approached the station, engrossed in watching the sun tickle the grass into a sparkle, she suddenly awoke her from her reverie and began a rush to the train. A man who was walking about fifteen feet ahead of her suddenly dropped to the ground, a sight she would have missed had she been walking faster, as was her custom.

A stranger to Rose, the man was surrounded by several companions who came to his aid. As she stood by in stunned silence, shaken to the core. the man was pronounced dead at the scene This was not someone she had known or would grieve, but the incident brought back with a vengeance the other sudden events of her life—the death of her small brother and Helen and their burning dwelling. The frailty of life again filled her mind.

The freakish day proved the only time that Rose ever arrived late for work. That she even got there at all is the bigger mystery.

The event played endlessly in her mind, a compulsion that refused to yield to reality. "He was a stranger," she repeated to herself. Though she could not picture him walking ahead of her before he fell, in her mind's eye she now saw him repeatedly fall to the ground. Reminding herself of the chance nature of the event, she knew that minutes could have placed her ahead of the small group; she would never have known of the incident. Why did it affect her? Old assurances that had sustained her through the sudden tragedies of the past now proved useless.

Depression overtook her. Though she continued to work, never taking time off, an emotional numbness overcame her. The job as well as the train ride now proved a drudge. Nothing seemed to matter anymore. Finding it difficult to attribute all this to a stranger's death, she felt confused by the feelings that so dramatically altered her mood—and her life.

Sullen and disinterested in her surroundings, she stopped cooking Sunday dinner as well as mingling with her sisters on the nights she arrived on the early train. She ate little and used the excuse of an exciting book to turn in early. Never a moody person, she was not herself, especially to her sisters.

Quickly her four sisters offered their takes. Similar to her prescription for most things, Anne counseled her to travel more—and to check on her employer's policy on early retirement. Marie continued her argument about job advancement. Billie, the sister who lived in another state for part of the year, recommended that Rose move from the house; the depression was merely a symptom of her disagreements with Marie. Only Maggie offered a different solution.

"Rose, I think that you need therapy. Lately, I've heard of people getting help from a different kind of doctor, a psychiatrist. Remember? Dr. Sunstein recommended one in Pittsburgh to Marie."

"Oh, I'd hate to think that I needed a head doctor!" Rose exclaimed.

Thinking that such specialists could only be found in Pittsburgh, making it a classier choice for her sister, Maggie had tried another tactic.... but failed.

In the end, Rose ignored all the advice and listened to her own drummer. And arrived at her own therapy—she would clean the atttic! The idea seemed an odd cure for despair, but such a bootstrap action would keep her busy, a state she had always relished. Unknown to all, she had long been curious about the mysterious attic, an unexplored space that separated the living quarters from the roof. Accessible only through the ceiling of her bedroom closet adjacent to her bedroom, the attic had been ignored by the busy residents since their arrival many years before. None of them had surplus in their lives; there had been nothing to store in this common area. But known to all was the fact that the attic was far from empty. After living near the puzzling trapdoor in her closet for twenty years, Rose decided to explore the attic on her own, welcoming this chance to be busy … in an unusual way.

Since work laws now required overtime pay for anything over forty-hour weeks, Rose had two free days instead of one to devote to her project. She found the space filled with old furniture, long forgotten relics left there by a previous owner. Knowing nothing of the value of her findings, she set them aside and proceeded with the awesome job of a soap and water cleaning on the abandoned region. The fact that the attic and its contents belonged to Marie—and technically Marie could have easily paid to have the work done—never crossed her mind. This was the house.

Finally with her sister's consent, Rose sold the attic treasures and donated the proceeds to the Church. The cleaning, as well as the financial payoff, took two months and left Rose with a feeling of achievement that was strong enough to right her emotional distress. The connection with the bygone era of the furniture served to lift the darkness brought on by the stranger's death. The change was as quick and peculiar as the bizarre incident that had brought on the despair, and she snapped back to her old self. With only a few alterations in her life.

Atlantic City vacations became a memory. In the future, her paid leave, now a month long, would be at the house. Other than the train rides and occasional lunches at work with friends, all socializing would remain within the family. Tightening the reins even more than she had in the past, she reduced the chance of surprise in her life.

Still, as she renewed her resolve to limit change in her life, stronger after this fourth unexpected event, the world at the close of the fifties was growing smaller. The new country was not as far from the old country as it had been fifty years ago when Anna made her lonely journey. Transcontinental television had begun at the beginning of the decade, and later, Explorer I, the first US earth satellite, went into orbit. The nuclear sub, Nautilus, made its first undersea crossing at the North Pole, and the first transatlantic telephone cable was activated. The first domestic jetliner opened service between New York and Miami. So in celebration of her victory over depression, Rose made a sudden decision to fly to Billie's during her next vacation. A short ride, the trip could replace Atlantic City with a family visit.

She had flown once in the past with friends searching for an alternative to Atlantic City; the group had once traded their former vacation mecca for the Florida sun, but the state had not lured them back. Public transportation came naturally to Rose's way of thinking; she had been influenced by the efficiency of her daily train commute and believed in mass transport. Never feeling any inclination to drive a car, she had had the train, which met her daily needs and also carried her to Atlantic City. Though too early to be a true environmentalist, she held to a mantra that proved on the vanguard of modern thinking.

"There are too many cars on the road," she firmly proclaimed on any occasion that seemed appropriate.

Now with a short winter vacation as well as a longer one in the summer, Rose chose a forty-minute plane ride from Pittsburgh to Billie's. Such a trip did not stretch her emotional limits. Seeking a swift mode of travel that would enable her to make visits in the future, she welcomed the possibility of a short trip, which would deposit her with family. Deciding to make a surprise visit laden with gifts for her nieces just as her Aunt Rosalie had done so many years ago, Rose felt elated. And the flight to Billie's proved a success. Pleasantly surprising the family, she had aviation to thank for the convenience.

Unfortunately, the return flight hit sudden turbulence, enough to have passengers screaming their prayers aloud. Rose, with her usual calm demeanor, emitted no sound, though the passenger in the adjoining seat advised her to pray for forgiveness: "for all the offenses you may have caused in this life," the woman repeated. Greatly relieved at touchdown on terra firma, Rose never traversed the heavens again. Just as the world had grown smaller, her personal world shrank even more. Left now with two forms of public transportation, as she had ruled out boats years ago, she assured herself that her future visits to family would be by either train or bus.

Though the harrowing flight likely produced a few white hairs, Rose hardly looked her age. At that age when women anxiously note the physical changes in themselves, she looked much younger than her fifty years. She refused to discuss age—hers or anyone else's—so there was no way to compliment her health or vitality. When the subject of age erupted, she had one comment.

"Age is a useless tag. It's how we *feel*, not the number of birthdays we've had!"

The two simple sentences abruptly ended any further conversation about aging—in a culture that wrote women off at age forty.

But far deeper than wrinkles and a loss of beauty lay Rose's fear that her treasured job would evaporate, forcing her into a retirement that held no appeal. The subject proved so frightful to her that she never explored the store's retirement plan, dismissing Anne's advice. Was there a policy that set a retirement age at the store? What was the severance package? These remained questions too scary for her to ask.

With more of her free time spent now at the house, Rose grew close to her sister Maggie. The sisters often shared the dinner that Maggie prepared and kept warm on her sister's late nights. And the two kibitzed about the day while Rose ate.

When Rose began taking her vacation weeks at the house, the sisters had time to deepen their relationship through feelings that appeared as they shared activities. Rose stepped in to help Maggie with such chores as hanging out the weekly laundry. Such a mundane activity provided the natural warmth of the sun. A joy that her celebrated job eliminated with air-conditioning. Clothes dryers were available at the time, but the two sisters considered the time-saving device useless, robbing clothes of the well-known outdoor smell. And their method provided more time to chat as they hung and folded clothes.

A kitchen dishwasher, also to become a household staple across the new country, was not installed during the remodeling because of plumbing problems. And the chore of washing dishes was also lessened by their ongoing conversations. Such bonding acts, eliminated by modern time-saving devices, filled their days in the happiest of ways.

Returning from work in the evenings, Rose carried a piece of the big city home in the form of stories. Usually about the eccentricities of customers, the tales added humor to Maggie's day. Rose, profited from her younger sister's insights into difficult customers while Maggie helped Rose move closer to the family that had long felt foreign to her. They attended Sunday Mass together and shared their favorite books, radio, and later, television programs. Together the two examined the details of novels, seldom finding fault in the other's choices.

And they had the joy of Maggie's daughter to share.

CRCRCRCRCRCRCRCRCRCRCRCRCRCRCRCRCRCRCR

As an adult now, I stepped into my aunt's life in a new way. At nineteen, I found that I could actually share that part of her world, which remained vague to me, as well as to the other residents of the house. Searching for a summer job at the end of my first year of college, I followed her suggestion to apply for work as a store extra. I had visited the department store many times in my youth, but my own job there through the busy summer months would be different. The position carried no benefits, but such dividends as hospitalization and retirement were far in the future and of no concern to me.

Thrilled with my first paycheck, I also had the chance to experience this mysterious side of my aunt's life. At last, I would ride the train as a commuter and explore the many departments spread over twelve floors with multiple escalators and elevators. In addition to the many departments, I soon discovered that the store boasted three large restaurants. The informal sandwich-dessert eatery called The Tick-Tock Shop to imply quick, counter style service lay at the back of the ground floor, while the formal dining area took up most of the fifth floor. A bakery occupied a portion of the mezzanine, unique in both space and wonderful aromas. All three restaurants spilled out luscious odors that when combined with the expensive perfumes of the cosmetic department created a marvelous smell that greeted me as I entered each morning.

Though my aunt had suggested the job to me, she never offered advice, and we seldom rode the train at the same time. I guess she knew that my mistakes, as they had been for her, would prove my most lasting teachers. I often reminded myself that she had started at the store three years younger than I was now.

Sometimes she suggested that we go to an eatery *outside* the store, an unusual proposal for her. There she would treat me to a healthy buffet that offered a choice of fresh vegetables.

At such times that the two of us shared an environment away from both the house and our workplace, our conversations changed. She often spoke of "women's rights." Just becoming aware of such social issues, I was surprised at her interest in the topic. Like her older sisters, she had been too busy with the task of survival when the woman's collective effort began at the beginning of the century; the Suffrage Movement would have consumed all their energy. But my aunt held definite feelings on the topic.

Recognizing the positive signs in the culture now, she spoke of women's colleges and the growing trend for women to retain their maiden names at marriage, even if only for professional use. The talks were about freedom.

"When young women like you stop needing the approval of men, you will have more choices in your life," she counseled—in 1956.

જીભ્જીભ્જીભ્જીભ્જીભ્જીભ્જીભ્જીભ્જીભ્જીભ્જીભ્જી

Rose hoped that as adults, all her nieces would settle near the house, but it was obvious that the house could not increase its residents and not even Marie proposed building an addition. So when the oldest of the second generation married and settled in another state and the third generation began to arrive, Rose, traveling on either bus or train, spent her vacation time with the family, eager to serve once again as aunt to a new generation. Proving an easy houseguest with few personal needs, she was eager to read to the children, just as she had faithfully done for their mother. In this new style vacation, she made no demands on her hostess. She enjoyed the nearby gambling casinos, but her passion in this never approached her sister Anne's. She found gambling, that constant chance to win, exciting but far from the thrill that she had known with her young friends on the coast of New Jersey. These now were *family* ventures that she valued at this point in her life.

14

The Resolute

Though grasping every opportunity to return to the house, Billie remained in her home three years after the divorce. The resolve, like her lease, required renewal: a discussion she annually held with herself. With the trips, the house claimed one-third of her year and continued to nurture her.

As the trips were defined by her daughters' school vacations, the house had become "recess time." Billie socialized more during her times there, though she also worked at The Joint. At their own home, the two girls had school, and she kept house in a routine manner with designated days for laundry, groceries, and cleaning; never missing a step even for her own dalliances, she always served dinner at precisely five-thirty. Her own residence implied duty and a structured lifestyle. Billie saw her daughters' formal schooling in a light that required a cadence—different than the house could provide. Determined to provide this, she followed a strict schedule at her home.

Life at the house was different, more casual. There were no school hours, so both meals and bedtimes could change with the whim of the moment. Billie, relieved of parenting duties as her daughters came under Maggie's guidance, waitressed at The Joint where her own schedule had parameters. Socializing in the evenings with Anne and Tom, she saw less of her daughters. But all three of the part-time residents were happy in the atmosphere of their extended family.

Such an arrangement proved financially good for Billie and filled her emotional needs in a different way. Marie, always happier when the three nestled in, juggled the schedules of her regular waitresses to fit her sister's trips. And Maggie was content to increase her family. The three were warmly greeted on their arrivals, but as this was frequent, no special arrangements were necessary. Nothing out of the ordinary was offered in recognition of their stays; they were not guests. No one planned outings or special foods. Billie, who had now begun to entertain family when they visited her home, found this fact frustrating.

"No one prepares for *our* arrival," she often complained.

But no one responded to her protests. Entertaining was unknown at the house where everyone was family.

Still, neither weather nor the brevity of the holiday interfered with the trips. The trips found Billie packing on the day that preceded *any* school vacation. As her daughters stepped out of the school door, the journey commenced. They had come to love the house and the family they found there.

But eventually peers became important.

"She's having a party. Can't we drive to the house tomorrow? Or maybe we can just wait 'til next vacation to go?"

Billie found herself defending their frequent trips

"I need the income," she'd say. "And the house gives us something to look forward to every few months."

"I love everyone there ... but I love my friends at school too," one of the two would reply.

As a single parent and without the liveliness of the life she had known at the house, Billie was lonely and needed the trips for more than income. Her daughters were young, and perhaps someday they would understand, she reasoned. Too close to see the whole picture, Billie had a split existence just like her sister Rose's. These two sisters went into the world and then returned to the house to touch base with their lifelines. The difference was that Rose's commutes were daily, while Billie's time away from her lodestar could be as long as three months.

Often in the lonely hours at her own home, especially in the dark of a winter's night after the two girls had gone to bed, she sat and listened to her favorite music on the Victrola, the record player that had been one of the couple's few luxuries in the early part of their marriage. On the vanguard of home entertainment, electric Victrolas (A brand name established at the beginning of the century when the phonograph had to be wound.) were not found in many homes in the early thirties. Even after Marie's renovation, the house had only a small radio, which the residents used on rare occasions for news alerts but never music. The family created their own sounds whose rhythm likely would have been disrupted by popular music emanating from the foreign box known as a record player. Such entertainment still came from the outside: from movies and the jukebox at The Joint.

But Billie, in her silent home, had to supply the music herself. With a wondrous voice of her own, she adored ballads. Songs that told stories and beckoned to dreamers were the favorites that got her through the lonely nights as she replayed them, quietly singing along. With repeated playing, the phonograph records soon acquired scratches, but in her loneliness, she ignored the poor sound. Replacing a *record* was unthinkable to her even in the best of times.

Intuitive and determined to solve at least some of life's riddles, Billie, recognized that something was amiss in her life. One late night as she nuzzled close to the Victrola, she admitted to herself that her home felt empty: cold and lacking in something other than material goods. Admittedly, she was finding motherhood difficult so far from her roots. Separated by more than miles, her home and the house failed to form a smooth seam in their lives. How might she create a homey atmosphere in her own home?

Oddly, the answer came through her past in-laws, whom she still saw on occasion because of her children. Though she had never warmed to Robert's parents, or they to her, she had unconsciously become Americanized through the bumpy relationship. Now searching for ways to change the ambiance of her home, she remembered wonderful dinners with them, where dessert crowned each meal. Such was never part of her mother's meals. Even Maggie, who did most of the cooking at the house, never offered dessert; the course did not exist in the family.

So Billie began to create desserts for her young family. Determined, she worked to create a perfect piecrust, and soon fresh apple pie became her specialty. Later she turned to cakes of all kinds; the one made with pink lozenges, known appropriately as Pink Cake, became her daughters' favorite. Making peanut butter or chocolate chip cookies to include in the school lunches, she extended the skill and even mailed penuche to her sisters one Christmas before the holiday journey. Somehow the mailing in holiday tins made the gift more official than delivering it in person. The luscious smells warmed her home in a new way and delighted her daughters, especially when they were allowed to lick spoons and bowls—only after the major contents had been removed with the new plastic tool known as a spatula! Baking cheered her home in aroma and taste. These were *comfort foods*.

But even as she solved one heartache, another emerged. The young woman, who had once sought challenges, now found more hurdles than she thought possible. Receiving minimal support from Robert who now lived fifteen hundred miles away, she had a small income. The divorce lawyer had made no provision for either the rising cost of living or her children's education beyond high school. Billie had no car, so groceries and Church, both necessities in her life, remained difficult. In good weather, the walk for groceries with her red wagon in tow became second nature, but walking to the Russian Church twenty miles away was impossible. Raised in the piety of her mother, Billie missed the Church in her life. She could rely on public transportation on Sundays, but transferring and waiting for bus connections required at least an hour and proved awkward for her young daughters, so she was forced to leave them behind.

The lifestyle that she struggled to provide lacked religious discipline. And she consulted with the family priest, just as she conferred with Dr. Sunstein over the miles. The same man had led the parish the entire time the family had lived at the house, and they were comfortable with the kindly man, though unlike the good doctor he had not been chosen by them; he had been assigned to the parish by higher authorities within the

Church. Having told him her dilemma, she asked his opinion on having her daughters attend a Baptist Sunday school very near her home.

"Why would you deny hungry children available food?" He wisely countered her question with his own.

The permission, so simply stated, inspired her to enroll the girls in a nearby Sunday school. With her own bus rides to the Russian Church well established, Sunday mornings took on the spiritual nature that Billie had remembered in her youth.

Still, the poor finances of the small family remained unchanged. Having discounted the possibility that Billie would maintain her own residence, Robert assumed that the lure of the house, coupled with Marie's insistence, would quickly win out, decreasing the financial demands on him. His defense from the beginning had been that her connection to the house had destroyed the marriage. Such reasoning relieved him of guilt so he pushed for a settlement that would aid his new family—that soon materialized.

Her sisters, including Maggie who now had her own child, remained generous with practical gifts, but the child support and Billie's income from waitressing were too small to support, at the very least, a car of her own.

Forced to admit that her house was often vacant during the year, Billie began to see things in a new light. She was paying rent on unused space. Perhaps the answer to her financial woes lay in tenants! Because they were so often at the house, it might be appealing to a boarder who at those times would have her home to themselves. She and Robert had leased the new two-bedroom brick house, strategically located on a large corner lot within five miles of the Nation's capitol. With a large kitchen, a breakfast nook, a full basement, and a large semi-finished attic that could be converted to more living space, she suddenly saw the property's potential. Her home could accommodate boarders! Though at first hesitant to share her home with strangers, Billie had culture on her side; tenants were common in the day. If she and the two girls shared one of the two bedrooms, she reasoned, the other bedroom could easily accommodate a lodger—or perhaps even a couple. Such an arrangement would leave the living and dining rooms, and the kitchen and bath as cooperative living spaces. Billie had not been raised with the luxury of space and so such a plan felt doable to her now.

The weighty question was who? Naturally, the answer arrived for her while at the house—where many of her questions were answered. One of her sisters knew of a man searching for a room in Billie's area. Newly married, he would be joined by his wife after several months. Hoping to become accustomed to the new area before venturing into home ownership, the couple welcomed the opportunity that Billie's home presented. Located near his workplace, her house seemed an ideal arrangement. So she met the couple, and appearing a good match, the three adults quickly reached an agreement on the space as well as the rent.

All living under the same roof, Billie and the tenants quickly became friends and began to socialize together. For the first time, she became friends with occupants who were not blood. New patterns often deliver outcomes different than planned. Having non-family in her home was new to her, but even more novel, the boarders provided her with a different worldview. She had met people at Church and in her neighborhood in the years that she had lived here, but socializing, now that high school friends had faded, had been confined to her siblings. Definite boundaries existed in relationships for Billie.... until now when she became, by necessity, a landlord.

She and her tenants had roots in the same city, so in the beginning, their talk was of mutual acquaintances, but conversation soon burgeoned to present interests and needs. Like Billie, the newlyweds were without a car. Quickly including her in their plans, the couple suggested that the three *bike* together around the area; such an experience would be new to them—as well as to her.

She had biked in her youth with the sheer joy of abandon, and the idea was exciting as well as practical. From the seat of a bike, Billie discovered an intimate view of her surroundings. Living in an area rich in history, she opened her eyes for the first time to its potential. For the first time since her move here, she felt energized *away* from the house. At one point, she even considered skipping a long weekend trip to the house but soon dismissed the odd thought. Fearful that her actions would be interpreted by her siblings as a rejection, she remained faithful to the family message; only family provided the second wing.

With the encouragement of her tenant-friends, Billie began to date, something she had not done as a single mother, though she was now only thirty-four years old. Attractive and full of life, she quickly found herself in a romantic relationship. Within two months, Brian suddenly presented an engagement ring. But the gesture proved too abrupt. Billie now understood the complexity of such a commitment; one did not marry a person. One married an entire family.

Her ten years of marriage, which had included not only a spouse but his doting parents and two aunts, had left her with feelings she chose now to forget. Even a determined wife like Billie, had no say in living arrangements at the time; she simply followed her husband's career. Feeling confused about the house and its relationship to her partner in those years, she was in no hurry to try again, especially now with the added responsibility of two children. Now marriage meant taking on a parent for her daughters as well as a life partner for herself. Not ready to wholly dismiss another try at matrimony, she played it safe for a change—at least for the moment. Though attracted to Brian, Billie ended the romance. She was not ready for a second marriage. Had he been patient, the answer might have been more to his liking.

Her time as a landlord lasted three years, long enough for the tenants to find their own place and start a family. Hugging Billie as their packed bags beckoned to them from the front door, the couple promised to stay in touch. Saddened by their departure, she was uplifted by the additional income which would enable her to buy a car. A car, though not as much fun as her trusty bike, would offer a bit more mobility—to continue her new adventures.

The secondhand car soon put the red wagon in retirement on grocery day, and she could now drive her daughters to the Russian Church, reinforcing the faith that had been so central to her own youth. The car also made trips to the house more convenient and cheaper than the train. Much had come from her years as a landlord. Her tenants had contributed more than money; they had expanded her horizons, which opened other doors for her. Billie began to take her daughters on day trips to places ignored until now. The nation's capital offered unlimited choices of museums and historic sites: Mt. Vernon, Monticello (a day trip), and the Smithsonian were only the best known—only the beginning of her discoveries. Such a large city had never been part of her life, and its vitality now astonished her. There were elaborate ethnic celebrations, including the Chinese New Year extravaganza in Chinatown each January, a celebration that proved a favorite for the three.

Still, even the larger world failed as a lasting replacement for the emotional sustenance the house offered. So the trips back to the homestead neither ended nor diminished. Nothing replaced family.

In the fifties, Billie's oldest daughter began to make college plans. The second generation in the new country would be entering the world through a different door than the first—through advanced education rather than the work force. Education beyond high school for women was looked upon then as a safety measure. Women might train for professional careers, but the goal remained marriage. If the need ever arose, they would have job training to *fall back on.*

The location of the college proved a prime consideration for the five sisters. They offered no overt counsel but saw the choice at this juncture as important. A state school, close to the house, would mean further connection to the family compound. Perhaps, as was common, the young woman would find her future husband there.

One of Pennsylvania's state colleges lay an hour from the house, and the cost was reasonable. Seven hundred dollars a year—one fortieth of the average college costs in the twenty-first century—included room, board, and tuition. The figure was for out-of-state students, as, technically, she was. In addition to placing her close to the house for the next four years, the college, *above* the Mason-Dixon Line, satisfied the existing attitude that the North educated in a manner superior to the South!

Though proud to see the first of the family prepare for college, Billie was saddened by the impending separation. Even temporary good-byes, such as this one, clearly pained the family rebel—and had for as long as she could remember. Simple to conclude that partings transported her back to the losses of her past: her unknown father, the death of Mary's infant so close in age to Billie's daughter, and the death of the marriage. But her pain seemed deeper than even these sorrows.

As the youngest in the family, Billie had spent more time alone with her mother than had any of her siblings. And she had absorbed, through an emotional osmosis of sorts, Anna's loss of both her family of origin and her homeland. Not one to victimize herself, Anna had never spoken of such grief, but this separation from the soil that had fed her roots for over twenty years could not be ignored in her unconscious. Likely, Billie's siblings also felt this unspoken loss of both country and lineage, but such sadness was buried too deeply. Only Billie the youngest visibly carried this grief, but as with other feelings, she never discussed the pain. This sadness lay hidden in the depths of her psyche and only erupted in tears at farewells. All her good-byes, even the temporary ones, forced her to relive a grief that even her intuitive nature failed to understand.

ଔଔଔଔଔଔଔଔଔଔଔଔଔଔଔଔଔଔ

For my entire life, I too felt a puzzling sadness at farewells of any kind, sharing my mother's heavy heart when faced with partings. The sudden tears and lump in my throat baffled me. As I prepared for my new experience of college, I braced myself for the good-bye between my mother and me at the end of the summer. She would head home with my sister, as the three of us had done at the conclusion of many summers. This time without me. For the first time, I would be headed north as she drove south.

Throughout the summer, she and I had been careful not to speak of the details of the inevitable day of parting.

As fate would have it, we were all to leave on the same day, she on her old journey, and I on my new one. The day before our departure, she offered to drive with me to my new school. Such a change of plans extended her journey by several hours. Though I wondered why she had not invited me to ride with her until we arrived at the campus, I was not surprised at her proposal to tag along. Originally the plan had been for Anne and Tom to drive me and my belongings; now with us the lead car, my mother and sister rode in tandem. Thus the caravan—befitting this milestone of the family's first college entrant—set off.

Our traveling day, a beautiful summer morning in late August, offered no hint of impending fall. Located in the Appalachian Mountains of western Pennsylvania, the school could only be reached on back roads. So the passengers in the two cars were treated with a smattering of towns, bucolic vistas, and neither traffic nor red lights ... for sixty miles. (The Interstate system had just begun, but even today, the trip remains untouched by time, identical to what it was fifty years ago.) On that particular day, I was in no hurry to arrive at my destination. This would be my home for the next four years, and I knew little of what to expect. My thoughts dwelt elsewhere so I briefly forgot the eventual good-bye to my mother and sister.

When we reached the college entrance, my uncle turned left onto the campus, and my mother, bidding her good-bye by waving from the car window, continued the journey home. This was my mother, eliminating the tearful farewell in one flourish of her hand.

ෲෲෲෲෲෲෲෲෲෲෲෲෲෲෲෲෲෲ

Unlike the house, where residency only seemed to increase with time, Billie's home was reduced now to two. With her youngest daughter still in elementary school, she had exactly six years of single parenting before her. Suspecting that Marie would encourage her permanent return to the house when her daughters were on their own, Billie looked ahead and pondered her response. These days, Marie often called to talk of her business. Of the four sisters, Billie had shown a lasting interest in both establishments. Indebted to Marie, who had been generous over the years, she was also bonded by blood.

But Marie's insomnia had returned, and the calls were frustrating, arriving at odd hours of the day or night, often when Marie was coming off the influence of the sleeping drug. Billie had idealized Marie since childhood but knew that she herself had become part of the family secret, by her silence. So though trying to comfort her sister during the agonizing conversations, she also tried to expose the unspoken reality.

"What are you taking? Do you have a prescription? How do you know it's safe?" Wanting direct questions that would avoid denial, she chose her words carefully.

"You're talking foolish," Marie replied with her usual denial. "Eddie just picked-up a mild sedative at the drug store, and I took it with some warm milk. There are no medical *prescriptions*."

"But you don't sound yourself. Your voice is strange." Billie softened her approach.

"And your imagination is even stranger!" Marie replied in growing anger.

Trying to understand the frustrating calls and calm her fears, Billie used her brother as a sounding board on his frequent visits. As always, he proved an easy guest—and a good listener. But he offered no solution.

"Eddie is her husband for god's sake. Surely he's aware of the risks of whatever she takes to sleep!" He responded.

Like her sisters, Billie placed her only brother in a category all his own. When he came to visit, she cleaned and prepared all his favorite dishes in advance. This way, the two were free to attend the horse races, sightsee, or merely talk for hours. What they actually did was always his choice, though Billie knew in advance that the one thing he would *not* do was attend Sunday Mass. Disliking leaving her guest, she refused to miss Sunday Mass but never left him for long and never criticized his lack of devotion. Many years ago, Andrew had made it clear that he viewed church as a *woman's* place and the declaration ended the discussion.

Male authority remained fixed for Billie. Though she silently questioned it in her marriage, she had her unusual name that endowed her with an inside track. People immediately viewed her in another way than they might have a Tiffany or a Grace. And as they have the power to do, the name caused Billie to feel strong. Though it might be said that it was all in her mind, feelings spur actions and actions define humans.

Hardly receiving their brother's royal treatment, Anne also visited in these days. Though Billie prepared special apple pies for Tom, cooking for these visits went no further than the luscious dessert. Anne insisted on treating for dinners in a local restaurant. Entertaining remained bothersome to Anne, and she could not tolerate her sister's toiling in the kitchen during the visits. But in Billie's eyes, generosity did not excuse her from attending Sunday Mass. For this guest anyway, such was the requirement, or Anne heard about it for the rest of the day.

Recognizing her sister's passion for gambling, Billie traveled with the couple to an adjoining state that thrived on the legalized pastime. But odds never charmed Billie, so she refused to gamble—at least not to the extent of her sister. Viewing the activity as wasteful, she often criticized Anne for not setting limits.

"Walk away when you're ahead," she would insist. To no avail.

Billie's sadness at her daughter's departure for college proved justified. The young woman never returned home. Finishing college, she married and moved with her new husband to their own apartment—a short distance from her mother. By design, the first of the second generation had attended a state college near the house. And though the school's enrollment was ninety-five percent state residents, she failed to be sufficiently enamored by a male student—from the state. Instead, the oldest of the second generation married a high school sweetheart, an act that immediately returned her to Virginia where Billie had lived now for fifteen years.

And the marriage became one in a series of changes in Billie's life, which eventually separated her from the house.

A year later, though convinced that at age forty-three, she was far too young for the new title, she became a grandmother. The third generation in the new country made his appearance; the first male since Andrew, born fifty-three years earlier. Three years later, a daughter bounced into the world, and Billie found herself grounded in the role she had previously contested. Her trips to the house continued, but with her youngest daughter now at college, the expected petition from Marie to return to the house did not arrive. Marie knew without asking that Billie was unlikely to leave her daughter and growing family.

Though she still journeyed to the house and waitressed at The Joint with the strong allegiance of a child of immigrants, Billie had finally acclimated to her own residence. She now participated in the life of the Church near her and consulted with the local priest rather than the one close to the house. She even discovered a local doctor whose services nearly equaled Dr. Sunstein's, though this shift in her life failed to classify as a choice; Dr. Sunstein no longer practiced.

Discovering entertaining games of bingo and poker near her home—games that required small wagers—she was still careful not to take heavy risks with money. When the stakes were low, her opposition to gambling vanished.

Billie had begun to feel settled. When Marie made her an offer difficult to refuse.

1963–1974

15

The Caretaker

Cherishing every moment of parenting, Maggie could not deny that her daughter at fifteen now stood at the portal of adulthood. The years had flown too quickly for the mother who had never expected such a gift. Accepting her child's growing need for independence, she saw that each day offered still another sign that her child was growing up ... and away from her. A childish nickname, acquired somewhere along the way, had become the young woman's newest contention; she insisted the pet name be replaced with her given name. Maggie read the plea correctly as something deeper than a name. She understood her daughter's desire to leave behind some of her protective ways—as well as the youthful term of endearment that had been used by all the residents of the house.

This difficult period of puberty was made even more trying by the times. The sixties saw adolescents leave their homes in record numbers to journey west and become the decade's "flower children." The existential writers implied that neither human nature nor the male/female roles within the species were defined, as once thought. In their manuscripts, these reflective thinkers suggested that humans were free.... and frighteningly on their own. This theme of freedom appeared in the words of popular music, remembered best in the words of the Beatles. Woodstock shocked the nation when a half-million people attended a four-day concert in an open field, a site with minimal facilities for hygiene and shelter. And the new contraceptive pill, "The Pill" as it became known, allowed for intimate relationships between the sexes without the fear of pregnancy. Unheard of in the past, unmarried couples began to live together.

But for Maggie, the teen years were not the nightmare of parental testing that plagued many parents in the sixties. An honor student through her school years, her daughter never neglected her studies, but now found time for additional interests that transported her from beneath her mother's protective cloak. Naturally, the new curiosities included boys and cars. And by the time she was seventeen, she was in love. Handsome, bright, and from a respectable family, the young man could hardly be dismissed on his credentials. And Maggie, long appreciating romantic love, could not deny this exciting period of first love to her young daughter. Even as she reminded herself that *she* had been in love at eighteen and married by twenty, seventeen now seemed far too young for eternal commitments.

Struggling, Maggie turned her thoughts to the future. Though finding the roles of both mother and wife honorable for women, she harbored no desire to replace motherhood with grandparenting, as often happens when the nest begins to cool. Hoping that future choices remained open to her offspring, in ways that she herself had not found at seventeen, Maggie presented a tolerant facade.

But such worries, which arise when the young begin to enter the world with their own wings, became obscured by a more pressing problem for the family caretaker.

Walter had been caught abetting criminals. The news, broadly flashed across local papers, proved traumatic and endless to his wife. Recorded in black and white and then sold throughout the city for a full week, his story was exposed in local newspapers that only embellished the tale—for all Maggie's acquaintances. As the sister who found human beings the most fascinating creatures on the planet, she now chose to avoid them. And thanked the hands of fate that long ago had released her as a waitress at The Joint where she would have faced curious customers every day. Even casual greetings to neighbors and fellow parishioners at Church troubled her. The discomfort extended beyond herself to her teenager, who Maggie feared encountered questions at school, perhaps heckling brought on by the ongoing publicity.

Maggie sensed whispers behind her back even in her limited trips from the house. And found herself surrounded by a publicized aura of wrongdoing. Whether it was real or imagined mattered little. They were real to her, and contrary to her goal since childhood to create the security of a harmonious home, the incident crushed her.

Others at the house shared only a small part of her pain. They all lived under one roof with the same address as the publicized lawbreaker. The city was small, and most people knew at least one person who connected them in some way to one of the residents of the house; associations were easily made. But the other residents, not sharing Walter's surname, casually dismissed the scandal with the attitude: "happens all the time in government; he was just unlucky."

Walter had been caught with invisible dust on his hands that had the effect of *egg on the face:* obvious and peculiar but soon forgotten after a good bath. Searching for a money trail, investigators, had put dust on certain bills to disclose whose hands had touched the cash, revealing a bribe. City government graft. After placing their hands under a special light, Walter and two other cops were identified as officers who had accepted money … to look the other way. As periodically happens, fraud in government needs to be exposed, and the event soon proved only a small piece of a much larger sting operation. A policeman for over thirty years in the city, Walter knew about the shady deals of the politicians and had, after repeated temptations, finally taken a kickback. Identified as a bit player, he was not asked to resign, but instead was suspended for six months. After the hearing, all the details were rehashed in the newspapers, reopening Maggie's shame.

Jaded by the acts of the city's powerful politicians over the years, Walter felt embarrassed only for his wife and daughter. He tried, during his months of suspension, to focus on the repair shop, which had done well in the past. But television technology had progressed, and the need for much repair of any kind had decreased, seriously affecting his profits. Running the small shop in the red made no sense, so he closed the business. Directing his energy into amends with his wife by making himself available to drive anywhere of her choosing, he now took all his meals at the house.

Walking on eggs for a time. After he returned to work and time began its healing work, life resumed a normalcy. People of the city, returning to the heartaches of their own lives, quickly forgot the incident.

But Maggie remained bruised by the publicly aired event. Though she forgave her husband, the small city that had been her world now felt foreign. Continuing to attend Mass on Sundays and holidays, she no longer lingered after the service to inquire into the lives of the parishioners, whom she knew well. Old interests such as window-shopping were now abandoned in fear of casual encounters, where prickly questions might emerge. She became a recluse for nearly a year, though dutifully seeing to her charges at the house.

No sooner had the incident faded from the lips of local gossips, and Maggie began to emerge from her shell, when her bachelor brother came in need of intense care. After major surgery for an aortal aneurysm, he required constant attention during a long recuperation. A nurse might have been employed, but when such family needs arose, Maggie volunteered all her energy. Only when he slept at night was her patient beyond the watchful eye of his sister.

Nor was his care confined to the house. When Andrew became well enough to travel, Maggie accompanied him. On the road to recovery, he chose to make a seven hundred-mile trip to visit their niece who had strayed with her young family far beyond the parameters of the house, and Maggie tagged along. To her brother, the trip would be an adventure, but to Maggie, it was an extension of her nursing job. She had agreed to play this role long ago and now felt content watching his return to health. The trip suited the family caretaker who had no intention of allowing her patient out of her sight … for an entire week. With the exception of the Miss America contest, her trips had all been motivated by family needs, and though she looked forward to seeing her niece in the new setting, priority was her patient.

As the convalescent could not drive, Walter, still making amends, volunteered. The visit went so well that the patient decided to try mowing the grass at his niece's new home. Physical activities, even recreational ones such as fishing, had been suspended in the days following the surgery. And anxious to revive his life, Andrew took the power mower and ventured across the large lawn, only to fall after a short distance. Though no immediate harm arose from the incident, and he insisted on completing the job, the event, witnessed by Maggie, from the back deck, provided her with an intuitive glance into the future.

"As I saw him going down, there was something about the fall; somehow I knew that death lurked close by," she later confided to her sisters. And the omen proved correct. Four months later, Andrew suffered a relapse and died within a week.

After the funeral when the grief endured by all the sisters began to subside, Maggie admitted to herself that the last years had been trying. She felt as Hamlet had observed on hearing of Ophelia's death: "One woe doth tread upon another's heel so fast, they follow as the day the night." Oddly, each difficult event eased the former one. Her brother's illness had transported her from her husband's woes, which had in turn lifted her from the inevitable empty nest. Each happening had proven an odd distraction from the previous one. Now with her brother gone and her husband back at work, Maggie's energy began to return.

Just as Marie involved herself in still another business endeavor.

Reluctantly, Maggie supported her sister's new venture, hoping that the bold move would allay the insomnia…. and eliminate the medication. As Marie and her husband excitedly enacted their plans, Maggie thrilled to see her sister glowing with evidence of her old self. And forsaking her initial misgivings, she embraced the huge project the couple had undertaken.

But in a short time, her hopes were shattered with evidence that her sister's old problem had returned now with a new symptom—a slight twitch of Marie's head. Undoubtedly, the medication she ingested nightly to induce sleep had damaged nerves in her neck, and larger health problems likely lay on the horizon. Maggie hid her suspicions and advised her sister to seek medical intervention. But again, Marie became defensive, and Maggie acquiesced to what seemed the inevitable—her sister was addicted.

Again she helped her sister through the difficult periods in the late afternoon, planning her days so that she was at the house at these times. Waking from her deep sleep each afternoon, Marie was unstable on her feet. Often the only other person there, Maggie listened anxiously when she heard her sister stirring each day. Did Marie understand the dangers, or had the addiction erased her reasoning power? Had Eddie looked into the side effects of the medication? Was it possible that her sister ingested a drug illegally? Without prescription?

Knowing that without intervention, addiction only grows worse, Maggie struggled with her doubts. Marie had not seen a doctor in years, and taking illegal drugs was wrong for reasons that included her sister's health. An accusation that included words such as *addiction* and *illegal drugs* identified criminals.

This was different than their past disputes. Over the years, there had been discord within the family; arguments were familiar. So many under one roof furnished fuel for smoldering fires, but the system had an instinctive nature that had worked.... until now. A division of labor within the house meant that no one resident was responsible for any one task. Sometimes Marie brought home prime cuts of meat from The Joint. Or Maggie shopped for groceries. Or Rose acquired a few delicacies on her way home from work. The three men shoveled snow or cut grass according to whoever saw the need—and picked up the shovel or mower first. Only politics or poker caused sparks to fly and then voices could be heard in protest

But to intervene in her sister's life would be more than a quarrel. It would force Maggie to confront both her sister and brother-in-law. And as such a showdown would disrupt the household in a new way, she hesitated.

Finally a respite came into Maggie's life as she prepared for her daughter's wedding day. Though shopping and organizing festivities for seventy guests hardly suggested relaxation, such a lifetime event excited her spirits.

Especially when she allowed her thoughts to hover on such personal details as a new hat for the mother of the bride.

Though hats, for both sexes, had declined since the forties, a hatless woman before the freeing spirit of the sixties was suspect. Especially to those already dubious of the notion of women's suffrage. But in the sixties, Jackie Kennedy stalled the trend by appearing in what came to be her signature pillbox hat. But by the seventies, hats were obvious only at formal occasions, weddings and church services. In the Russian Church, women were required to cover their tresses—though the decorative hats drew more attention than the hair itself!

Women's hats, colorful and bold in design, were gradually fading, robbing the culture of a certain frivolity. But Maggie, schooled in the past, prepared for the wedding by shopping for a *chapeau*, as she fondly called the accessory. Such a search was a favored pastime, and the prospect of wearing the new hat on the special occasion made the task even more thrilling to her. In her city in the early seventies, there remained stores that sold women's hats exclusively, and Maggie could compare a favorite in one shop with a close choice in another.

Many such decisions needed to be made for the ceremony: clothes, food, and entertainment, and her old favorite, window-shopping, now had the most exciting of goals—the wedding party of her only child.

The bride-to-be and her high school sweetheart had completed their academic degrees and were now headed for a life they had planned together. Maggie had come to adore her future son-in-law, feeling secure in the coupling. Witnessing firsthand the pain of both her niece and sister's divorce, she hoped now that this union would be strong. And such a hope, she concluded, had the best chance if the couple postponed a family. It appeared an odd desire for someone who had waited so many years for a child, but observing people over the years had endowed Maggie with a postulate: couples need to develop their own relationship under one roof before adding new, complex variables—such as children.

Shortly after the exquisite wedding and a honeymoon in Hawaii, the couple secured teaching jobs two hours from the house. Hopes that they would remain close had been a dream that Maggie had held for only a fleeting moment. Witnessing her nieces leave the nest, she accepted that the house no longer served as a family sanctuary. And two years later when the young couple decided to buy their own home miles from the house, making their separation from the nest certain, Maggie bowed to the change, offering her help in the momentous move into a first home.

When it came to family, this was Maggie's nature. With a goal so close to her heart, she would have worked endlessly to aid them in settling in the new space, but midway through the move, she found herself, without explanation, anxious to return to the house. Walter had come along to help, and she confided in him her desire to return home. This urge to leave stunned her, and she fought to keep the odd feeling from their beloved daughter. Helping to ready the place as best she could, and not departing so quickly as to cause concern, she endured the mood.

She felt that a finale had occurred in her life, as though she were closing a book after a satisfying read. Her job, the one much bigger than the unpacking, was done. Trying to make sense of the gnawing feeling, she assured herself that this was all natural. Simply part of the classic empty nest that many mothers experienced at such times. Still, as she unpacked boxes, cleaned drawers, and stocked shelves, the feeling of finality weighed on her, leaving her physically weary.

Returning to the house from what proved her last family contribution, Maggie slept late for an entire week. In the past, one day beyond eight in the morning was rare for her. She fought to regain her energy, but when, after several weeks, all methods failed, she sought help.

Medical doctors in 1974 were not yet probing into patients' lives, so there was little effort to connect illness to lifestyle; had they inquired, they would have discovered that the last seven years had been difficult ones for Maggie. But only physical causes for her fatigue were pursued and a series of tests were ordered, and within a month, she was diagnosed with the dreaded disease of cancer. The malignancy was confined to one organ of her body, so hope emerged with immediate plans for surgery.

But optimism proved short-lived. The operation caused a diffusion of the malignant cells throughout her body. And offering no hope to the family, the doctors only advised that she be made as comfortable as possible—the most dreaded of medical counsel. One oncologist suggested that she be taken on a trip of her choice, a place she had always longed to visit. The man, of course, did not know Maggie, who seldom journeyed far from the house in *good* health, unless someone needed her. And she would not leave now as she fought the dreaded disease.

Even in the twenty-first century, the diagnosis of cancer is a dreaded one. But in the seventies, the prospect of recovery from it was nearly non-existent. Such a diagnosis came close to a death sentence for a patient. Even the president of the United States at the time proclaimed a War on Cancer. Like many others, Maggie had secretly feared the malady. Little was known of either its genesis or replication of the mutating cells; even transient bruises became suspect. Concluding for such reasons that the true nature of her mother's illness must be kept vague, her daughter pleaded with the attending doctor to temper his words when in dialogue with the patient. Not the trusted Dr. Sunstein, who would have counseled from a long history with the family, the new doctor only complied with a frantic plea from a distraught daughter.

After the surgery, Maggie returned to the house expecting a slow recovery. But she was not herself, and this fact could not be hidden … least of all from her. Lacking energy, and worse, motivation, she began to suspect that full disclosure of her illness had not been made. Described to her as mere "precautions," the radiation and chemotherapy treatments following the surgery failed to arrest the rapidly spreading malignancy. After three months of no visible progress, she returned to the hospital.

This stay proved different than the previous one that had held a glimmer of hope. Maggie now understood her condition and refused all medication.

Her four sisters faithfully gathered at the bedside. They agreed—something rare when the sisters worked towards consensus of any sort—that this drama ought to be played out at the house instead of a hospital. Such had been the case when their mother's illness had reached a similar juncture. But surrendering to the notion that modern medicine could provide the best care for their sister, the four carefully divided up their visits to assure a constant presence in the sterile atmosphere of the local hospital.

For the size of the city, the hospital was well equipped and staffed with experienced doctors and nurses, many of whom the family knew personally. Though some cases doctors referred to the prestigious hospitals in nearby Pittsburgh for experimental treatment, Maggie's prognosis failed such optimism. And the local hospital, a mere mile from the house, provided the sisters easy access.

The chances of recovery dimmed along with each day's dusk but the sisters tried to lift her spirits. Though with serious doubts about recovery, they were still convincing in their suggestions to their ailing sister.

"You know this year's Miss America contest is only two months away. It will be my treat. I'll look into advance ticket sales tomorrow," Anne said with her usual smile.

Marie, who had watched her sister's delight with customers at The Joint many years before, had created an ideal position. "There's going to be a new kind of job at the restaurant," she said. "I know that you tired of waitressing, but this is a hostess position. Someone needs to oversee the tables." With this proposal, Maggie would feel needed but without a real workload Marie reasoned.

"Lately, I've been thinking about our old movie night "It was such fun. I think that we should revive it." *Rose* was suggesting change? As the sisters stared in surprise, she added, "I think that television has lulled us in a bad way."

Finally, Billie, the sister with whom Maggie had shared her childhood and later the wonders of motherhood, entered a petition with her obvious signature. "Maggie, you know they've been married for three years, own their own home, and both have good jobs. I'll bet it won't be long until you become a grandmother. You need to get your energy back."

Maggie listened and smiled at each suggestion. She recognized the ardent attempts by the four to pull her into the future.

Though lovingly offered, the pleas failed, and the stricken sister grew weaker. A mere four months after the initial diagnosis, she died. The entire event passed as though someone had pushed the fast forward button on the machine of life. According to recent profiles on the ailment, Maggie proved the classic cancer patient, too often sacrificing her own needs for those of others.

The family gathered to bid their farewells to the sister who, in one way or another, had nursed them all. As with Andrew, the wake took place in a modern funeral home rather than the living room of the house. Just as she had failed to do in life, Maggie left no final requests of her own.

16

The Entrepreneur

In the beginning, Marie was afraid to try the medication that Eddie brought home. Never having taken anything beyond aspirin, and seldom that, she longed for the approval of the old family physician, Dr. Sunstein. But the good doctor had long been retired, desiring to spend his old age in a warmer climate. Although Marie had been thrilled that they now had a *family* physician, other than impending death and babies, Dr. Sunstein had seldom been needed. Consulted by phone on small matters over the years, he had been a resourceful friend. The residents, who never considered regular check-ups, only needed his *assurance* at times. As Marie now did with the medication. But he was gone, and desperate to return to a normal sleeping pattern, she began to take the dose prescribed by Eddie's friend.

The sedative proved an instant solution—for both partners. Having used it now for five years, she welcomed the deep sleep into which it never failed to lead her. It also provided Eddie the quiet he craved when he returned to the house in the wee hours of the morning. But when her mind cleared in the afternoons, Marie recognized that life was slipping out of her control, undoubtedly as it had for her cousin Mickey when he died in the asylum. But such thoughts, rather than insights that prompted change, created fears that made sleep more difficult, and a vicious cycle ensued. Night fell, and she reached for the sedative that delivered sleep—and freedom from anxiety.

Though arriving at The Joint in the afternoons nowadays, she seldom stayed until closing. Her presence there was different than it had once been. In the beginning, she had subbed as needed, as cook, waitress, auditor, and occasional bartender. Now she circulated among customers making friendly chitchat. Such surface conversations, though likely good for business, failed to fit her intense personality. Marie felt unnecessary, and her abbreviated hours granted most of the authority to Eddie.

Though enthused by his newfound power, Eddie had become aware of a growing loneliness. At the beginning of their relationship, he and Marie had a social life that focused on their shared love of dancing, but the business had soon overshadowed their intimacy. Finally, the demands of a growing business, which had then evolved into two establishments, dominated their lives. Still, watching with his wife The Joint's success, Eddie had shared some of the accomplishment … until he found himself in need of something more.

After his return from the war, Marie had tried to rekindle a closeness between them, but both were too set in their work routines to make significant changes in the relationship. Occasionally, they tried to take Sundays off, a privilege they had never allowed in the past, but eating a meal in a glamorous setting, they wound up *talking shop*. The dinners were feeble attempts at change, and hardly enough to encourage intimacy. Growing a husband-wife connection required more energy than either partner knew how to give.

For intimacy, Eddie nurtured a group of friends at The Joint.

Unlike many men caught in a midlife crisis, he did not seek a younger female. Womanizing was not his thing. As the youngest of three children and the only boy in the family, he had received his share of female attention in childhood. Now in this, the middle of his life, it was male recognition he craved. A gathering of friends at *his* bar seemed to fill his need. Each day five or six patrons formed a tight circle generally over drinks, Eddie himself abstaining, and discussed their jobs, local politics, and families. All on a surface level of feeling, as was common for men of this generation. The discussions were never so personal as to appear "unmanly." Over time, the group grew in importance to Eddie.

Hardly naive to the gatherings at the Joint, Marie referred to the men in her husband's life as his *cronies,* which broadened the definition of friend to include *sidekick* and *associate.* When less good-natured, she called them his *henchmen,* which included other less flattering synonyms such as *lackey.* All the words could be applied to this odd group that Eddie fostered and which changed in membership over time. In addition to friendship, the group had a practical side. Anytime maintenance was required at The Joint or the house, jobs for which the three male residents pleaded ignorance, Eddie found someone among his cronies to carry out the project and rewarded them with either money or free drinks. Such is how the inner circle worked; one man supported the other, as their backgrounds allowed.

Never probing, Marie was puzzled by these men who were forever hovering around her husband. Over the years without close friends, or even one to whom she could confide her buried feelings, she failed to empathize with Eddie's actions. That his faithful group substituted for missing elements of their marriage never occurred to her. Marie understood survival, not contentment; one did what needed to be done, regardless of outcome.

Unknown to her, a pharmacist in the group, on hearing Eddie's complaints of his wife's insomnia, provided the sedative.

Oddly, this life that Marie and Eddie had created for themselves was changed by the city's planners. The city council decided that The Joint and the attached little store occupied a prime location for the planned city park. Such had been rumored, but Marie had lightly credited the talk to councilmen with no better ideas for spending taxpayers' money. Until the notice reached her by certified mail.

Their city had not evaded the changes of the sixties; even the Roman Catholic Church had transformed itself through the Second Vatican Council! Just as her father's death had changed the trajectory of her life years ago, the notice from the city first delivered anguish and then.... a different direction. The kind of concrete goal that Marie understood. The city seized the land by the legal action known as eminent domain, paying fair market price for the two businesses.

Invested properly, the lump sum could have comfortably sustained the husband and wife, now sixty years old, for life. And there were no children to consider. Of course Anne advised that they take the money and travel; to Anne's way of thinking, their time as entrepreneurs a 24/7 job, needed to end, and the city nicely concluded it for them. Other family members, sensing that Marie was not ready for retirement, suggested that they open a business closer to the outskirts of Pittsburgh, where suburban strip malls now hinted of the future.

Beginning to blur the lines between urban and rural life, suburbs, malls and the fast food industry had begun to prepare for liftoff when the city seized her two businesses. So the advice to consider the outskirts of Pittsburgh was sound. But the observation that McDonalds had successfully established itself in the *center* of their city went unnoted by the couple.

At the time, the new fast food chain was no threat to The Joint but eerily modeled the little store with a simple menu of tasty, inexpensive hamburgers at its core. Though never abandoning the little store, Marie had focused all her energy on The Joint. Unable to think outside the lines as she had done so creatively in the past, she failed now to visualize a model of the little store in the suburbs of Pittsburgh. She understood her long-time patrons, many of whom represented a first generation of immigrants like her. And her brief forays into Pittsburgh had convinced her that the tastes and habits of the large city's inhabitants were different, and she was unprepared for such a change. With thoughts now only of a larger version of The Joint, she dismissed the little store.

Had she noted the telltale glimmers of the fast food explosion, as well as growing rumors that the steel mills would be leaving not only her small city but the entire country, her decision to replace The Joint instead of the little store might have changed. Instead, with the cash from the city, which represented the hard work of over a third of a century, Marie decided to open a variation of The Joint—in another location.

Marketing experts would not have supported such a decision, and likely would have cautioned her with three words—"location, location, location." To move the business closer to Pittsburgh could force Marie to leave the house, or at least endanger the living arrangement that she had established for the family of which she remained the patriarch.

During demolition of the structures that had once been the little store and The Joint, Marie and Eddie made their plans for the new establishment. The restaurant emerged less than a mile from The Joint's old location—and closer to the house. The office building that they bought, though in good condition, required considerable renovation for transformation into a restaurant. With the firm decision to stay with an enterprise similar to The Joint in the same city, Marie found a bit of her old spirit, aligning herself once again with the determination of her youth. She had a job to do, and the new goal revived her. No longer dubbed The Joint, the new establishment, she concluded, would be classier, a step above the previous one, just as The Joint had outclassed the little store.

Reasoning that the location, décor, and bill of fare, would produce fresh patrons, she began her final creation. The menu would include a variety of fresh seafoods, elaborate entrees, and delicate pastries, as well as an official wine list. The space, physically larger than The Joint, had an upstairs with the potential for private parties, even conferences if the need arose. When she finished with the interior decoration, the new enterprise boasted an exciting ambience and upscaled The Joint by leaps. Though her previous customers would be welcomed, she planned on a clientele far above the city's *hoi polloi*. (Marie liked to use the curly phrase to remind herself of the time it applied to her and her family.)

As she hoped, professional doctors and lawyers were soon eating stuffed shrimp and filet mignon on the dining side, and unlike The Joint, customers now had fancy mixed drinks as well as vintage wine with their dinners. As before, Marie set high standards of freshness for all the food and worked to keep prices reasonable. The bar section too, gained new customers, but also retained previous ones, including Eddie's cadre of friends.

In the beginning, the scheme worked.

One change over The Joint, but not decided by the owners, proved major in the new establishment. Dictated by the federal government, black patrons *must* now be served; they could no longer be turned away by owners with the words, "Sorry, we don't serve blacks here."

In the past, both Marie and Eddie had informed blacks of their policy at the entrance. At the Joint, such a statement was only necessary in the bar area because black customers lacked the confidence to enter the dining room for a complete dinner. High in the social consciousness of the time lurked the attitude that black patronage degraded businesses; even in the North where blacks were said to be welcome, racial divisions remained clear. Having their own neighborhoods and schools throughout the nation, the blacks "stayed in their place," and small businesses like Marie's had been within their rights to reject them with the *separate but equal* apology. Until 1966.

Though energized by their classy restaurant, Marie and Eddie were soon daunted by the effects of racial integration that followed the race riots of the sixties. James Meredith's historic bid to be the first black student at the University of Mississippi hastened change and would finally overturn the U.S. Supreme Court ruling of separate but equal facilities for members of the once enslaved black race. The new country now had a black senator, a black cabinet member, and a black Supreme Court justice.

Haunted by memories of being fed in her youth by kind members of a black church, Marie still retold the story of their generosity in her time of need. Though conflicted over the years at the social prejudice, she was unable to overcome the fear that a black clientele would discourage white patrons. Now the law had changed and she had no choice. Her solace came from the fact that black customers only entered the bar side of her new establishment. At least for the moment.

Additional employees were needed in the new restaurant, and Eddie immediately found the ideal opening to hoist his sister and nephew into the business. Without children of his own, he welcomed them as paid employees; *his* family would now be linked to the new establishment—and to what had become his life. A pastry chef in her own right, his sister became one of the three main cooks, and her son one of the four regular bartenders. Though he had never kept a closeness to his family of origin as had his wife, Eddie had not forgotten his two older sisters who lived in the same city. With Marie's two sisters working in the previous businesses, and Billie waitressing at the new one, Eddie had always felt eclipsed. But keeping his feelings to himself, he never complained and compensated with jokes, his medium in all conversations.

The inclusion of his sister and nephew now inspired Eddie, and he began to seek further recognition for himself. Never having received much attention from his busy wife, for thirty-six years, he had quietly gone along with any role she designated for him. Though his group of cronies supplied some of the prestige he craved, Eddie posed the soul-searching questions of himself.

He continually asked, "What have *I* done in my life?"

Translated, he yearned for something that he could claim as his own. Over the years, Marie had reminded him that *she* had purchased and succeeded with the original establishment—without his help. But Eddie needed to create something on his own. So, inspired by the idea of one of his cronies, he became a sponsor for a potential cooking gadget. The timing as well as the product proved an ideal combination; Eddie might at last define himself.

The electric gadget, named, for an unknown reason, the Keggie Machine, cooked six hot dogs in less than a minute. The microwave oven was not yet in widespread use, so instant cooking was revolutionary in the late sixties. (Wieners, cooked before packaging, can be eaten right from the grocer's case, but general preference is to "cook" them in some manner.) Grilling, boiling, or frying all expand the compressed meat, but the Keggie Machine had wires, which, when inserted into the franks, caused them to double in size, making them especially juicy. Though likely healthier than frying, such an asset was not touted at the time. Both the taste of the wiener and the short cooking time of the contraption captured Eddie's interest—as well as his ego. Eddie himself had not invented the gadget, but after listening to his friend and examining the product, he took on the paper work, wrote the check and applied for a patent. He anticipated its use both commercially and in private homes, and all his energy flowed into the pursuit. Managing a bar, even a new one, had become second nature to him—and dull. The idea that he could be part of such an exciting innovation absorbed all his waking moments.

But the Keggie Machine failed the patenting process; someone else had taken the lead with a similar invention. Soon Eddie's cronies offered other possibilities; his reputation as a generous sponsor had grown, and after many endeavors, the breakthrough that he expected would bring him fame arrived. A cure for cancer. Far less intrusive than any medical therapy for the dreaded disease at the time, the remedy would be taken by mouth. But the liquid concoction, arrived at by one of his ingenious friends, also failed to receive a patent.

Marie did well with goals of necessity. Absorbed in the third business, she found that her insomnia lessened for the first few years; perhaps her determination affected her endorphins in some way. But when the poor sleeping pattern returned, she turned to the old remedy only to find that an increased dose was required to bring on sleep. Decreasing again her hours at the restaurant, she accepted her role there now as maitre d'. The new restaurant, though classy, remained far from this, but Marie accepted the pointless role. Her addiction now controlled her decisions.

In its sixth year, the new establishment began to falter, but both Eddie and Marie held to the hope that it would simply take time. But the gross continued to decrease, and Marie lacked the creative energy to explore the reasons for the decline. Working for ten years before opening the little store, she, like her husband, had tired of the nearly forty years of ownership. She had toiled for fifty-two of her sixty-six years with little time off. And was now depleted.

Perhaps her sister Anne had been right about retirement.

"You've worked long enough. You can't be thinking of opening another business!" Anne had warned when the other restaurants had been bulldozed.

"Of course I am. I have no plans to retire when I still have energy—as you so foolishly did." Marie had always trusted her oldest sister's opinion, though she had never understood Anne's ongoing desire for freedom.

But to sell a business at this low point made no sense financially; in addition to the structure itself, she would be selling a *name* that was well known in the city—surely this had worth. She clung to the hope that the tides would change and concluded that she only needed a diversion that would allow her to ride the waves. Though enjoying the speed and classy nature of airplane travel, often making quick trips to Billie's, she had never acquired a taste for travel; the business had always needed her attention. Her assertive personality would have fit well into local politics, but her gender, at least for the times, limited her involvement in city government. Even volunteer work held negatives for this first generation of immigrants. Unheard of among the immigrant families whence Marie sprang, volunteer work was lost in the motto; *charity begins at home*. Unable to find a satisfying diversion, she reverted to an old standby. Shopping.

And decided to buy a car.

Actually, the purchase took no browsing. She had held a car of her dreams for years. A *Cadillac* proved her instant choice, and she quickly bought the newest model. The price was not a factor. At this point, she needed no silk stocking for the acquisition. As always, she dealt in cash, paying the salesman the sticker price in hundred dollar bills. Though in the past her badge of wealth had been clothes, furniture, and even the new business, in the culture, cars remained the most visible status symbols.

Contrary to Marie's taste, the car was loaded with what she had always labeled "gingerbread." The array of needless extras included hidden armrests and ashtrays, elaborate lighters even in the backseat, though no potential passenger smoked; there were headlights that automatically dimmed in bright light—which only frustrated the driver when they dimmed under *every* streetlight in the city—and luxurious seats designed for ultimate comfort on long trips, which she never took. The only trip Marie took these days was to her sister's, and then she flew. The car hardly matched her needs.

At six months, the vehicle had brake problems that suddenly and frighteningly showed up on the descent of a hill. Though the brake failure and all the pointless gadgets frustrated her, nothing could change the power of the name. It was a *Cadillac*, a car driven only by the wealthy.

Marie had never paid much attention to cars and had bought a name rather than a car. In the past, her determined nature had secured a driver's license, and later a jalopy at a time when women drivers were considered oddities. Her interest in cars never ran beyond the practical. And after the hair-raising brake incident, she never drove the car again. On the few short trips that she made afterwards, she designated Billie as the driver. And soon the Cadillac became a collector's item, just like the furniture in the living and dining rooms of the house. On occasion, one of the men of the house used the car, but twenty years after its purchase, the odometer had recorded fewer than ten thousand miles.

"How *does* the other half live?" Marie now asked herself. The car, the last in a list of symbols, had failed her and in the end had provided no joy. She had struggled to become wealthy—by her own definition, a simple test of her own design meant to distinguish the rich from the poor. To her, the rich ate white bread while the poor consumed what she called "black bread," when they could afford bread at all; the rich owned nicely decorated homes in the city while the poor dwelt in the country as tenants; the rich dressed in stylish clothes of good quality, never overdressing in a gingerbread style; the rich were educated and the poor were not; the rich were chauffeured in large fancy cars and finally had fewer children than the poor.

These rules had evolved from the poverty of her youth, and she had faithfully followed the dictums. She had bought the house in the city that had become the hub of all their lives. After decorating it, she had paid full tuition for the four-year college educations of her nieces. And she now possessed a *mink* stole and a Cadillac. And only white bread ever came into the house. Though she could not apply her regulations and limit the size of the second generation, Marie's generation of six finally produced only three children.

Having faithfully followed the formula, she knew with the failure of the Cadillac that something was amiss in her definition

She knew that, even under the democracy of the new country, life was far from classless. To Marie, there were two classes of people, rich and poor; such was the binary nature of the feudal system that she had learned from her mother's tales of Galicia. Her three restaurants had risen up the social ladder, but Marie had never *felt* rich. Or the acclaimed state was not what she had expected. For immigrants, success was about money, and now, even as the third restaurant faltered, she could buy what she wanted but found her personal desires alien to her. In her quest for survival—of her entire family—she had repressed her own needs. And no cultural definition of social class could ever dictate what actually made *her* happy.

Lacking now even a definition of "rich," Marie harbored anxieties that were more unyielding than the poverty she had known. Her creative nature, once galvanized by the family's need to survive, now proved static. Although not as reclusive or anywhere near as rich as the famous Howard Hughes whose money also haunted him, Marie had eccentricities reminiscent of the famous billionaire of her time. In his youth, Hughes had personal strength, building planes and single-handedly flying around the world in a record breaking four days. But as he grew old, paranoia gripped him, and the fear of germs or flaws of any kind, paralyzed the celebrity. Marie's anxieties were of death, heightened by her cousin's untimely one. Unlike her, the famous Hughes had been born with a silver spoon in his mouth, but they both had learned from the Great Depression, which had poked them from the rear and fostered a distrust for institutions of any kind.

Like Hughes, Marie was an eccentric, who stored all profits from her businesses—in shoe boxes. From the nightly cash intake, she allowed Eddie a generous amount for his needs and to pay bills, but the remainder of the cash she *packaged*, carefully taping each cardboard box as it reached capacity.

The boxes, which had once held new shoes, she then stored in a wardrobe in the house, a frame structure without security against fire or burglary. The closet's only qualification as a secure safe was that it could be locked. And lay within the house. In Marie's mind, the closet was as indestructible as the structure itself. But even without the threat of fire, the shoe boxes, reminiscent of the silk stocking that had once held her precious savings, hardly proved effective *investment* devices. Unlike vintage wine and antiques that grow in value with the passing of time, money stored in such a manner loses value as the cost of living rises; and it produces no interest. Her cash stored in the shoe boxes, sadly worth less each day, cried out for investment. But from the early days of her business endeavor, cash had been Marie's medium of exchange, and she had no trust in either banks or accounting systems for even simple checking—let alone long-term savings.

From their early days, the second generation had proved Marie's best diversion. Buying toys and clothes, she enjoyed, along with them, their childhood delights. And in the next season of their lives, she generously paid college tuition. Though footing the bill, she never influenced their choices of career. Teacher, secretary, and nurse were the common choices at the time for young women. And all three chose to teach. None of the residents ever doubted that she would shoulder this bill; such an act was simply part of her old message to preserve and protect the family. Happily, when the third generation began to appear, Marie started the process anew. Once more, there were toys and clothes to buy and childhood delights such as circuses and amusement parks for which she had not grown too old. When the first of the third generation proved a boy, she welcomed the opportunity to now encourage male pursuits.

The first of the third generation in the new country rekindled in Marie the lifelong hope that a family member would eventually take over her restaurant. Unlike her own aborted education, she dreamed that he would go off to a school, study business management and take over the reins in a professional manner. And a family business on a different scale would emerge. But such a desire was short-lived. The third establishment would be gone by the time the young man reached maturity.

In the seventies, Marie's addiction grew, fueled by the frailty of her newest enterprise. A variety of circumstances marked its demise. Once blacks began dining there by federal law, she lost, just as she had feared, her white clientele. Racist attitudes flourished in her city, as they did across the new country. The steel mills pulled out of America, and the fast food craze reduced the interest in elegant dining—at least in her city. Each of these proved a barrier, and the combination dealt the lethal blow.

Disillusioned, Marie seldom went to the restaurant in those days, though it remained open. More and more, she found her way only from the bedroom to the sitting room of the house in mid-afternoon and turned on the television instead of dressing for work, as she had done even in the short period she served as hostess. Retiring to her bedroom around nine in the evening, she did not take the drug until after the late television shows, and then the medication led her into twelve hours of heavy sleep.

Just as it seemed that matters could not get worse, the one person who had always watched over Marie, though unofficially, fell ill. Maggie was diagnosed with cancer and quickly succumbed to the dreaded disease. The death reinforced Marie's deepest fears—the fears that had begun with her cousin Mickey's doom. Having long focused on the money that would secure and finally define the immigrant family, she now felt powerless. And the arch collapsed.

17

The Mediator

The animated life of the sixties did not escape Anne's spirit. Gaining inspiration from the times, she decided to open a conversation with Marie about the insomnia. Though convinced of her sister's growing addiction in the last years, Anne had hoped that the energy required for this third restaurant had changed matters. In the beginning she had argued against the plan to relocate The Joint, but with the new business now established, Anne, forever the optimist, hoped to hear that the endeavor had supplied a magic cure.

"I still think that you should have retired and traveled with Eddie. You may not be healthy enough to do it later. But the business seems to be going well. How are you sleeping these days?" Anne cautiously asked.

"Anne, I feel better than I've ever felt. I fall asleep as my head hits the pillow at night." Marie reassured her.

"You're not taking anything to help you sleep?" As her sister had always denied this, Anne thought she would double-check, as directly but softly as she could.

"*Not this* again! I don't know why the four of you are stuck on such a silly idea. I don't take drugs, and I'm sleeping just fine."

Exactly what Anne had hoped to hear, she returned home delighted with the news.

Life-long Republicans, neither Anne nor Tom had voted for the winning candidate for president three years earlier. Though they could not deny his charms, the couple would not desert their party for the Democrats, who in their eyes were *big spenders* and promoters of big government. With a reputation for being tight-fisted at the time, Republicans guarded their hard-earned money, and Anne admired such thrift. Tom agreed with the Democrats' support of the union in his own workplace but recognized that his wife as self-employed had had no experience with organized labor. Tom disliked any discord in his home, so spoke little of politics there. The electrifying period was personified in the young president's vigor and enhanced by pictures of his young children frolicking at the White House. Such lively images inspired Tom as they did many who had failed to give him their vote.

The vibrant tone of the sixties roused Tom to act on a recurring thought. Deciding to retire from the mill after forty-two years of service, he was encouraged by his wife to join her in the freedom that she continued to enjoy. Finally making the two a retired *couple.*

Anne had sold her business eighteen years earlier, and although they had frequently traveled, Tom's job limited the freedom that she coveted. His longtime employer supplied him with a full retirement package for his years of devoted service, and he needed little persuasion from his wife. Hale and hardy at age sixty, Tom, recognized the transitory nature of life at this stage and happily joined his wife.

Though fully retired and without a work schedule of any kind, the couple made no visible life changes. No smaller residence. No retirement village. No move that brought them closer to relatives, already so near they could hardly improve location. No equipped RV. And no exotic travel plans. Cruises or planned vacations of any sort had not reached their present popularity, so this was not an option. A trip on a large cruising vessel that allowed gambling would have undoubtedly captured Anne's attention. Such an excursion met her criteria for enjoyment: gambling, adventure, and prepared meals!

The social attitude towards retirement had just begun its gradual shift when Tom left the mill. This season of life was still viewed as a slowing down period with little emphasis on either travel or exercise. Elderhostel was unknown. Aches and pains were interpreted then as the natural consequences of aging, rather than annoyances that could be controlled as one reached for a second wind for the remainder of the journey. By retiring at age forty-two, Anne had been on the vanguard of changes that would eventually define retirement as a *new* period rather than a terminal state—which only delivered physical woes. Her father had died at age fifty in the early part of the twentieth century with no hope of retirement in his latter years. When Tom left the mill, exiting the workforce while one remained healthy was just becoming a viable notion, strongly supported by organized labor

For Anne, retirement was an earned part of life and needed to be enjoyed in as many ways as possible. Though shopping, especially for household items, had never been among her favored choices, she proposed a new piece of furniture for their home in celebration of Tom's decision. The cabinet that came to rest in their living room was quite ordinary. Television sets were in nearly all homes in the mid-sixties, but this was the couple's first. And it was color. Today, purchase of a fourteen-inch television without benefits of either cable, satellite dish, high-definition or surround-sound appears trite, even funny. But to them, this addition in honor of his retirement was a huge happening.

As a child, Anne had known no home entertainment of any kind, except that which she and her siblings could create with their imaginary games. (Youth failed to *be* entertained in these times and amused themselves.) Her struggling mother could not consider even a radio. Much farther up the list of necessities for her family was food. So Anne's first radio came when she bought it as equipment for her shop. Concluding that her customers deserved to be entertained during the personal service she rendered, she had selected the newest of its kind. But not until Tom's retirement did she consider the luxury of *home* entertainment, nor did she dream that television would be only the beginning of such an industry.

Having something as lively and varied as a television set in her living room mesmerized Anne. Comparing the compact box to a movie theater, without the cost of either tickets or a trek to the theater, she also could boast the educational value of the set, something she had demanded of her travel. At the time of the purchase, Educational Television (now PBS) was just making its debut with such programs as Julia Child's, *The French Chef*, and Anne delighted in having this resource at her fingertips—without charge beyond the initial cost of the set. Forever searching out mysterious facts in magazines, almanacs, and encyclopedias simply for her own knowledge, Anne now had it all on this wondrous screen.... in her own living room!

The set did encourage the retired couple to do what the culture dictated for the retired stage of life—to slow down. Whether social attitude towards aging influenced them, or real aches and pains began to intercede in their plans, the two idled away more time than in the past. And though they continued to travel, even this activity changed.

Less interested now in exotic trips, Anne opted for visits to relatives, and Tom, growing tired of flashy casinos and restaurant food, gladly went along with the change. Though still evident, Anne's attitude of *giving it a try* had also been diminished by age and its demand for less risky initiatives. The home of her sister Billie continued as a favored trip for the couple. And Anne's grown nieces, with homes of their own, now welcomed them, offering new places to explore as well as the intimacies of home.... in the evenings. The two now enjoyed the comforts of *home,* wherever they might be after dark. And with Tom retired, they had the privilege of staying away for longer periods.

Anne remained upbeat in her life. If the headaches of aging intruded, they went the way of all negatives in her life, remaining invisible to the observer.

With his additional time, Tom became an active member of his long-time favorite, the Moose Club. In the past, the club had served both he and Anne as a convenient social gathering, but now having more time to join friends for a mug of cold beer, Tom began to participate in the community projects sponsored by his local lodge; often too tired in the past after a shift at the mill, he knew little of its social actions. Now he volunteered, helping members of the small city less privileged than himself.

The Moose Club became the heart of his interest in these retiring days. Though always the devoted husband, never losing the original adoration he held for his wife, he enjoyed this new role. Unfamiliar in the past with the national programs of the organization, he now became interested in two of them: Mooseheart and Moosehaven. True to the club's mission, these two programs offered a helping hand. Mooseheart provided a home and school for dependent children of needy members, while Moosehaven supported a residence for retired members whose income had generally shrunk at retirement. Located in Florida long before the retiree boom in the Sunshine State, Moosehaven quickly planted an appealing thought within Tom. The cold winters of western Pennsylvania were beginning to trouble him in ways they had not in the past, and the possibility of warm, sunny days all year long appealed to him. At the right moment, he planned to suggest to his wife a place for their eventual old age.

While Tom was busy at the Moose, Anne often *visited* friends and relatives. Though it had begun its decline even then in the culture, visiting was still a popular activity that she enjoyed. Some visits were spontaneous and unannounced while others were planned: one was an invited guest. Generally there was no agenda, other than a cup of coffee or tea over conversation. Anne often visited at the house, but as she qualified as a resident an invitation would have been redundant.

She especially enjoyed visits with her cousin Rose who lived a half-hour drive away. So often before going to the local Moose, Tom dropped Anne off at Rose's. The two spoke little during these drives as they remained a stark reminder of her failure to pass the driver's test. With a license, she could have dropped *him* off at the Moose. It would have saved time and gas money, but as Anne had once said, it was not to be.

Similar in age, both the oldest in large immigrant families, she and Rose had followed disparate lifestyles, but a magnetic force drew Anne for frequent visits with her. Rose had married young and quickly spawned a brood of five. And rather than going it alone in the business world as Anne had done, she had become a business partner with her husband. Opening a small bar and juggling its demands with family life, she had worked hard, just as Anne had done. And now in their sixties, Rose and her husband showed no signs of slowing down and even now failed to consider retirement—a surprising choice in Anne's thinking.

Perhaps the two women complemented each other or perhaps the blood bond between them was especially strong because they were daughters of immigrants and had so few relatives. But the two cherished the visits when they shared memories of their youthful escapades together. They had never lost touch and now embraced the future through their long talks. Anne had stood as godmother to Rose's four daughters and son who managed to make his appearance as the caboose of the family. Her godchildren were now grown with families of their own, but Anne had taken seriously her spiritual vows to mother the five should anything happen to the parents.

Anne had experienced motherhood from afar with her three nieces and Rose's five and felt no loss as she caught glimpses over the years of this state that had dodged her. In fact, she felt lucky to have had these chances to see them all grow; even here Lady Luck had watched over her. She had never fostered melancholy seeing such a condition as a hurdle in her determination to enjoy life.

As fate would have it, Anne found herself at her cousin's on the most crucial of days. As the two sat talking, catching up on yesterday and tomorrow even as their mothers had once done, the ringing phone suddenly aborted the conversation. Rose's son had been found dead of an apparent heart attack at age thirty-five. The caller left Rose frozen to the chair. Anne held her cousin in her arms and, as Rose later said, was the perfect person with whom to share such shattering news. Consoling the stunned mother, Anne reminded her that quality mattered most in life and far exceeded quantity, regardless of the pain a shortened life bestowed on survivors. And Johnny's life had been wonderfully full.

She remained with Rose through the wake and the difficult moments after the hectic days of the funeral. Though the bond between the cousins had grown over the years, Rose detected something in her cousin now that the past had never revealed. Anne's counsel was less about Johnny's heavenly home and more about the wonders of his life on earth—the deep love he had for his parents and the young family that he left behind. Having been raised by devout sisters who practiced the religion of the Russian Church, Anne and Rose had often attended Mass together, and Rose had never thought of Anne as a zealot. Far from it, Anne's church attendance, unlike her younger sisters, was sporadic. Missing Sunday Mass or holy days was no calamity for her. So now, Rose was surprised by Anne's intense spirit, and never forgot the wondrous gift of her presence throughout the painful period.

Still, Anne's gift to her cousin that day would not have been made at least not easily, had Rose not been family. Anne, like her sisters, drew a line between strangers and blood. Only Maggie had reached out to those beyond that line—and by doing so had ignored the family message.

After nearly ten years, the blush of the color television in the living room had barely begun to fade when the modern age gave Anne another wonderment to fill her free time. Fast food and shopping malls had emerged. Though neither activity would have classified as an adventure in her youth, at seventy she found them entertaining, casual and not at all demeaning—as did her sister Rose who viewed only fine dining and a Pittsburgh department store respectable!

To Anne's dismay, their city, having become a suburb of Pittsburgh, had only two malls. Forever at the top of her list of necessities, convenience seemed the password at these modern shopping extravaganzas. Parking was simple and the wide variety of stores opened the door to one-stop shopping! The malls offered a leisurely afternoon just as "downstreet" once had for her…. with less effort, no weather concerns and enticing food courts. Never a true shopper who constantly looks to purchase *something*, Anne meandered through the indoor complexes. Too young in 1904 to attend the World's Fair in St Louis where ice cream cones were introduced into the culture, she now relished the wide variety of flavors atop these edible containers.

Especially enjoying the new sensation known as "pizza pie," later short-ened to "pizza," Anne watched pizza "huts" spring up throughout the malls as well as in her city. (The word "hut" implies that a small dwelling has been put up quickly and proved the perfect description for these fast food eateries). As the new food was simple and appetizing, Anne knew without the aid of a calorie counter that pizza must be fattening, proving, like the ice cream, her long held claim that the tasty things in life were fat-tening. Less enticing foods carried no such price tags. Doubting that pizza duplicated, as advertised, any authentic Italian recipe, she concluded that neither this fib nor the calories would restrict her enjoyment of the new delight. These days, she would take her adventure where she could find it.

Still another hobby that now fit both Anne's age and personality was coin collecting. Like the malls, this new interest satisfied her ongoing hun-ger for new experiences, and the pastime aligned with her thrifty nature, which had never embarrassed her.

"I don't like to waste" she often proclaimed when confronted with her inability to throw anything away. Admiring the sparkling mint proof sets that the Treasury Department now made available to the public, she faith-fully collected them each year in hopes that their value would increase with time. This natural blending of savings and hobby fascinated her. Her life had slowed, but even after years of retirement, she found much to capture her interest.

As Anne walked up the alleyway to the house one fall day, she noticed that her right sandal was wearing in an odd manner. Her two smallest toes appeared to be moving without her direction and rubbing away the inside leather of the shoe. When she arrived and related the incident to Marie, Anne heard the words of someone who had never forgotten the education she received in the doctor's office fifty years before.

"You've suffered a minor stroke. Maybe you should see a doctor," coun-seled her sister, who was never one to frequent doctors.

"Oh, I haven't had other symptoms. I doubt that's the case."

"It was too small to get your attention at the time, Anne. But it's left a trace."

Never one to argue, Anne smiled to acknowledge her sister's diagnosis. Even in the days when the family had its own physician, doctors played little part in Anne's life, and she was determined not to change the family message around health—pay symptoms little attention, and they like other unwanted things in life will disappear. But her age now dictated caution … of some sort. The condition worsened over the year, as could be deduced from the wearing of the inside of her right shoe. But Anne soon forgot her disobedient toes.

The family's focus had become Maggie's health.

Maggie's returned home after surgery, and Anne was constantly at her bedside. For the first time, she broke her housework rule. Knowing her sister as a meticulous housekeeper, Anne dusted and vacuumed Maggie's side of the house. Though the gesture astounded all the sisters, it proved a one-time happening. Confirming her earlier conclusions about housework, Anne paid in the future to have her sister's home cleaned.

Maggie did not recover, and Anne sadly attended the first funeral of the five sisters. She, like all her sisters except Billie, controlled her tears. Though Anne often claimed that tears came *too* easily to her, even when viewing movie cartoons, they were never visible. She may have felt sadness but others seldom saw any telltale evidence. With handkerchief close in hand on any occasion that might prove emotional, she quickly swept tears away before they traveled too far. And such was now the case as she greeted friends at Maggie's wake

Within a year of the funeral, Anne's toe problem grew to an entire twitching foot. And when she noticed her right hand begin to involuntarily shake, the signs proved more than she could deny. Practical, she knew that the time had come to call in the experts. The diagnosis of Parkinson's came exactly three years after the initial clues. But Anne, as she had throughout her life, took even this diagnosis in her stride. Though medical science offered little help for the terminal disease in 1974.

Quickly deciding that Anne was too passive in her acceptance of the disease, Billie rebuked her sister.

"Anne you aren't active enough. Just move more!"

"You're not around all the time. I move a great deal."

"Well, I think that you should take at least three thousand steps a day. It won't cure it, but I know that it will help," Billie continued

"You think that I'm going to start counting my steps? You've gone crazy," Anne replied with a laugh.

"Just listen to me. Walk to the house more often; don't take the alleyway. Take the longer path. Hang clothes outside more often. Activity will be good for you."

Even as she offered the last suggestion, Billie thought of her sister's aversion to anything that even approached housework. And Anne, who had grown used to her kid sister's unsolicited counsel, subtly changed the subject or tuned out the family rebel.

"If you can't beat 'em, join 'em," Anne thought to herself. Though less sure this time of what "joining 'em" would mean in the case of Parkinson's.

18

The Constant

Sitting in the front row near the altar, where the open casket could clearly be viewed by family through the service, Rose forced her thoughts to ramble. Though her brother had seldom attended Sunday Mass during their mother's lifetime, after Anna's death, he never went to church. So now, his burial rites felt curious to her as she sat rigidly in the pew. It took death to get him to church, she thought. And she could feel the irony now as clearly as she could hear the choir.

Smelling the familiar mixture of burning candles and incense in the nave of the church, Rose, with the others in the family, sat on the men's side of the church. Exceptions were made during funerals so that families could remain together during this taxing time. Ordinarily the church separated parishioners by gender as they entered the space made sacred by the altar—a practice similar to many Eastern religious sects. At an ordinary Sunday Mass, males sat on the right side and females on the left. So she never had sat with her brother at a service, but she wondered now how it would have felt over the years to even have him across the isle from her.

Hoping to dodge the heavy sadness of his death, Rose continued with her mental meanderings.

She realized for the first time, the paradox of Church attendance. Far more women attended than men, twice as many at a regular Sunday Mass. But only males were allowed into the priesthood, and even those who *assisted* the priest were boys; women were not permitted behind the altar in the sanctuary, the most sacred of spaces. Even at baptisms, which took place when infants were only six weeks old, only male babies were carried behind the altar. Unlike the Roman Catholics, priests in the Russian Church were allowed to marry. Though after becoming a priest, a man could rise in the church hierarchy to become a bishop or a metropolitan—only if he remained free of a wife. And, Rose pondered, the women who more faithfully attended Mass had expectations placed upon them while in the church. Required to cover her hair with either hat or scarf, a woman could not reveal her "greatest physical asset." A woman's hair could not be flaunted—or even clearly seen as in Muslim sects.

Feeling now a touch of resentment at such sexism, she called herself back from the reverie, pushing her thoughts into the present and more relevant facts. Her brother would be the first to join their mother in the large cemetery plot the family had purchased twenty years before. The parcel, a mere mile from the house, held space for twelve caskets. And Rose wondered for the first time where his body would be placed in the family plot, secured so many years ago. Next to her mother? Such arrangements mattered little to her, but she considered their effect on the others. Who would be the first to sleep—a verb often used by the Church to lessen the pain of death—next to their mother?

They had buried Anna twenty years ago, and, Anne had insisted then that they locate their father's unmarked grave and transport his body to the newly acquired plot. In her usual way, Anne had insisted on equality.

"It's not right to forget Papa. He loved us too."

"Anne, we don't know where his grave is," Rose replied.

"Well, let's try and find it!"

"You have time to search. I don't. I'll help pay, whatever it costs," said Rose trying to support her sister's long held hope. Finding and exhuming her father's body only to bury again was hardly something she had ever considered.

One parent in a manicured cemetery, someday to be surrounded by her children, and the other lying in an anonymous grave, haunted Anne. And though Rose and the others agreed with her, the sisters in those days felt far from death. For them, there remained time to carry out the idea, but it soon lost the energy it needed for fruition. Now, Andrew's death returned the discussion to Rose.

Eventually, her brother's death led Rose to the practical thoughts of her own savings, all now in U.S. Savings Bonds with Andrew's name as beneficiary. She would attend to the official paperwork, designating other heirs; she would replace his name with those of her three nieces. Though such paper matters flustered her, more complicated than necessary, she often complained, they never slowed her down. She would take care of the matter as soon as she returned to work.

At the close of the funeral rites, Rose remained tearless. The musings had blocked her sadness: a practice at which she had become expert.

"There's nothing I can do about it," she thought. This time, the *it* in the sentence referred to her brother's death. Such reasoning over the painful matters of her life came easily to her.

In the five years following Andrew's death, two weddings reduced the residents of the house to nine. The family tradition of elopement had come to a halt with the colorful wedding of Rose's second niece. She, as well as her sisters, had begun to sense the benefit of a public celebration; others could share the excitement of the newly joined couple. When her youngest niece followed suit with vows witnessed by many invited guests, Rose again felt the pain of her brother's absence; as the bride's godfather, his presence would have been honored at the wedding celebration. But he was gone, and the sad thought overshadowed the otherwise happy occasion. She consoled herself with the fact that adulthood and death were absolutes of life. And fighting them was futile.

Even as the residents dwindled, Rose was determined to go on as usual. She still had the *other* half of her life; the wondrous job in the large city, accompanied by the interesting commute, had never grown stale. The only change at the department store had been the policy that eliminated commissioned sales in the coat department. Though this shift also meant an increase in her base salary, unrelated to what she sold, the loss of the commission troubled her. She was good at what she did, and the commission reflected this. Commissions established a gauge among the salespeople and felt right to Rose. As a first generation in the new country, she needed this barometer as support.

Still the loss of the commission had no effect on her standard of living. The gifts to her nieces and their families, her vacations, and the personal

services for her hair and nails never wavered. And she faithfully contributed to the general upkeep of the house with a monthly payment, which
included her food. The monthly fee originally posed by Marie proved
unusually small for room and board—and had not increased in forty years.
Though these two sisters seldom agreed on much of anything, it was clear
that Marie wanted Rose at the house. Other than the small payment and
her savings, why else did Rose need money? She did not drive, and material items, even for entertainment, held little appeal for her. Marie's clothes
buying had created a vast wardrobe, and Rose began to wear her sister's
hand-me-downs; like Anne, waste of any sort bothered her. But remaining
true to her own tastes, she chose only those castoffs that fit her style, which
given Marie's wardrobe made her choices nearly unlimited.

The money Rose placed in savings was a guarantee for her future independence. And with this kind of nest egg, she would rely on no one.

And then Maggie's diagnosis of cancer arrived.

At first, Rose tried to encourage her sister to eat better and focus on the
positive and not permit lack of energy a top priority in her life. Though
sound advice, after surgery, radiation, and chemotherapy brought no sign
of improvement, Rose found herself unable to shrink the situation with
her old standby—"nothing I can do about it." But this method that had
insulated her from crises of the past now proved useless. The three months
between the initial diagnosis and her sister's death shook Rose's system like
an electric shock, destroying all her defenses. Though the doctors had
offered little hope after the surgery, it was as though Rose had never heard
them. The death returned the other unexpected events of her life.

Managing to get through the hours at her sister's bedside, at both the
house and hospital, and finally at the funeral, Rose never visibly went to
pieces. Her mother had taught that lesson at her cousin's death. Except for
the four days she took off for the wake and burial, her work schedule never
varied. But once the friends and relatives dispersed and she arrived at the
house from work that first night, the grief set in with what seemed like

massed revenge. The methods that she had used to rationalize her feelings had now stalled.

Without Maggie, she could not deny that her life had changed.

Assuring Rose and her brother a hot meal, regardless of their arrival times, Maggie had always been there. Even in those early years after their father's death when Anna and the older siblings had been forced to work outside the home, Maggie had been there as surely as the break of day. And now the lack of meals provided only a material reminder of her loss. Rose missed the intimacy that the two sisters had shared, though repeating her disbelief at the suddenness of the death became the only overt sign of her gloom. She went on as she always had: work, train commute, church, and vacation.

But shattered by this fifth sudden blow to her system, her resistance shrank. The evenings after work proved unbearable. And Rose began to drink. In the past, she had been a self-disciplined social drinker and would have only her standard rum and coke on evenings when she had no work the following day, which nicely allowed for vacation time. Until Maggie's death, the rule remained hard and fast with no exceptions, but now a new nightly ritual of a few drinks after work cut the pain of grief and seemed harmless. Sleeping through the night, she still started her day promptly at six in the morning, never missing the train. Working in the same place for fifty years, never using sick days, she had no intention of tarnishing her sterling record.

Recalling the warning signals of alcoholism, she tried to follow the cautions and never drank alone in her bedroom. Going upstairs after a few drinks meant a bath and then sleep. Though the old trick of reading a boring book to put herself to sleep no longer worked. In fact, all novels were forgotten. The sitting room, where the family had ritually gathered over the years, was now occupied by Marie and Kate as they watched the evening news. So Rose found herself drinking in the evenings on Maggie's side of the house. Maggie's daughter had her own home, and Walter arrived long after Rose had forced herself to bed. She was alone in this space where she had spent so many hours with her sister—enveloped now in memories. Basking in the calmness that the nightly drinks bestowed, she thought of her sister and their many years together.

She had objected to Marie's renovation after their mother died, but the change had brought Maggie and her family to live at the house; for the first time, Rose felt indebted to Marie and actually thanked her sister, a first! Perhaps alcohol could be beneficial in ways other than dulling pain, she smiled to herself.

Obeying the "don't drink alone" rule by never carrying drinks to her bedroom, Rose was not one to deceive herself; she saw that she *was* alone in a way that even the house could not erase. And her evening libation increased. There were days when she considered for the first time calling in sick for work. And this startling thought finally brought her to the reality that alcohol would eventually control her.

In the struggle to again take charge of her life, she thought of an alternative for her evenings. Admitting to herself that the notion had lagged in its arrival, she welcomed this bolt from the blue. Her sister Anne lived less than a minute away; why not walk to Anne's in the evenings after work?

There, Rose could regain some of the companionship she had lost with Maggie's death. And her visits would be company for the three of them, she reasoned. Anne had been retired for years and Tom now over ten. When the two were not traveling, which lessened with each passing year, they were home after dark, a dictate of the aging process. So they would be around on most evenings. In the past, Rose had casually visited Anne on her days off, but this would be different. These would be regular evening visits, ending the solitary drinking that brought on the nightly nostalgia.

Her relationship with her oldest sister was good, certainly better than with Marie, and the thought that her self-invitation would be rejected by Anne never crossed her mind. They were blood.

And she was right.

Anne welcomed the chance to help her sister. She had not made the suggestion, but her house, from its initial purchase, had been meant for exactly such a circumstance. Arriving evenings *after* dinner, Rose knew that her sister had never been inclined to entertain on any level. And there remained a mutual acceptance that made communication between them easy. These two had more in common with Aunt Rosalie than with their mother, so they understood one another in ways that made words unnecessary.

"How was the day? Any interesting customers?" Anne generally began.

"Just one. She told me that she knew exactly what she wanted. But after searching through every coat and color, and trying on about twenty, she complained that our stock was low. That our styles were outdated!"

"Rose, you've been there for how many years now? Maybe you should think of retiring. I would be so tired of waiting on those kinds of customers day after day." Anne was cautious with such questions but wanted her sister to consider it.

When the chitchat between the three found a natural end, they settled into the night's television offerings. Rose left at exactly eleven when Tom walked her to the corner of the street, intently watching as she made her way up the cobblestone alleyway. Out of his sight, she was within seconds of the house, in the nightly ritual.

The visits did not prove miraculous. A sudden choice of abstinence was not the case. In fact, Rose stored a limited amount of rum at Anne's. But the evenings placed her back in control, and returning to the house in the late evening, she never drank. She kept no alcohol there—just to assure such resolve. Not allowing melancholy to encase her in the evenings at her sister's, Rose understood firsthand why drinking alone was considered harmful by the experts. At first, she was satisfied that her evening visits simply decreased her drinks and hoped to eventually restore her old rule: no alcohol preceding a workday.

Anticipating a workday, which began with a walk down a steep hill to a half hour train commute, eight hours of catering to often finicky customers, another half hour train ride back, and finally a walk *up* the steep hill, Rose found perfectly natural. At nearly seventy years of age. Even the wintry days that caused her to clutch anything in sight for support presented no problem. If the oddity around this scenario ever struck her, she never discussed it, simply taking work as the given of her life. So the people around her came to accept Rose and her lifelong job as part of the same tapestry. Though she and her sister Anne were alike in matters of style and appearance, their attitude towards work stood in glaring contrast. Anne, seven years her senior, had retired over thirty years earlier. But Anne believed that everyone had a right to their own lifestyle, and Rose and her job had become linked over the years in a way similar to marriage partners.

So Anne's hints of retirement diminished with time. Until the thief stepped out of the night.

Even as she aged, Rose made the nightly climb up the hill to the house after the train commute without complaint. Lightly placing the required ritual in the exercise category of her life.

"It's all in how you think about things," she would explain, tossing away most of life's petty annoyances.

In the heat of summer when everyone around her complained of high temperatures, she remained relaxed and cool. The only concession she now made to age in her nightly walks was her shoes. No longer the spike heels she once wore, regardless of the hike, her shoes were now practical and flat. Though she quickly returned to the high heels when on the job.

But Walter, not influenced by her talk of exercise, worried about the walks in the dark of winter. He often met the late train and drove her up the hill. Until one night, attending an old friend's retirement bash, he failed to appear, and Rose walked her familiar path up the hill to the house. At the age of seventy at ten in the evening, she walked alone with her large purse flung over her shoulder. A calamity waiting to happen.

The city's economy, now without the steel mills, had reached an irreversible ebb, and there were few jobs for the inhabitants. Aside from the economics of the loss, the light from the blast furnaces, which had once eased the darkness of night, was gone too. As Rose neared the house, she sensed a presence behind her. Keeping up her usual brisk pace, she glanced to one side, and at once felt a hand from behind, in one experienced motion, shove her shoulder and grab the purse. She fell to the ground but quickly stood and walked to the house, a mere five houses away. Managing sufficient courage, she swore at the fleeing thief, one of the few times she was known to use vulgarity. Luckily, the only damage was the loss of three hundred dollars and a bit of courage. The purse contained only cash and nothing that would reveal her identity—neither checks, credit cards, nor a driver's license. As always, she traveled light.

The mugging did little to change the pattern of her life. She insisted on the same agreement she had had with Walter in the past. If opposing plans arose during his day, he would not meet her train; Rose asked for no guarantee of a ride at night and always walked up the hill in daylight. But after the mugging, frightful by all accounts, Walter felt negligent and now met her more often, even in the early dusk of winter.

The robbery also allowed Anne to reopen the discussion of retirement. But even Anne's easy manner proved futile.

Rose continued the job that she had so joyfully accepted fifty years before.

19

The Forerunner

Billie's youngest daughter, now a working woman, remained with her mother, but such an arrangement was soon due to end. Meeting her fiancée the previous summer while at the house, the young woman planned to marry. Her college choice, unlike her sister's, had not been close to the house, but she assured her future connections to the family nest by marrying a man who had grown up three miles from it; but there was little work there now. And the couple could find no logic in making their home where the economy appeared dire. Before the nuptials, he had secured a job near Billie, and this had added to her connections to the area. The family rebel had freed herself of a few ties to the house—consistent with the freedom the sixties brought.

This was the decade of change all over America. Similar to the twenties, the sixties were about free will. But while the twenties saw disregard of custom, in the sixties, laws would change—immigration quotas were abolished, and the successor to the slain president waged a new kind of war: a "War on Poverty." In the seventies, the twenty-sixth amendment to the Constitution lowered the voting age to eighteen, abortion became legal, the Equal Rights Amendment went to the states for approval, and the cultural attitudes that accompanied such changes in the sixties were strong enough to continue through the seventies.

Having *two* daughters and their growing families nearby had caused Billie to at last feel at home—in her home of nearly thirty years. Her awareness of the area had disclosed the Chesapeake Bay that offered an eating experience like she had never known in the mountains of western Pennsylvania. And closer still was a wharf sporting a daily catch.

Learning to eat shellfish of all sorts, she became a fan of the plentiful Maryland blue crab. At first, Billie simply watched from a distance in amazement as diners expertly shelled and ate the steamed crustaceans on paper tablecloths. (The crude table coverings allowed waitresses to wrap the shells in the paper and cover the table with a new one for a rapid restock of the delicacies for the same diners, who shelled many crabs at a sitting) Could she eat those? Could she eat those *like that?* Dipping the white crab meat into vinegar before eating, partakers ate little else at such repasts. Appropriately known as crab *feasts,* one meal could number two dozen crabs and was accompanied by only a minor suggestion of starch—saltine crackers. Though it had taken her several years to muster the courage to order such an odd meal, Billie found herself now enchanted by the food, as well as the ritual that accompanied it. The character of the festivity appealed to her nature—a nature that continued to seek what others found curious.

The area had grown on her, encouraging a sense of permanence. And she now considered the purchase of her home—not even a passing notion in the past. Her landlord, aging and in poor health, had offered her the first option to buy. Having moved in when it was newly built, Billie had been his only tenant for many years. Still, buying a house would be a major step for her, a permanent act that would undoubtedly deliver a message to her family at the house; she would never again reside there. Would they, especially Marie, see her as having deserted the nest?

There were also finances to consider. A saver by nature, she now possessed a nest egg that allowed her to seriously consider his generous offer. But Billie had never taken risks with money; what if the market for houses fell? Unlike Anne, she was not a gambler. Though open to challenges in her life and often relying on her intuition, Billie never depended on the throw of the dice in money matters.

She had rented her home for $55 a month. And the owner, a generous man who viewed her as a struggling single mother, had never raised the rent! Now with his generous selling price, his virtues shone even more brightly. The amount, only to his faithful tenant, was eight thousand dollars, an amazing price in 1963. The price, he claimed, was due to the fact that she had always paid her rent, exactly 264 times, on time on the same day of each month. His selling price was what it would have been had she purchased it in 1942, the time of the initial lease. How could she refuse such an offer?

Still, she hesitated. Such a decision felt heavy and about more than money.

As had happened in the past, destiny stepped in to plant another variable in the decision. Both her sister's restaurants had been seized by the city, and Marie's emotional state would surely profit from Billie's presence. As the only sister who had ever shown an interest in a family business, Billie had taken the reins whenever she waitressed over the years, helping Marie to relax, at least as much as this sister ever could. Complicating her decision now to buy her home was her sister's state of affairs as she relocated and began anew, at what for many was retirement age. Marie would need her youngest sister for support.

Marie, without children, had confided her plan to eventually place Billie's name on the restaurant deed of ownership. Such serious conversations had occurred only between these two, but as yet no legal change had been made. And now, Billie had heirs of her own to consider. If Marie put her name on the deed, Billie could leave the restaurant to her children. But this would mean that she would devote more hours to the enterprise; Marie was more likely to transfer ownership if Billie resided at the house. And this would mean less time with the two budding families—a double-edged sword

The new restaurant and the fact that she no longer had children to raise made the time right for a permanent return to the house. Yet, with her two daughters and their families so close, a rejection of her landlord's generous selling price felt naive to her.

Close to a decision to accept his offer, she saw the variables change again! Just as she had worked through a strategy to help Marie with the transition and still make the purchase, Billie's oldest daughter unexpectedly moved—six hundred miles away. Abrupt, the action landed Billie back at the drawing board. Her second daughter, newly married, could also move in the future. Who knew what the future held? Never known for ongoing doubts on much of anything, she found herself in turmoil. Should she move back to the house to help her sister with the new business? Or buy her home as a logical investment and continue her many trips, perhaps increasing them? Perhaps it was not an either, or decision.

Finally, her intuition sided with the purchase, and she acted on the old adage: best not to look a gift horse in the mouth. The purchase was real while Marie's words were only possibilities. In the past, her sixth sense had been a reliable tool. The advice she had given her four sisters over the years, governed mostly by intuition, had been frighteningly accurate, though her dictums often stirred things up at the house for days.

Billie accepted the landlord's offer and bought her house. In addition to the amazing price, after so many years she had begun to feel at home away from the house. And this feeling of belonging in the new space strengthened her decision.

Though she knew that Marie would be disappointed, the offer to bring her into the business had been a tenuous one and would likely be stalled by the family image of her as the rash rebel. And secretly, Billie questioned the reality of her sister starting over after so many years. Forever in awe of this sister, she wondered now if Marie possessed the energy for such an endeavor at this point in her life—the sleep-inducing drug had created health problems larger than the insomnia. As she did with all her sisters, when their choices seemed wrong to her, Billie confronted Marie with the tangible evidence—this twitch in Marie's neck that now could not be ignored. But as in the past, Marie scoffed at Billie's suggestion of addiction and ended the discussion by storming away.

Even with such denial, Billie planned to support her sister, continuing to act as head waitress and also patronizing the restaurant in her free time. Over the years, she had convinced Anne and Tom to return with her to The Joint in the evenings to socialize with the customers.

"Anne, aren't you going to The Joint tonight?"

"I get tired of the same atmosphere. Tom and I are going to the Moose Club."

"It's important to Marie that we go. That she knows we care about all the work she's put into it," Billie countered.

"She doesn't care one way or another where we have a nightcap. She's never there at that time anyway," Anne said, defending her preference.

"I think Eddie tells her if we've been there in the evening. Why spend your money someplace else? Marie has been so generous with the kids. Sometimes I don't understand you."

"We've gone many times this summer. I need a change." Anne stood firm in her verdict.

When Billie's decision to buy her house became firm, she considered increasing her trips to support Marie's new endeavor. The trips had become second nature to her. A seasoned traveler, she now packed for one, rather than three. Packing was a learned skill, she held, and after so many years of practice, she had developed a "science of packing." For the summer trips, though necessary to take clothes for nearly three months, her clothes were similar; there were no erratic weather changes as at other times of the year. Placing a metal bar above the back seat of the car and hanging much of the clothing on it, she could quickly transport, via hangers, a vast amount that would otherwise require packing and ironing after arrival. This way, a tiresome task was reduced, with less *un*packing at either end. Over the years, she had acquired many aides to her travel, her most recent purchase, a trunk that resembled a foot locker, had drawers for her small articles and fit into the rear of the car. The trunk could also be carried into the house and used as a bureau throughout the stay. The years had nicely reduced the task for her.

Such packing skills were useful as she now made visits to her older daughter. The new trip was nearly triple the journey to the house, but Billie's nature never permitted the option of a motel room along the way. Even as the lone driver, she refused to allow the long trips more than one day. But she was rewarded by two grandchildren who excitedly welcomed her arrival at the end of each long drive.

At the bank closing for her new home, Billie came face-to-face with an old issue. Money transactions had become more complex, and she lacked what seemed most important—identification. Having neither social security nor credit cards, or ownership of anything, except for her used car, she lacked the most revered proof of identity, a birth certificate. As there had been no consequence to this deficit in the past, she had never pursued a solution with her usual determination. Before this major purchase of real estate, the bureaucratic actions of her life had been her marriage and driver's licenses and the children's birth certificates. On these occasions, her baptismal document had been sufficient, and never traveling outside the country, working only for her sister, she had found the paper adequate. The lack of a birth certificate, proof of citizenry, generally caused a variety of questions, but her persuasive powers always won out. But now in this major exchange for property, the old question arose. Was she a U.S. citizen? Where was the evidence?

She and her siblings had all been born in their parents' dwelling. Which had changed, depending on the location of the coal mine that employed her father. A certain *radius* of the seven births dwelt in their memories, but a hospital for simple inquiries did not exist. A hospital was not even a thought for any of the births where midwives were luxuries in only two of them. Home births were not rare at the start of the century, but doctors who signed birth certificates had a certain status; they were connected to hospitals regardless of where the delivery occurred. Her parents could not afford such assistance; their link to the outside world came only through the Church. Regardless of where the family dwelt, baptism occurred at six weeks of age; well documented, this act was certain. Like her siblings, Billie had her baptismal paper signed by the attending priest, but without a doctor's signature, the document was frowned upon in larger legal matters.

Her siblings had similar frustrations in their transactions. But people all knew each other in their small city and overlooked certain formalities. But in Billie's area, five miles from the Nation's capitol, government reigned and laws were enforced. Buying her home, she suddenly felt a challenge between herself and the governing powers.

Having lived at the same address for twenty-two years, she managed to win the debate at the closing but vowed to finally obtain an official birth certificate. She *was* born in the new country and had never left or re-entered it! A birth certificate would eliminate such debates in the future. Surely she had an innate right to be acknowledged as a citizen; she was a child of immigrants and a first generation American. Writing numerous letters to a variety of offices and even visiting town halls within the vicinity of her birth, she pled her case. One authority led to another—who led to another.

Though she could have gone on indefinitely, after a two year crusade to prove herself a citizen of the new country, she finally admitted the futility of the quest. She had no birth certificate and never would. Billie consoled herself with the thought that the search had endowed her with an unexpected payoff: a parable that would prove useful in future discourse.

"Without my birth certificate, I really have no age," she proudly began the homily, happy to reveal the irony that had snuffed out her age.

"Don't take things for granted. I can't prove I was born here, though I've never left this country," she would continue as she expanded on her theme. "Surprising events defeat the best of schemes and plans *of any kind* are arrogant and tempt fate."

Any of the statements could be integrated into the discussion, as she tailored her tale of the elusive birth certificate to fit the situation. When she had begun the search for the document, who would have guessed of such philosophical results?

The core of her message reduced to *expect the unexpected* in life. Feeling that others pompously made plans based on the unknowable, she claimed that her own plans were always tenuous and open to the hand of fate. Marie's promise of future ownership of the new business fell into such a category.

Following such rational adages, Billie often comforted others: "You never know how things will change from one moment to the next." Her statement served to release friends of lingering guilt over all the *shoulds* of their lives.

But such counsel provided little solace for her when Maggie's alarming diagnosis arrived without warning. Like all her sisters, Maggie had always been the picture of health. At first, Billie believed that her sister would recover, though this time her sentiment was not her usual *prediction*, only a fervent *hope*. Spending every free hour that summer at her sister's bed-side, she watched life slowly ebb.

She sat in what seemed endless vigil in the hospital room, though she later realized that the time between the diagnosis and death had been very short. Towards the end, when hope could no longer be kindled, she began to see death as freedom for her sister; Maggie's protracted pain would be gone. Though the thought delivered temporary respite at the time, the death produced such grief that her sister's release from earthly pain was soon forgotten.

From the beginning, these two sisters had been bonded to each other in a different way than the others. They had traveled similar paths. In their youth, they had been left to keep house and play together when the others became wage earners. Maggie and Billie had been the only two of their generation to receive high school diplomas and to bear, nurse and raise children. And because their sights were never far off one another, even when Billie's life took her a distance away, the two thought of the other when problems arose. It was Maggie's gentle criticism that often caused Billie to reconsider impulsive acts made in anger. And Billie's farsighted advice tempered Maggie's romantic side. As a young child, Maggie had been her youngest sister's keeper—and later, her confidante.

Now, at Maggie's death, Billie felt a void. Though such emptiness negated the Christian teaching that her sister dwelt in a heaven free of sor-row. But perhaps this grief surrounded by loss and love held meaning for her; perhaps the death was a sign that the time had come to move her own life away from the house. Recalling her own words about the unexpected

in life, Billie thought of her own home, and the comfort this brought energized the healing process. Maybe in creating a life beyond the house, she
would nurture her spirit in a different way. The traditions she inherited
from her mother and built upon with her sisters would be with her forever,
but now she would encourage buds that were her own.

After Maggie's death, Billie still traveled to the house, but now her
times there were truly visits ... rather than her life.

C8 C8 C8 C8 C8 C8 C8 C8 C8 C8 C8 C8 C8 C8 C8 C8 C8

Feeling that I had either witnessed or heard all of the events of my
mother's life that conveyed her daring nature, I required no further persuasion when they were all surpassed by what has become my favorite. Her
house, which she long occupied and finally bought, had neither carport,
driveway, nor garage, so she forever fretted over a parking space, at least
close to her home. Unlike ordinary streets where residents politely leave
space in front of another's property, Mother's included a church that held
daily services, and parishioners, focused on their worship, often left no
parking space for others.

One might expect a house of worship to endow a certain sanctity to its
surroundings, but such was not the case. Time had taken its toll on the
street; the neighborhood was no longer safe. So, Mother's constant concern for a parking place carried a modest element of anxiety, which proved
justified.

One evening, she returned home to find a man walking the street with a
baseball bat in his hand. Rather than a mere symbol of his attachment to
the game through recent participation, the bat was now being used to
smash the windshields of parked cars. Such actions may have been the
result of a lost game, but his motivation failed to interest my mother, as
she turned onto her street to witness the bizarre spectacle. Even her
thoughts of finding a parking space vanished in the moment, and,
stunned, she turned her car around and headed for the local police station.
But as her thinking cleared, she realized that the location of the law
enforcement agency was unknown to her; she had never been there, and

the short drive delivered this fact. Now less fearful than she had been when first sighting the lunatic, her true nature returned.

She declared "I will not allow a madman to drive me away from my home." For the second time, she maneuvered a U-turn and headed home. Arriving there a mere fifteen minutes later than the first 180 degree turn, she found the villain gone—and a parking space in front of her house.

As the listener in this extraordinary tale, which even delivered a happy ending, I could not allow it to conclude without a daughter's speculation.

"What would you have done if he had still been there with his lethal bat?" I anxiously asked.

"I would have run him down with my car." Her instant reply betrayed the fact that she had considered such a possibility.

Without the aid of the elusive birth certificate, I calculate that she was at the time in her late sixties. Signs of the aging process, both physical and emotional, and evident without the legal record, generally include increased caution, but such was not the case with my mother.

1974–1990

20

The Extremist

Marie was now a constant presence at the house. It might be concluded that she had at last reached a deserved retirement. If her addiction were not so evident. The drug had taken a toll, the extent of which was only suspected by the other residents. The situation contained only two facts: Marie was not under a doctor's care, and her head often moved slightly outside her control. A twitch of sorts had appeared in her neck. By definition, she was not ill, and she had no disease. The sisters had no medical terms for any drugs or proof of anything beyond these realities.

But after so many years under the same roof, they knew her well enough to make a fair deduction. She had become addicted to the remedy for the insomnia. Though she often stumbled on the steps in the afternoons, unable for hours to resume a normal day in either speech or physical activity, they never managed to get past her denial. Without ownership of her bizarre behavior, there remained little for them to discuss.... or do.

And Eddie, busy at a restaurant that no longer required much attention, failed to comment.

The third restaurant now flailed in its death throes. The elaborately decorated second floor designed for private parties had been Marie's pride and joy. But this space, which had once pushed the new establishment up the star rating scale, now remained dark. Though the first floor dining room stayed open, dinners were no longer served, only sandwiches and short orders of fries. These, reminiscent of the little store, now existed only as a courtesy to the drinkers in the bar, who sought nutrition from time to time to absorb the alcohol. Only the bar still produced revenue—and provided a gathering place for Eddie and his cronies.

Startling everyone at a time when both her health and business were in disarray—Marie suddenly decided to take a trip. Forever enjoying such extreme actions, she now stunned her family and delivered memories of the days when she wore her bathing suit in the cold basement—to do laundry.

In the past, she had flown more than her sisters, always to Billie's, a short, fifty minute flight. Lauding the benefits of this modern mode of travel that others still found a bit frightening, she had never used it for travel. But displaying the courage to test current trends had often been her delight so she casually announced her plans to fly *alone* to visit her niece, whose new residence lay seven hundred miles from the nest. Choosing to live three times further than any family member had ever wandered from the house, the young woman had forged a distance that now worried her aunt. So with a glimmer of her old nature, Marie made the trip to assure herself, not about plane rides—she had done that years ago—but about family.

As she had hoped, the trip erased two worries. The distance to her niece's by plane was far shorter than it appeared in raw miles, and she herself could still manage such a dramatic act. Not a trip any of her sisters would have made alone by plane, the flight was a success, and Marie felt comforted on her return; a member of the second generation was secure in a new setting. Perhaps her role as patriarch was still intact.

But even such a feat failed to erase her personal pain. The reality of the failed business, her own health, and the house without Maggie—all weighed heavily on her. Maggie's absence was like a phantom limb to Marie; all the sensations of her presence remained, but the member herself was invisible.

Still, she kept such feelings to herself. And distracted herself as best she could with thoughts of the third generation, which now numbered three. Though she spent far less time with this generation than the preceding one who had been literally teethed at the house, the future of the third generation now felt secure to her. No member would ever beg for food she assured herself.

Unlike the early days, schedules at the house varied little now. And with them vanished the excitement that such outward discord once delivered. No longer working shifts, residents were around the house more. Eddie closed the business in the late evening, rather than abiding by the legal two in the morning curfew for serving alcohol. Walter, now with a desk job rather than a beat, worked regularly from eight in the morning to five in the afternoon, after which he generally had dinner with a friend and then found his way to the house just in time to greet Eddie. In the past, the men had only nodded as they passed in the night, sometimes only once a week; now they would sit and chat over the late news. Kate worked a few days a week at the dying restaurant, arriving home in the early afternoon. Only Rose's schedule remained as it had been, with one revision. After arriving home from work, she quickly ate and then left for her evening at Anne's.

During the daytime hours these days, Kate offered Marie companionship in the form of city gossip and updates on the customers both had known over the years. Trying to conceal the bad news of the business, Kate sensed that Marie knew the truth, and such a topic never arose between the two. Marie could appear at the restaurant anytime she chose, but her visits decreased with each passing week.

In this atmosphere, three months after her impulsive trip, Marie sat in the abiding comfort of the sitting room while Kate busied herself in the kitchen, making tea for the two of them. As had become her routine, Marie attempted to shake off her drug-induced sleep in the late afternoon. When Kate entered the sitting room and handed Marie her cup, she realized that something was frightfully awry. Marie, though her eyes remained open, failed to respond by reaching for the teacup or even looking in Kate's direction. Frantically, Kate made the necessary calls, and Marie was rushed to the local hospital, luckily a short distance away. As she no longer had a family physician, she was assigned a doctor in the emergency ward who immediately called in the appropriate specialist.

The cardiologist diagnosed a stroke. Marie could not speak and appeared paralyzed on one side of her body. But the prognosis was hopeful. There had been no remarkable damage to the brain. The doctor cautioned that while the paralysis would likely disappear, normal speech would only return through therapy. Having seen such warnings trivialized by previous patients, he emphasized the perils. Rehab was a necessity—not a choice.

Marie quickly regained awareness, though now uttering only garbled sounds. Her actions made clear that she fully understood everyone and wanted only to return to the house. She offered yea and nay head movements, and other appropriate responses shown through her expressive eyes. Within a week, the paralysis disappeared, just as the specialist had predicted, and she was released from the hospital. The remnant of the stroke remained her speech, but hospital staff could do no more; she would require therapy.

Throughout her life, Marie had spoken energetically, gesturing with her hands and arms, and the physical mannerisms had not changed with the garbled speech. Responding with facial expressions that showed she grasped the words of others, she seemed herself in all other ways, even energized by her rapid recovery.

"Don't assume that the speech will return as simply as the paralysis disappeared," the physician warned for the third time. "Her brain must *re-learn* how to form words. And this can only be accomplished by therapists trained in the process." He assured Eddie that with determination, a quality that Marie had once displayed a lion's share of, her full recovery was within reach—at that time.

But Eddie refused to force the rehab center. Physical therapists at the time were just coming into their own and only available in institutions where patients remained for an extended time. Eddie stood firm on the assertion that it remained *her* choice not to leave the house, even for a short period. And her demeanor supported his claim. Why would she choose to journey to a strange establishment at a time when she could not make herself understood? Even her sisters responded to her in odd ways these days.

Fettered to her old fear of death, Marie was hardly in a position to make such a decision for herself. Institutions of any kind had been frightening to her in the best of times. Even without the benefit of the spoken word, her anxieties over such a possibility were obvious.

When approached by the three sisters as to his intentions, Eddie repeated, "My Mamie doesn't want to go anywhere." Marie had always been the decision-maker in the marriage, and Eddie, now forced into this untested role, hesitated. Was he faithfully abiding by the wishes of his frightened wife? Or was the lure of power too tempting? Or were the two motives too tangled to tease apart? Even *self*-intentions become knotted in the complexities of life, and Eddie's now were impossible to separate.

Disagreeing with his decision, each of the sisters presented her own argument.

"I've been diagnosed with Parkinson's. And though I can still get myself around, I know how horrible it feels to be helpless." Anne, the least con-frontational of the three, also knew that too much pressure would put Eddie on the defensive.

"Eddie, she's too confused She's not lucid. That's why you have guard-ianship. Look at her there in front of the television when she could be learning to talk again! This is ridiculous," cried Billie.

"She needs professional help," Rose said, "and there's no one here who can give that to her. It's that simple." Rose, who generally stayed out of such disputes and seldom agreed with Marie anyway, now came to the aid of her silent sister.

But when all the arguments failed to sway their brother-in-law, the sis-ters stopped short of their one recourse: taking Eddie to court to relieve him of custody.

Their case would have been strong and direct. The husband had failed to follow the doctor's orders in behalf of his ward. But the court system intimidated the three sisters. Even Billie had had little luck in entering into the male bureaucratic order when she searched for her birth certificate.

Throughout the new country, women were slowly stepping into powerful positions of government. But filing suit against an in-law of fifty years, whom their sister now as never before appeared to lean on, was too far a stretch for the three to make. Unable to venture beyond their fears, the three sisters finally took no legal action.

Undoubtedly, Maggie would have sided with her sisters—and then taken over Marie's care. She had lived to see Marie's decline, though not long enough to see her without the speech that had been her lifeline to the world.

In the months ahead, the family found it more difficult each day to react to her. Though she seemed to understand them, they had no hint as to the meaning of her responses. Hindsight, with the arrogance of time in its corner, could have predicted the eventual outcome. A year after the stroke, Marie stopped responding in any way. The sister who had received attention for her flamboyant acts now fell silent.

Eddie invited Kate to change her job description as his employee at the restaurant and give Marie round-the-clock care, trading a three-hour job for a twenty-four-hour one. Though the offer included a salary increase, it was far from an even exchange, but Kate accepted, never commenting on her new role. She undertook the task and tenderly cared for her patient. Having worked in all three restaurants, Kate remained grateful to Marie for the jobs and shelter she had been given over the last forty-two years.

But Kate's new job lasted only four years. Conversing with others had always been one of Marie's joys, and she could not survive without interaction. Nothing left for her creative spirit, she withdrew from the world. Sitting in front of the television in the sitting room for hours on end, she appeared unaware now of both herself and her surroundings. She had no visible interest in anything, including food. Eventually, Kate force-fed her charge; the only way to insure nutrition of any sort.

The world that had once held so much allure had simply vanished for Marie.

Other minor strokes may have followed the one that robbed her of speech and contributed to a spiral into oblivion. But none were obvious enough to require hospital stays. Though full immobility never occurred, Marie finally showed no interest in even the natural act of walking. There was no place she wanted to go. It became more difficult to get her up the stairs to her bedroom—ironically the same steps that had proved danger-ous for her to descend in the months preceding the stroke. A hospital bed was moved into the ornate dining room, presenting a stunning contrast to the room she had so lavishly decorated.

With nearly no physical movement of her body these days, her lungs became congested from a winter's cold. And five years after the stroke, pneumonia set in, and she died Her old fear of dying in an asylum, as Mickey had done, had not come to pass, but her final days paralleled his torment. Again, she had gone to the extreme: from the independence that money bestows, to the helplessness that illness delivers.

The business quickly folded after her death. Perhaps she had been right in forever saying that her husband "had no business sense." Though she had not been a real presence at the new restaurant for several years, it had been her dream. Without the drug, her old energy may have created a plan that aligned the business with the changing times.

After the death of both his wife and the business, Eddie turned to alco-hol and religion. Admittedly, the two pursuits were odd bedfellows, but they had one thing in common. Both were firsts for him. Until now, be had never taken a drink or gone to church. Boasting in the past of his dis-dain for both alcohol and religion, he now sought to catch up on lost time in both endeavors. In addition to joining a fundamentalist church after Marie's death, he spent his days at the house enthralled by the popular television evangelists of the times.

Eventually, Eddie donated the remnants of the fortune to the religious movement that captivated him, claiming, "I feel guilty for selling booze to innocent people for all those years." Guilt seemed a factor, only its source remains uncertain.

Still, perhaps such a conclusion gives Eddie an unfair rap. Marie had sought a place in the world as a lone businesswoman and had become the patriarch of a family before women in the new country had even the right to vote. Shortly after her death, a woman was appointed for the first time to the U. S. Supreme Court, and the new country saw a female on the ticket for the vice presidency of the nation. But even in the eighties, America was not ready for powerful females—the Equal Rights Amendment failed. Though Marie met her goals and undoubtedly found comfort in ensuring the family's survival, she paid the price for straying so violently from the female norm of the day.

Can humans painlessly ignore the culture and remake themselves to fit their larger dreams?

21

The Seeker

It could safely be said that Billie had now left the nest. At last, she felt "at home in her home." And her longtime energy endured. No longer waitressing, she knew that her spirit needed a replacement for the old job. Unlike her sister Anne, and with one of the few values that she shared with Rose, Billie had no interest in retirement. Her need for income was less than it once had been, but she now sought an interesting pastime, which would also offer monetary compensation. She would give all her vigor to an endeavor but wanted at least a minimal paycheck. Given the life as the seventh child of poor immigrants, such was her need. This need for a monetary return eliminated such possibilities as traveling or gardening in her large lawn, but the emotional rewards of such pursuits were unknown to her.

Working for *spiritual* satisfaction, belonged in the Church's domain for her. And she now extended her church attendance beyond the Sunday Mass, to which she had forever been faithful. Mass, the ritual of a literal union with the Divine, was celebrated once every day in the Russian Church, not simply on Sundays. Daily Mass, preceded by the Matins service to greet the day, was followed by Vespers to end it. Though Matins had never enticed her, when feeling a slump in her mood these days, she frequented the evening service and occasionally a weekday Mass, practices that she had never considered in the past.

Completing the shift to her own residence, she searched for employment—close to her home. Suddenly aware of the local newspapers and regional happenings that had before eluded her, she read the want ads and made inquiries.

When the right signals are sent into the universe, things fall into place, and she soon learned of the area's large tourist trade, which had enticed antique dealers from all over the world. Though knowing of the rich history that surrounded her, she had not connected this fact to tangible things such as antiques. Her visits to the surrounding historical sites had never revealed the large antique trade. *Life* in the new country had consumed her energy, not its relics. Billie had been busy learning the customs of a land that had not been part of her heritage, and collectibles had meant nothing to her.

But the antique shops of her area sought clerks. Material goods had become important to people, and sales of all kinds were on the rise. A cultural shift had occurred; shopping was now entertainment. Throughout America, it was now more important to spend money than save it, as was her family message. Most of the wealthy still recognized that it took money to make money, and those large purchases—homes and college tuition—took sums that needed to be amassed over time. Buying now seemed the draw of most citizens. It had become so important, that credit cards were now carried instead of cash. The new country had moved from a creditor to a debtor nation. America no longer dominated the world economy, as imports exceeded exports.

To Billie, all of this was new. Neither she nor anyone at the house had ever owned a credit card. But she took the new life in stride and soon discovered a quaint antique shop in need of a clerk, a short distance from her home. She quickly admitted her inexperience. Waitressing for her sister had been her only job, and antiques, which required critical judgment, hardly seemed the ideal place to start such an endeavor. But still open to challenges in her life, she talked to the owner who erased her doubts.

Immediately sensing the applicant would commit herself to the new job, he counseled, "Experience will be your teacher."

Billie threw the intensity of her personality into the new venture and soon learned the trade. Her friendly nature combined with a fervor that when ignited fascinated both clients and dealers. Entering into intense conversation with the shop's owner, she was warmly welcomed into the antique community of her area. Antiques, as do such hobbies for their devotees, washed her into a different world.

Quickly becoming a social as well as business venture, the job filled Billie's needs. Talk of antiques continued through many evening gatherings, which were enhanced by gourmet delights and rare wines. Though the setting was different, this mingling of work and play came naturally to her. In her years of waitressing, she had often returned to the restaurant after her shift to socialize with both her sisters and the patrons. And once again, her job and the social side of her life quietly meshed. Still, she recognized from the start that her frugal nature would never permit her to become either a serious dealer or a collector of antiques; a nest egg remained her interest. Still she was mesmerized by the new job—and also reimbursed in cash for her services.

Now making limited trips to the house, Billie knew that neither Anne nor Marie would ever travel again. No longer acknowledging those around her, Marie made no attempt to speak. In the beginning, when chances of a full recovery seemed possible, Billie was hopeful; her sister seemed to know her. But within a year, hope faded, and Billie found herself without a hero.

There had been times when her sister's denial of the sleeping sedative and its effects had enraged Billie. But Marie had been at the helm of every significant family action, for as long as Billie could remember. In her younger sister's eyes, this sister had managed miracles. Now as she observed the necessity of Kate's constant care, Billie pondered what lay ahead, at the house and with the business. The family enterprise that Marie had hoped to build now belonged to Eddie, and as her guardian, he made all decisions. And, as far as Billie knew, the couple had never discussed the possibility of her name on the deed to the restaurant. With her sister now unable to speak, the time for discussion had passed. Billie herself had proclaimed all plans foolish, and accepting the fate of the enterprise was less difficult than seeing her champion so helpless.

At Marie's death, the trips to the house ended. Billie traveled occasionally to see Anne, staying at her house, but visits to the house with Rose at work all day made no sense.

"My traveling days are over" she announced. But this proved only half true.

When traveling to visit the daughter who lived hundreds of miles away, Billie invited Rose to join her. Her relationship with this sister had been clouded over the years, but Rose was blood, and Billie worried over her sister's fate; with neither partner nor children in her life, Rose now had only the house and her job. Claiming that she never understood this sister, Billie had seen her as more attached to her own needs than those of the family. Unlike Marie's family enterprise, Rose's beloved job remained far outside the orbit of clan. But Billie dutifully shared parts of her life with invitations either to her own home or travel.

Spending much more time with Rose now than in the past, she struggled with her disparate feelings of duty and resentment. She pondered the fates that had paired her in the end with the sister with whom she had not felt close. But her belief in providence had been real, and undoubtedly, the karma between the two needed to be worked through—far from the familiar surroundings of the house.

Though she missed the house, her absent sisters and the whirlwind of her younger years, Billie now had the thrill of four grandchildren and her newly discovered world of antiques. And her trips these days could be classified as vacations!

Finally, just as the decade was about to close, she held her first *great*-grandchild. The first of the fourth generation in the new country. She adored the little girl at first sight, and judging from the child's alert nature at so early an age, Billie declared that the tiny being would surely be America's first woman president! A stretch for someone who had forever felt that power belonged in the male corner. Even the resolute of the family could change her mind—on the right occasion.

Now with a *great*-granddaughter, Billie was forced to accept her age. The elusive birth certificate no longer allowed her to say she "didn't know how old" she was; how much could great-grandmother's stretch the point? But on the issue of her death, she remained definite. She desired a swift departure—when the time arrived. Thoughts of lingering, dependent on others with no hope of recovery repelled the independent spirit that had guided her over a lifetime. At the time, euthanasia and assisted suicide remained vague, and no one placed such desires in the black and white legal jargon of a will. But a rapid demise was clearly her one wish.

CRCRCRCRCRCRCRCRCRCRCRCRCRCRCRCRCRCRCR

I had arrived for a visit with Mother, but she was still at the antique shop. Waiting for her in my car in front of her house, I regretted my forgetfulness. I had not packed the spare key that she had given me for just such an occasion. Traffic had been light, and I was simply early. Working in the antique shop for full forty-hour weeks, she was due home in an hour. She expected me and would be on time. Actual clocks could be set by my mother; she was always on time.

So I sat in the car thinking of the next few weeks. At the end of my visit, she would join me on my return trip home where she would meet the second of the fourth generation. As I waited, I thought of other trips that Mother and I had made together. Different than the many trips I had made with her as a child, our journeys now were sight-seeing tours without specific destinations. With my children grown, it was just the two of us, And though they were wondrous sojourns where we came to know each other as fellow travelers around New England, they lacked the anticipation of the trips of my youth when the residents watched for our arrival from the windows of the house. Mother had forever complained that the greeters never prepared for us: special foods to welcome our arrival. But food had been a minor consideration for me in those days. We had made the trip to the house so many times, it was the excitement of those at the house as our car pulled to the curb that remained with me.

Casually waiting for her now, I knew that she arrived from the antique shop at five in the evening, so I picked up a novel to pass the time. But when the clock on the dashboard flashed six o'clock, I began to wonder how our plans had veered in different directions. A thunderstorm had blown in, so I concluded that she had gotten caught in the traffic that such acts of nature often bring. As Mother had declared over the years, Mother Nature interferes in the plans of us humans, forever reminding us of Her presence.

I found myself regretting that I had not taken an alternate route to her house, placing me on the very city roads that she traveled from the antique store. If I had, I'd now likely be in the snarled traffic created by the storm. And we may have even met along the short route, I thought to myself as the hour grew later.

My mother's determined nature had made her immortal to me, and though I still had no fears about her safety, by seven o'clock my reverie abruptly ended. At this stage of my wait, I felt the hunger that I had been denying. Dissuading the pangs so that I could later have dinner with her, knowing that regardless of the snafu, she wouldn't eat without *me*, I now admitted that something bigger than a traffic backup had occurred.

Deciding that the heavy storm had involved her in a fender-bender, I found a pay phone to inquire at the local police station and at hospitals. Discovering after six calls that she was on no one's list, I returned to her house, only to find it still dark and lifeless.

At this point, I could clearly hear her reprove, "If you had the key I gave you, you could be inside—and reachable." It was 1990, and neither of us even knew of such things as cell phones, which may have clarified my questions.

Finally, after driving by the antique shop, which was as deserted as her home, I tried to rethink our plan, now peppered with possible obstacles. Now four hours past her usual arrival time, I found my mind unusually clear. A fog had miraculously lifted on the stroke of nine, allowing me to answer my own questions. In my earlier calls to the local hospitals, I had not asked for the *emergency* room and had spoken instead to receptionists at registration desks. Though there were several hospitals in the large area, only one facility lay along her daily route home from the antique shop. So now I made *one* call—and asked the right question. Mother was there, and they strongly advised me to get there as quickly as possible.

When I arrived, the emergency room doctor who had treated her met me. Though he tried to be gentle, his message was far too short to provide much emotion.

"Yes," he said simply. "She was brought in three hours ago, experiencing severe chest pain. An aneurysm ruptured, and she died at nine."

Nine o'clock—the exact moment that my mind had cleared.

He continued to speak in his professional manner, but I heard nothing beyond the time of her death. I learned later that hospital staff had made calls to my sister and son, the closest of kin at local numbers. Mother had gone off the road while driving home from the antique shop and had briefly regained consciousness at the hospital. Of the two numbers that the staff had taken from her in those lucid moments, neither had reached a family member. No one was home at one, and the second number was incorrect by one digit. So no family member was with her when she died.

Later, I discovered that while still at work that fateful day, Mother had left a phone message for me.

Calling to say that she was expecting me, she mysteriously added, "There's to be a big storm, but don't worry."

A natural storm *had* come up, but my mother had never been fearful of such events, hardly taking note of them her entire life. The real storm behind her warning was her death. Unconsciously, her intuitive nature managed what she had wished for in this inevitable moment. A rapid departure. And I, like the two who never received the hospital calls, would not be present to protest her resolution.

22

The Optimist

After Marie's stroke, matriarchy fell to Anne It was a position that she had never sought and did not welcome now. Never threatened by Marie's competitive nature, Anne had allowed her sister to serve as head of the family with neither regret nor resentment. In fact, she enjoyed the freedom such an arrangement granted her. That Marie had always trusted her older sister's judgment sustained Anne's ego. But now with Maggie dead, Marie disabled, Rose struggling with drink and Billie with her own home, Anne stepped up to the plate. She proposed that Billie, when there, use her home as an alternative to the house that had become eerily quiet. And welcoming Rose each evening, Anne had always planned her home as a surrogate. Just in case.

Providing both company and outings for Marie, while she could still communicate in actions and gestures, Anne treated her stricken sister to the new malls and her discovery, pizza pie! Marie did not object to using a wheelchair, and pushing it also helped Anne to walk longer distances. Remembering Billie's counsel to simply move as much as possible with her own progressive ailment, Anne struggled through daily walks to the house and quietly sat with her silent sister. Such exercise did not halt the crippling Parkinson's but slowed its progress. And the house still endowed Anne with a security, which she now needed more than ever.

Tom brought up the possibility of Moosehaven but had gotten, as he expected, an immediate rebuff. His wife would not consider a move of two thousand miles, accompanied by a plan for permanent relocation, though in its own way, her growing immobility seemed to increase the distance from the house each day. Fortunately, the ailment spared her mental alertness, and she remained cheerful, hiding her growing anxieties about the future.

Now armchair travelers, the couple allowed the television set to serve as a tour guide; after nearly twenty years, the small set continued as a welcome dividend in their lives. In addition to entertainment in the comfort of their home, Anne reassured herself that they had each other, shelter, and food. The last was helped along by the Meals on Wheels delivery each day. Rose's nightly visit also brought the outside world into their home with tales of the daily routine at the department store; the stories of the customers lightened the tone of the evenings that the three continued to spend together. The visits seemed to meet the needs of the three as they faced the difficult years of aging. Even so, Anne would not have sustained such a ritual had this not been family; her attitude towards hostessing had not changed. The evening sojourns ended with the news, when Tom faithfully walked Rose to the corner of their street.

Within a year of Marie's stroke, Anne began to have trouble rising from her chair. Once standing, she had to force her feet into a gait. These were difficult actions, but once the walk began, she had a momentum that made the process easier. Someone at her side offering reassurance always helped. Of course, it was Tom who faithfully extended the extra hand and provided the muscle needed for her upright stance. Just as he had done for so many years, he remained at his wife's side.

But Anne began to sense that Tom was less attentive to both her and his surroundings. At first, she interpreted his forgetfulness as a small footprint left by the aging process—or perhaps the natural response to her constant need. But such speculations quickly changed after he had a series of fender-benders when visiting the local Moose Club. No one was hurt in the mishaps, and their car insurance covered most of the damages, but Anne began to reason that the time had come for the couple to live without a car. Only using the vehicle these days for the Moose, Tom could easily walk downtown for necessities, she reasoned.

She knew that without transportation his old haunt would be lost. And though saddened by this void in her husband's life, Anne imagined frightful possibilities with him behind the wheel. Which accompanied by her own growing helplessness presented a dim future.

After eating lunch one day, she settled into the most erect chair in the living room. Rising from a seat had become her priority, so she sacrificed comfort and forever chose the straight backed chairs these days. Tom remained in the kitchen to tidy up after the meal, and suddenly Anne began to smell smoke. Unable to get to the kitchen without help, especially in her now anxious state, she repeatedly screamed, "Tom, I smell smoke. What is it?" To no response.

Leaving a gas burner on high, Tom had wandered outside with the trash and was now chatting with a neighbor as the flame ignited a nearby dishtowel, which in turn lit a pile of newspapers as its firey remnants fell to the floor. Eventually, he heard his wife's frantic cries, and with minimal damage to all but Anne's sense of safety, the incident was soon brought under control.

More aware of the possibility of calamity than her husband these days, Anne struggled now to see the glass half full. Neither she nor Rose, her only confidant during the trying days, knew of community services available for the elderly. The sisters, as the first generation of immigrants, had raised their living standards, and the ethic that encouraged such actions was *work hard and don't look for handouts*. The possibility that there were social agencies in the city, designed to help its elderly citizens who found themselves in the couple's predicament, never crossed the mind of either sister. Both had worked lifetimes to prove themselves independent.

Three months after the fire, Tom was diagnosed with Alzheimer's disease and died of the dreaded disease a year later. His loss of memory combined with Anne's physical disability made their last year together an anxious one. Seeing the inevitable long before his death, she grieved the loss of this man who had been her constant companion for nearly fifty years. For the first time in her life, Anne found it impossible to conceal her sorrow.

Ironically, her physical helplessness offered the defense she needed to get through the days following his death. Claiming that it would be too difficult for a funeral director to handle her wheelchair on the steep concrete steps in front of her home, Anne declined to attend the burial rites. But the truth lay much deeper than the many steps leading up to the front door of her home. The blithe woman of the past had finally come up against feelings that she could not bluff with a smile. Alone, she could deal with the grief of Tom's death, but her longtime image of good spirits was beyond her reach. So Anne depended on her faithful family to represent her at the funeral. The grief had wounded her in unknown ways.

Within days of the funeral, she knew it would be impossible to remain alone in her home. Though his memory had failed him long ago, Anne had depended on his abiding presence. And now he was gone. She researched nursing homes through repeated calls accompanied by her pointed questions. Her lifelong focus on savings and investment, as well as gambling in case the other methods failed, endowed her now with welcome choices. Even in a vulnerable state, her thrifty nature studied the services each home offered. She could not make visits and examine the facilities firsthand, but having no intention of being frivolous this late in her life, she would ask the right questions.

Finally taking no leave of even such beloved friends as her cousin Rose, Anne chose to *slip out the back door*. Quietly, she asked Walter to drive her and moved into a nursing home within two hours of the house. From outward appearances, the move appeared impulsive. Simply filling a suitcase with personal items, she made no attempt to empty her home of its contents. Recognizing the minimal value of all her furnishings, by her own design, she packed only the necessities required in the new setting.

All of her life, Anne had claimed a dislike of good-byes, those wrenching moments of departure when parting is inevitable. The sentiment likely came to her, as it had to Billie, from their mother. Anna had harbored in her unconscious an unspoken grief over the loss of her homeland—of her roots; though that departure had been voluntary and her journey's goals had been realized, the pain was deep enough to settle into the first generation, without the aid of words. Over the years, unlike her youngest sister,

Anne had managed to hide tears. Always spoken in her light manner, her complaints over farewells were never taken seriously by either friends or family. Until she permanently moved—without warning.

Forever declaring experience more valuable than possessions, Anne now proved her lifelong claim. Safely stored in memories, special happenings of her past required no packing. Accepting, as she always had, the hurdles of her life, she made her silent farewell to her home and the house.

Marie had died before Anne's transition to the nursing home, so Rose and Billie were the only sisters the matriarch had to consider at her departure. Billie was settled in her own home and even had a new job. And thinking of Rose who remained at the house with two aging brothers-in-law, Anne never doubted that this sister would continue her job as long as such an act remained in the realm of physical possibility. Over thirty years older than Anne had been when she sold her business, Rose still showed no interest in retirement. And Anne had no intention of debating the issue with her again. Anne had carried out the job of matriarch as best she could and would now retire from this job as well.

Birch and evergreen trees, robins, hills, valleys and meadows all weave their way into the official names of nursing homes, conjuring gentle images of the natural world. Though nature also has a frightful side, names such as Volcanic Cavern or Thunderous Den are not likely to entice potential nursing home residents. The gentle picture of nature is intended to present the elderly a comfort, available to them.... as spectators. Words such as "villa" and "estate" are often coupled with flowery adjectives in hopes of achieving a prestige that denies the truth. Participation in life is over and even mystery fades for the inhabitants of these final stops.

Anne, at age eighty, became a resident of Scenery Manor. Small, the residence promised the security she sought. But like her disease, the home was terminal—she would live here until her death, and Anne accepted this fact. There were similar establishments closer to the house, but as she was now incapable of getting anywhere on her own, she made comfort her priority. The fact that her youngest niece lived nearby strengthened her choice. For the cost, Anne knew that the private home would take care of her physical needs and sought convenience for her niece who had graciously assumed responsibility.

In the beginning, Anne received unexpected visits from those she had failed to contact at her departure. Some took offense at her hasty departure from the city, which had been her home for nearly sixty years, and refused to connect; but others, like her four goddaughters, declined to let her go without a loving closure. Her cousin Rose had also fallen ill and could no longer travel, so the goddaughters drove without their mother to the nursing home. Even after the visits eventually dwindled away, they frequently wrote and made calls to the godmother who had been so kind over the years.

After the first year, Anne's only visitors were her two remaining sisters and three nieces. Though lonely, she accepted the reality of this season of her life and worked to find things to enjoy in the terminal space. Cared for by a friendly staff, she adjusted to the strangers who surrounded her each day, recognizing that her worldview must shift—if she were to endure. In a dull environment and ill, she still chose survival and quickly made friends with aides, nurses, and fellow residents. Nearly everyone warmed to her cheerful manner. In addition to the humans in the new space, there were the birds to watch as they hungrily gathered at the window feeders and the Wednesday and Friday bingo nights to look towards. None of the residents were permitted cash in their rooms, so bets were unknown in games of any kind. Still, the once ardent gambler tried to follow her lifelong dictum—to enjoy it all.

附 CR CR CR CR CR CR CR CR CR CR CR CR CR CR CR CR CR

My visits to Scenery Manor assured me that my aunt felt safe there. Not happy, but safe. Spending two years with Tom's senility and her own immobility, she had grown fearful in ways that differed from her old self; she had become insecure. I could see that she was lonely but as always hid her sadness. Fearing any expression of these feelings would place expectations on me or others of the second generation, she told me at each visit of her satisfaction with her new home. And when her spirits began to fall, she would think of her abiding luck, still good after all the years. She was safe here in this clean space staffed with friendly attendants. But I knew her too well not to recognize that life's mysteries had vanished for my aunt, who had forever looked to the sunny side.

She never complained, showing nothing but delight when aides helped her into my car, and we drove around the town where she now lived. Forever looking for wonder in life, she luckily lived now in a town with two great assets: Colonel Sander's Kentucky Fried Chicken—and several of the haunts of her youth. We would collect a bucket of the Colonel's deep-fried, which nicely fit her old test for tastiness, and then find places where she had once gone with old beaus. The crispy chicken mixed with the memories helped to erase the monotony of the nursing home—for a moment.

In her sixth summer at Scenery Manor, I admitted to myself that she was in the homestretch and very close to the end of her journey. She began to talk of Church. The nursing home provided ecumenical services, which never having been the most ardent of churchgoers, she seldom attended. I knew she longed now for the *Russian* Church, with its wondrous stained glass windows, the smell of candles and incense, and the familiar icons. Seven years since she had been to her church, Annie yearned now for its comfort. So I offered to drive her to a small Russian Church that I knew of, twenty miles from the nursing home.

At first, she was reluctant. Generally, we didn't stray this far on our outings. And with just the two of us, how would we manage with her infirmity, she asked with eyes that revealed her real desire to make the trip. I knew nothing of the church schedule, and a weekday when we could not depend on a Sunday service, I offered no assurances, only a willingness to make the drive. She finally agreed to "give it a try," the familiar phrase that restored some of her old self to me. The closer we got, the more excited she grew. On arrival, she remained in the car while I surveyed the grounds to find no one at the rectory, but the door of the church open.

Light as a feather now, she proved easy for me to carry the short distance to the door of the church. But she chose not to stay. With both of us strangers to the surroundings, she feared that our presence would be viewed as an illegal entry. So we left before she could absorb the essence of this space that was sacred to her.

"So close but so far" she exclaimed as we returned to the nursing home; even at our failed attempt, she remained cheerful. I remember well this day, which proved the last I would ever see her. Three months later, she died. The Parkinson's had made her vulnerable to a variety of lesser ailments that finally proved fatal.

જીભ્રજીભ્રજીભ્રજીભ્રજીભ્રજીભ્રજીભ્રજીભ્રજીભ્રજીભ્ર

In light of her lifelong attraction to gambling, a paradox in the treatment of Parkinson's cannot be ignored here. Twenty years after Anne's death, researchers found that medication used to treat Parkinson's astonishingly turned patients into compulsive gamblers. When the drug was withheld, all interest in gambling ceased. Such a correlation proved too great to ignore by those interested in the effects of the medication, and the fact was reported in the New England Journal of Medicine in 2005. Anne had done no real gambling after her official diagnosis. But on hearing of such unique research, undoubtedly she would have concluded the termination of her lifelong passion a mistake. Proclaiming that the drug would have treated the ailment as well as render her additional luck, she would have declared with a twinkle in her eye: "two birds with one stone."

And her fascination with gambling left telltale evidence. Her considerable nest egg would be divided among the generations.

23

The Dynamo

Rose continued with her life in the same immutable way she had always done. Though, except for her own schedule, everything had changed. The residents of the house now numbered five. Her brother and Maggie were gone forever, and Kate, who had always worked at one of the restaurants, now cared for Marie. Actually, it could be said that Marie, too, was gone; nothing of her old self, not even her voice, endured. Only her frail body offered a faint sketch of what once had been. Billie now owned her own home and stayed at Anne's on her rare visits. The three members of the second generation had homes of their own. Walter remained in his part of the house, only to put in a rare appearance in the evening. Eddie outwardly continued to attend to the doomed restaurant, but its demise was accepted by everyone, only the death certificate needed a signature.

Eating with Kate and Marie only when she rode the early train, Rose walked to Anne's after the meal. Marie had always been the most talkative at all gatherings, and to sit at the table and hear nothing from her sister, felt irreverent to Rose. The conversations between these two sisters had never progressed much beyond mutual criticism, but their comments, easily classified as sibling rivalry, hinted of mutual caring; the two simply saw the world from different vantage points. On Sundays, Rose went to Church and still cooked a dinner, but the meal, rather than the basis of a family gathering, provided her own dinner for the upcoming week. On her second free day from work, she cleaned Maggie's side of the house. Walter paid little attention to such details, and Rose disliked the neglect of the space that had once been her sister's pride.

At Marie's death, more changes punctured life at the house. Kate, who had lived there since Anna and her family moved in fifty years ago, decided now to leave—as she no longer had a job. She had cared for Marie and previously worked at the three businesses, and now, without work, felt misplaced. In Kate's mind, her residency at the house was indelibly linked to her job—company housing of a sort. Though she had participated in family affairs over the years and loved the others, she had always felt that she owed the family something. If she would have had a job at what was now Eddie's business, Kate might have stayed. But though the restaurant remained open, it had reached a terminal point, so Eddie could not make such an offer. At age sixty-six and unmarried, Kate needed a job that included housing. Such had been the pattern of her entire life. Her own aged mother, who now lived with Kate's brother, needed care, so she packed her bags after Marie's funeral and joined another household. Leaving the house forever.

Highly unusual for Rose to make requests of anyone, she asked Kate to reconsider and remain at the house. Though their opposing work schedules over the years had never allowed for much talk between them, the two had lived under the same roof for decades, and each would miss the mere presence of the other. But finally admitting to herself Kate's determination to go where needed, Rose accepted her cold feet. The house would be left with three residents—herself and the two husbands of her dead sisters. Still, she had Anne and Tom down the street at the alternate house—a short-lived comfort.

Soon after Kate's departure, Tom died, and Anne moved to a nursing home, which could only be reached by car. The nursing home, nestled in the Allegheny Mountains of Pennsylvania, canceled Rose's previous praise of public transportation; without a car, she could not visit her sister, so Walter often volunteered to chauffeur her on either of her days off from work. Anne's rapid departure had left her home devoid of life, but it was eerily filled with furniture and clothes—the trappings of daily living.

With her free time, Rose took on the job of property manager. Because of the city's poor economy, real estate sales were nearly nonexistent, so Rose looked after Anne's house and quietly paid the taxes from her own paycheck. She faithfully cleaned, just as she did Maggie's side of the house and packed any additional items Anne needed at Scenery Manor. Recalling how lovingly Anne had welcomed her after Maggie's death, Rose now sifted through the remains of the two lives.

Though busy, she knew that the time had come to make a change in her life, but her thoughts were not about retirement. She needed something social to fill her evenings—as her days were covered. Sitting with Eddie in front of the TV screen filled with evangelists while he consumed his drinks, Rose knew she could easily revive the habit that she had finally conquered. Trying for awhile to convince him of the pitfalls of the alcohol abuse, she finally gave up. She could only speculate as to his part in Marie's addiction, now a moot point that she had no intention of reviving. Too, such accusations she felt below her dignity.

What might fill her evenings? Perhaps she would remain in Pittsburgh at the end of the workday, but at age seventy-three, this felt wearisome; such was an impulsive choice of youth. She might invite fellow commuters she had known for years to the house, but as she had never entertained strangers, non-blood by her definition, this too felt awkward. In the end, Rose found a poker group who were looking for another player. Not within walking distance of the house, the games had players happy to give her a ride. The arrangement proved simple and filled two evenings a week.

Unlike hostessing, poker was not a new activity for her. Having played in the kitchen of the house with her siblings many years before, Rose liked the idea of now reviving the game in the lonely evenings after work. She knew that the atmosphere this time would be different, more restrained. In the past, nothing like poker in the kitchen could get blood running hot, she admitted to herself for the first time. These games, which included any resident who was home at the time, had helped release the steam of sibling rivalry. All of the pent-up anger over other matters was allowed to fly during the games, though the language had been such that Rose later banned certain words from her vocabulary. Controversy in these events abounded over *every* move in the game, and nothing went unnoted by players.

"Who raised?" Maggie quietly posed the question as the game began.

"Who reneged on the last bet?" Marie's voice rose, matching the heat of the game.

"The deck was not cut by the last dealer; that's a misdeal!" Anne offered in her constant search for equality.

"Watch the discards; didn't you notice the last play?" said Billie, aware of every card.

Such comments promoted a game that strayed far from a friendly family pastime. Though embarrassed even now in her thoughts of the expletives used, Rose cherished the memories. Even as she joined the new group of card players, a poker revival was beginning to sweep across the new country. America had begun what would become a deep enchantment with the game that Rose adored. The Internet later introduced the game to young people, and to attest to its popularity in the twenty-first century, television carries poker tournaments, world series, and world tours of the game.

Because of her longtime image of refinement, it might be reasoned that Rose would have searched for a bridge club to fill her evenings, but such was not the case. Unknown to Rose, poker has two elements that made it appealing to those of her generation who were spawned by immigrant parents. Poker draws from its Western roots and is about optimism, more about luck than skill. While bridge, which evolved among the wealthy from the old English game of whist, has little to do with cash. Poker offers the art of the bluff, providing hope to immigrants who often find it necessary to fake their way through the unknown. Depending more on luck than skill, poker is played to amass cash. And money affords the first generation a grounding, a safe place on which to stand.

CRCRCRCRCRCRCRCRCRCRCRCRCRCRCRCRCRCR

In the summer after her sister moved to the nursing home, I thought that Ro must be lonely and decided to visit. Knowing that she still had her precious job, I hoped that the initial sadness at Mame's death and Annie's departure had passed for her. I knew that she would never complain but was hardly prepared for what I found. With her new poker group and the additional duties around Annie and Aunt Marg's she seemed happy.

Though her new duties were alien to her, she liked to be busy. In the past, my aunts and mother had often reminded her, in not so subtle a manner, of her innocence in maintaining a home. Standard duties of bills, grocery shopping, and general house repair, had never been hers. Though the jobs that she had taken on now hardly matched those of the average home-maker, she felt a pride in watching over the three residences of her sisters.

I suspected that in addition to keeping things in order, she kept a part of the past alive through her efforts. And it reminded me of how she had once cleaned the attic. I knew that my aunt thrived on goals—and finishing them. Only idleness stumped her.

In the week that I spent with her at the house that summer, she had her usual two days off from work. On one day, we went to see Annie at the nursing home, and on the second day, a hot July day, we cleaned the basement of her abandoned house! Cleaning a basement, even with her enthusiasm, had not been one of the intentions of my visit. She had not directly asked for my help, but seeing the scope of her newest project, I offered. Over the years, Annie had thrown nothing away, and as her home had no attic, unused items all eventually landed in the basement; she forever felt that regardless of the article, *someone* might *someday* need it.

In fairness to my aunt's frugal nature, I might add that in those days, material goods were less disposable, less replaceable, especially for the children of immigrants who searched for permanency of any kind. But faced with the gigantic task of cleaning that basement in one day, I was less profound. I just wanted to get the dusty job done.

Knowing Annie would want us to discriminate and pass useful items on to the second generation, Ro and I carefully examined everything before declaring anything "rubbish". And the things that had the slimmest possibility of future use by one of us, we boxed.

Our task was enlarged by the coal dust. This was western Pennsylvania where the prolific coal mines provided heat for the majority of homes. Years of coal burning along with the still obvious coal bin in the basement left us now covered with the black dust. Exhausted after seven hours there, I questioned whether I could walk up the alleyway back to the house. But I managed. Though slightly behind my aunt.

ଔଔଔଔଔଔଔଔଔଔଔଔଔଔଔଔଔଔଔଔଔ

Rose never considered a move into Anne's furnished house. As she had so little that was truly hers at the house, such a move would have been simple. And in a practical sense, she would have been a bit closer to her daily train ride. Privacy, in the truest sense, would have been hers in this space that her sister had left behind. As the second floor had been a rental space as long as Anne and Tom had lived there, such a suggestion had been made in the past at those times when her style clashed with Marie's

"I don't understand why you don't move into the apartment at Anne's. You'd have privacy," Billie had often insisted.

"I've been at the house for so long; it would feel strange, even with Anne and Tom downstairs," Rose said in a manner that revealed that the thought had crossed her mind.

"Well, of course it'll feel odd in the beginning, but it's like anything else. You'll get use to it," replied Billie as she thought of her own struggle over the years, living so far from the house.

"I know the apartment is empty now I'll look at it next time I'm at Anne's," Rose, anxious for the conversation to end, replied.

And now Anne's whole house sat vacant.

But Rose had never sought solitude. The people sounds at the house had been the background music of her life. Though such noise could no longer be heard, she refused to consider a move into the empty structure.

Until the stranger arrived to live at the house.

Rose, Walter, and Eddie, vestiges of another time, remained together at the house. Leading lives that demanded only casual interaction. There were no meals when three, or even two of them, regularly convened. But each of the residents rendered the other a sense of security reminding them of their shared past. Now the three lives moved more slowly through the daily task of living with a cautious sense of acceptance rather than the eager anticipation for life that they had once held.

Walter, now retired, continued old friendships in the police force, which took him from the house just as they had in the past. Still, he continued his ritual of meeting Rose's train whenever he could and happily drove her to visit Anne on any of her free days from work. Eddie had finally given up the ghost of the business, and except for the time spent with his religious community, he was a steady presence at the house and often engaged Rose in conversation as she ate her evening meal.

Rose, the only one of the three who continued a structured work life, became an easy subject of discussion between the brothers-in-law. Now in her mid-seventies, she had altered little her work-commute schedule since she was sixteen. And the incredible fact provided the two men with constant gossip.

"Can she go on forever on the job?" "She's gone against all the odds." "Will the store simply tell her that it's time to leave?" "But surely, they won't; she's such a faithful worker." "How old is she, really?" The men bantered the questions between them.

Though the tone of their conversations remained funny and casual, their queries were real. But knowing that such talk evolved from curiosity rather than malice, Rose took no offense and answered outlandishly. As laughter among the three proved rare these days, such diversion came as comic relief and made life bearable.

The trio had found a way to survive under the same roof. But out of the blue a change occurred. Walter decided to invite a tenant. Alone in six rooms on his side of the house, he felt it wasteful to pay utilities that could easily accommodate two people. Another presence in the space that had once been so filled with life hovered as his real motive, though he would not have admitted such sentiment.

Instead, he introduced Roger to his two housemates as "a friend, down on his luck, who can help me a bit with the bills."

Roger proved more than *temporarily* down on his luck. He was a city vagabond whom Walter's humanitarian side had pitied. Fortunately, Walter's instinct affirmed his good judgment, and the new resident proved quiet and respectful of the others, never intruding in their lives. Holding down a menial job in the city, Roger was grateful for his space at the house. When spring arrived, he planted a vegetable garden in the back-yard, happily sharing with the other residents the late summer fruits of his labor.

But, indifferent to Roger's attributes, Rose refused to accept a non-family member at the house. In addition to his status as a stranger, his presence changed the male-female ratio to three-to-one, placing her even deeper in the minority. She had forever lived among a majority of females, but had Walter's choice been female, her objections likely would not have diminished. In her mind, Roger had no *right* to live at the house. He could claim neither blood nor marital connection to it. And he was obviously of a social class much lower than Rose could accept—in a space she occupied.

One of a first generation of immigrant parents, Rose had labored her entire life to raise her social class through work, associates, appearance, and speech. And she now found Roger an insult—an embarrassment, a desecration of the house itself. In the past, all residents except Kate were related through blood or had a marriage partner who was. But known to the family *before* she became a resident, Kate, like Rose, was of a first generation of immigrants. So Rose had accepted her as an exception to the rule.

Nothing Roger could do changed Rose's attitude. Sometimes when Walter could not meet her late train, Roger, who did not drive, appeared at the station to accompany her up the hill—on foot. Walter had, of course, asked this favor of his housemate, but Rose knew that the man could have declined the request. Though she thanked him on such occasions, she detested this new living arrangement. Could the house have come to this? A "flophouse?" Convinced that his presence could change the living standard that she, as well as her sisters, had worked so hard to raise, she remained inconsolable.

She considered moving into Anne's abandoned home. After several years on the market, the structure's sale seemed unlikely. Though the move would remove Roger from her life, the prospect of such a change frightened Rose; she had never lived alone. And over the years, her city had changed. With the steel mills gone and unemployment high, drifters were now obvious. And recently, the entire country had begun to feel dangerous to her. *Terrorists,* a new word for Rose, had abducted fifty-two citizens from an American Embassy. Previously, hostages—a word until now heard only in Hollywood Westerns—had been murdered at the Munich Olympics. Such an atmosphere did not inspire her to change her residence. A growing anger seemed to be building against America

So after two years with Roger at the house, Rose's practical side won out. She *would* get through this; she had survived more difficult things in the past. And legally, the house was not hers, and she had little to say in the matter. Once she dispelled her anxiety with reality, she realized that her path and Roger's seldom crossed anyway, except on the few occasions he met her train. And this act, so clearly for her benefit, caused her lingering resentment to fade. Determined now to ignore the intrusion, she went on in her customary manner: commute, work, and church, adding now to her routine, poker and the care of the three homes. Often, Walter drove her to visit Anne in the nursing home, and for her vacations, she visited either Billie or one of her grown nieces. Life goes on.

Four years after Roger materialized; he vanished just as suddenly—at Walter's death. Walter had been his channel into the house, and without him, Roger felt awkward. With Anne and Eddie's death following a year later, Rose became, by default, the last resident of the house.

And after Billie's death, Anna's last living child.

Reluctantly, she decided to leave her beloved job. Though at age eighty, she still managed a forty-hour workweek and the care of the house and Anne's, her common sense prevailed. She would retire both her job—and the house.

In the sixty-four years of her devoted service, the trustees of the department store wisely never questioned her age, and simply regarded her as a remarkable employee. Other than her personal savings, she had not planned for retirement and had only a vague idea of the store's policies around it. Such neglect was not her style, but leaving her job had been too unthinkable to search out the details of retirement. Rose had assured herself over the years that her respected employer (which now consisted of a board of directors) would not abandon her in the end. And she was right.

Her severance package proved extraordinary. She received a monthly pension of $1200 for the remainder of her life. The store's personnel policies capped at fifty years of service, so the inspiring figure would have been identical had she retired fourteen years earlier. As commissioned sales had stopped long ago, her pension now would be greater than her actual salary in those last years. But, as the residents of the house had always known, Rose had emotional ties to her job. And this attachment carried no dollar figure. Refusing to attend any kind of recognition dinner at the store, she randomly declared one particular day as her last—after returning one night from an ordinary workday. The decision to leave had been difficult, so she made a departure devoid of fanfare.

She had a second heavy task before her. Exiting the house. Maggie's daughter had offered Rose the opportunity to join her young family, so she now accepted the invitation and had much to do in preparation. The sister who had always felt different from the others, was now left to close the house. Perhaps somewhere in the remnants of the nest lay the reason for this odd turn of events, though Rose accepted the task without such conscious speculation. Theorizing slowed her, forcing her to step out of the business of the moment—packing the house.

Legally the house had belonged to Maggie and Marie. So Rose packed a home that was not her own, as she had done at Anne's and later would do at Billie's. Her sense of family was stronger than property deeds. Though this task of sorting and boxing would be different.

1990–1998

24

The Survivor

As Rose packed, thoughts of her mother's journey arose in her mind. It had been nearly a century since Anna had left her homeland. How difficult that voyage must have been. Though America continued to be flooded by immigrants, they no longer came from central Europe; refugees were now arriving in large numbers from Asia and Latin America. Rose was saddened by the fact that she would now leave the house and wondered how her mother had left family and homeland. She would be joining her niece, and the comparison of this departure and Anna's struck her as absurd; there *was* no comparison. She forced herself from the reverie and quickly restored her practical nature. There was much to be done.

An arduous task, this dismantling of so many years kept her busy for two months. But determined that she would do this, she contained the sadness that tried to meddle in her chore. Forever good at focusing on the moment, Rose did well with busyness. Making calls to see who wanted what, and finally sending packages to members of the second and third generations, she tried to salvage remnants of the family that might prove of value—to someone.

At the deaths of Maggie and Marie, the house had gone to the closest heir, Maggie's daughter. And it would now be sold at auction. The city's economy had continued its downward spiral, and as an alternative to an ordinary sale, owners were offering their homes at public auction. Buyers seldom lived in their acquisitions. Interested only in investment, the new owners encouraged multiple tenants rather than single families. Knowing she could not prevent such an undignified end, Rose accepted the fate for the house. She could have purchased the property from her niece and lived alone in the large structure. But such a decision seemed impractical, if not absurd, given the age of the property—and her own age. So, in her usual way, she released the painful thought of the auction and threw her energy into the task of packing.

From the time Rose had moved in with her mother and five siblings six decades before, the house had served as a substitute for Anna's homeland. The new country, unfamiliar to immigrants, offered nothing familiar that parents could pass on to children in the natural way of simple stories. Anna's brood lacked memories, a source of constancy to growing children. The Church had helped with some of this, but intimate details of their parents' lives were unknown to Rose and her siblings.

"I once worked this old field. This is the path I took to my friend's house. I could view the river where I learned to swim from here. I walked to this place and then just stopped and let my thoughts wander for awhile," such words were never heard. Though all appreciated their mother's difficult journey and the promise it had given them, until they moved into the house, life had been unsettled, and the space had grounded them.

T. S. Eliot once wrote, "Home is where one starts," and the house, which Rose would now abandon, stood as her start in a country alien to her parents.

Though the house had not been emptied of all material items, she now readied herself to leave. Her task of sorting, packing and cleaning was over. The dwelling would be bargained away along with the remaining furnishings, and Rose had no intention of attending this terminal process. Her part was done, and her farewell would be taken now. Sending her niece ahead with a few small items to wait in the car, in the heat of summer, Rose stood alone at the front door with her suitcase. As in the past, there was little in material goods that belonged to her, so the large suitcase stood as her only real baggage. Closing the front door for the last time took all the determination she had learned to muster. Significant by all accounts.

Gazing at the large oak in the front yard, she realized that the tree likely bore the same age as the house. It had stood there when the family moved in as tenants and served as a beacon when she approached on her evening arrivals from work. More aware of the tree as she herself aged, she now realized that she had watched the mighty oak shed its leaves, only to sprout tender new ones in the spring—over sixty times. But there were no tears now, only the swift reflection of a lifetime. As she stood in reverie with her hand idly on the doorknob, Rose suddenly felt other hands grasp hers. The silenced hands of her mother and siblings joined her to pull the door closed in quiet gratitude.

Rose's determined nature was put to the test as she struggled to endure all the changes that now fell like dominoes in her life. The house and her job, the lodestones of her life, were followed by the loss of the interesting train commute, the Church she had walked to for so many years, and her latest foray into the local poker games. In moving two hours away, she would break *all* the patterns at once. After consciously trying to avoid change her entire life, she was now forced to play catch-up; so many shifts at once rendered the defenses of her past useless.

In spite of her excellent health and energy, Rose would not have survived the move without intervention. Destiny saw to it that her niece, whose household she would join, gave birth only weeks before Rose's permanent arrival. The child, the second arriving twelve years after the first, would create a new family that could more easily embrace Rose, another newcomer. As infants often do, the child encouraged Rose to look forward; her retirement now included a new life. The infant girl arrived exactly on time to greet the other new arrival and proved a gift to the woman who had always relished the title of *aunt*. Once again she would play her cherished role for a new life.

The wonderful stages of childhood would unfold in front of her, just as they had with the child's mother. Now with another generation, she, as a spinster, was permitted to experience the wonders of grandparenting. Though she left the title of "grandmother" to Maggie, its rightful owner. And clung to her own—Aunt Rose.

Considering the shattering changes that occurred all at the same time, Rose did well in the new setting. Though absorbed with her great-niece, she protected herself so that her own life did not revolve around the little girl. Taking long walks alone these days, she assured herself of daily exercise, as she had had in the past in her hike to and from the train. Now she walked to the bank with her retirement checks and quickly found the local Russian Church. Having walked to church her entire life, she was disappointed to find this one beyond walking distance; but the trip from her new home proved easy for the drivers in the household.

Quickly, she made friends among the congregation, a new behavior for her. In the past, it had been Maggie who casually chatted with others after Mass. While Rose and her sisters had forever been in a hurry to get on with the remainder of their only day free from official work. Slowly adapting to this new freedom, she discovered a friendliness in herself that delivered unusual results. A widowed member of the new congregation felt sufficiently close to her to make a surprising offer. Having been a member for only a short time, Rose was invited to join the woman as a companion in her now *empty* home.

By accepting the proposal, Rose would live in a small town where her church would again be a short walk; she would have need for neither car nor driver. And the bid would provide her a peer, someone with whom she could share activities, restoring some of the independence she had known in the past. The dividends of such a tempting offer gave her pause. Once again the opportunity to leave family raised itself just as it had with Anne's empty home—and Jim's proposal. But in the end, though flattered by the invitation, she declined. She could not make such a quantum leap from family.

The one thing that seemed matchless in the new setting was a good poker game. An evening's entertainment that she could look forward to throughout the day, poker appeared non-existent here, at least among her connections. Making inquires at every opportunity, Rose finally accepted the reality that poker now belonged, as did many other things—in her past. Hiding feelings of disappointment, she thanked the fates for the family that now surrounded her.

ଔଔଔଔଔଔଔଔଔଔଔଔଔଔଔଔଔଔ

Hearing the emotion in her voice as she relayed memories, I smugly decided to take her back—at least physically. It seemed the least I could do for this, the last of the generation that had nurtured me. On several occasions, I drove her by the house after the auction, but the bed sheets hanging in the front window, hung by indifferent tenants, did little to brighten her day.

Then there was the time I planned a trip back to the department store where she had worked for two-thirds of her life. She had not been to Pittsburgh since her retirement five years earlier. I did not tell her of our destination until it became obvious where we were headed. Feeling anxious, even before the disclosure, I was uncertain of the source of my fear. Trying to warn me, my intuition knew this would not be a welcome surprise. My aunt was shocked to be back in Pittsburgh and flatly refused to enter the familiar store.

This part of her life, the store and the large city itself, lingered in her memory as exciting and vital. The job had kept her young, and few people could have guessed that she was eighty years old when she finally left. Now Ro recognized that the years of retirement had aged her. How could she face people who might not even recognize her? I had nearly destroyed the memory that even now nurtured her spirit.

But unwilling to relinquish my hope of restoring, even briefly, a past joy, I remembered her vacations. Deciding to try again, I concluded that Atlantic City would prove a better choice than the old workplace. When she vacationed there with her friends, the allure was the sun on the white sands of the Atlantic Ocean and wonders such as the world-famous Steel Pier. But as with vacationlands everywhere across the country in the eighties, Atlantic City had needed more unique attractions to compete, so developers had turned to gambling casinos there. By the time we visited in the nineties, her old vacation retreat had evolved to the Las Vegas of the East Coast. Like most things, the city had changed.

Still, I felt the changes were not that far adrift from her interests. The idea felt viable, at least to me and would hopefully work better than my previous fiascos had. Her interest in gambling had never equaled her oldest sister's, but like her, Ro was fascinated by the chance to win large sums of money—to enlarge her savings.

I knew from the start that the sun and water would hold no allure for my aunt. But in a city she had once loved, there might be a chance for her to enjoy the slot machines. Especially now that she lacked even an exciting poker game. And her excitement at returning to the youthful haunt thrilled me. She was easy to please. But the fifty years that had passed since she viewed the city through the eyes of a young woman frolicking with her friends on a paid vacation from a job she adored, had altered the space for all she could see when we arrived was change. Though the city *had* physically changed, the real change occurred in her own eyes. She saw the city now through eyes at the end rather than the beginning of the journey. And this was the difference.

Due to my effort to bring her here, she did her best to praise the convenience the casinos provided. There was easy access to silver coins in all denominations, buckets to carry them in, and a large booth in the center to quickly convert winnings to paper money. At her insistence to bring me into the excitement, we played as partners. At times, the one-armed bandits got the best of us, and we had no coins to convert to greenbacks—and carry back to our hotel room. Still, our conversion from paper to the silver that fed the machines occurred less often than the reverse, and we ended ahead of the game.

As we left Atlantic City that summer, I knew, though my aunt never expressed disappointment, that this city too ought to have remained sculpted only by her memories. No spell that I could weave could retrieve the past for her.

Finally, life stepped in and erased all her memories. After ten years of retirement, the last of the first generation in the new country succumbed to Alzheimer's disease.

At her death she was older than any of her siblings, but Ro was always reluctant to announce her age. Her hesitancy was generally covered with a favorite remark, "It's not yet my time to leave the earth," she often proclaimed. Her observation implied that destiny still had work left for her, and she would live until that task was done. Without detail but with conviction, she knew there was a larger plan.

At her gravesite, exactly one mile from the house, I recalled a conversation that I had had with her at one of the previous burials. Perhaps trying to release me, who lived so many miles away, from a future duty, she said, "I won't be here when I die."

Baffled, I replied, "But Ro, it's a family plot, and I thought that ..." Unable to complete my question, I wondered if perhaps her words had to do with her place in the family that had shadowed her for so long. But she smiled, and I knew then the meaning of her claim before she spoke.

"Only my body will be here," she softly added.

Unlike her physical lifetime that had remained so constant, her spirit had other places to travel.

Epilogue

Life would be no better than candlelight tinsel and daylight rubbish if our spirits were not touched by what has been.

—George Eliot

Rose's death marked one century since Anna's arrival on the S.S.Kensington, a landing that rendered life to the young immigrant and her descendants. An emblem was needed to mark the close of the hundred years, and the death of the last direct descendent of the determined settler did just that. Rose's declaration, when she retired from her cherished job ten years earlier, "It's not yet my time to leave the earth," proved correct. She lived just long enough for her death to mark the anniversary of her mother's courageous voyage.

Nor was this the only one of her conclusions that proved true. Forever praising her longtime employer, she did not live to see the acclaim solidly justified. Three years after her death, the store sent her next of kin a sizable amount because of a "faulty" retirement plan. Not sufficiently detailed, the plan had not met legal standards. Likely a loophole that the store's Board failed to tighten, the event is notable. With retirement packages crumbling at every corner in the twenty-first century, the fact boldly reinforces Rose's contention—she had had a remarkable job

Anna's children, this first generation born in a new country, were sobered by their mother's raw courage. And survived her illiteracy as well as the loss of the designated breadwinner. Managing to raise social class for themselves and the generations that followed, they depended only on themselves or occasionally each other.

The five sisters wove a cocoon around themselves, insuring an emotional security that they could not find elsewhere. All were industrious, determined, thrifty, and self-disciplined. But each uniquely broke one rule of the tight system that bound them together. Anne refused to allow work to deprive her of freedom. Maggie sought the excitement of strangers. Rose indulged herself with personal services. Billie allowed feelings in the form of tears. And Marie displayed a sense of the dramatic. Such strays could have weakened the order.

But each sister also possessed a quality that contributed to the success of their mother's endeavor. Learning to live in a land foreign even to parents, the first and natural guides of children, the first generation in a new country must remain hopeful. Anne, keeping her own life sufficiently light, stayed cheerful in the tryingest of times. But optimism by itself is not enough. It took Marie's fiery nature to deliver the solid nest that would embrace them all. And even a sound nest is cold without the warmth of the home fires that Maggie lovingly stoked at her post. Over time, all dens eventually become musty, so it's urgent that one member scout the outside world and report back in some fashion, just as mother birds do with their offerings of food to the chicks. Rose completed this contract as faithfully as she did her paying job. Finally, it falls to one member to model the art of leaving the nest.... for good. Though finding it easier to take small steps, Billie bravely accepted the role.

Their roles often dealt personal pain, but the collective of the five sisters established Anna's lineage in the new country.

Though immigrants continue to flock to the new country in the twenty-first century, even challenging its immigration laws, American materialism has become suspect to the religious extremists of the East. Taking matters into their own hands, terrorists without a national identity have begun to wage a new kind of war. The World Trade Center was bombed and five years later an American Embassy in Africa saw the loss of three hundred lives; suicide bombers, another new phrase born of the times, have become common. The immigrants entering at the millennium know that the new country is not the promised land as it was once echoed. But even subject to the same waves of good and evil that have existed through all human history, America still holds the dreams of many.

The house burned to the ground in less than a year after Rose's death, leaving only the old oak tree as testimony to what had once been. Anne's house never sold, and eventually the city assumed it to cover back taxes. Speculation among the second generation as to the origins of the fire still abound. It may have been carelessness by tenants. Or perhaps the city found the property ill-kept and dangerous, or the new owner, greedy for the insurance money, was his own arsonist. But regardless of the reason listed in the legal records, which no one in the second generation cared to research, the truth is that emptiness brought it down. After losing all the energy that had once danced within its walls, the house collapsed, just as lifeless people finally do.

The spirits of Anna and her children undoubtedly remained in the space for a time, but finally the neglect of the uncaring tenants released them—to another repose.

CRCRCRCRCRCRCRCRCRCRCRCRCRCRCRCRCRCR

Though the house, like its residents is gone now, my dreams often return it to me. These nighttime fancies, where fears and hopes entwine themselves, place me there, alone and frightened by the silent rooms. But the awe of the gift I was given soon quiets all my fears.

1928 Photo

1928 Billie, Marie, Anne and Maggie. (Of course, Rose is in Pittsburgh.)

Map of the Journey

From the Carpathian Mountains of Galicia to Antwerp, Belgium: 750 miles

From Antwerp, Belgium to the harbor of New York City: 3500 miles

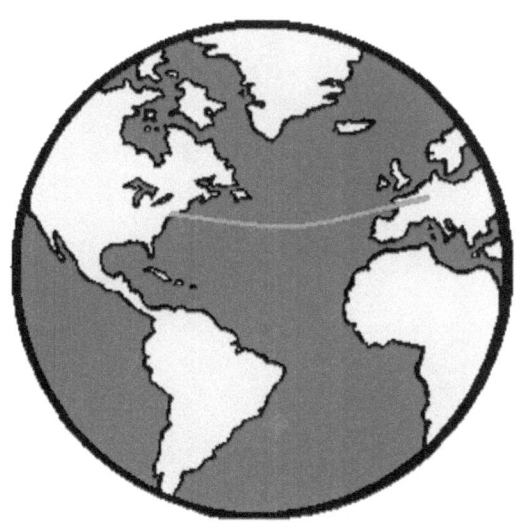

978-0-595-45713-7
0-595-45713-4